I0416666

The Fetal Issue

The Devolving Human Condition

By

Guy Cavet Myhre

© 2004 by Guy Cavet Myhre. All rights reserved.

No part of this book may be reproduced, stored in a retrieval system, or transmitted by any means, electronic, mechanical, photocopying, recording, or otherwise, without written permission from the author.

ISBN: 1-4140-4175-6 (e-book)
ISBN: 1-4140-4176-4 (Paperback)

This book is printed on acid free paper.

1stBooks – rev. 12/03/03

Dedicated to my son,

Franck Guy Myhre,

who created the image for the cover.

Foreword

From the very beginning, *The Fetal Issue,* a futuristic sociological novel, sets a blistering pace. It is an extraordinary, big, rich novel set in a disintegrating society of the future. Its multi-faceted content is exquisitely crafted in meticulous fashion such that its fifty-six chapters have something exciting for everyone—murder, intrigue, romance, sex, conspiracy, compassion, jealousy, sorrow, and greed. For those readers less interested in human emotions and foibles, Myhre interjects sections of futuristic science and technology, which, in their plausibility, enhance the credibility of this engrossing story.

The heart of the story is about a mother and daughter, each of whom births a deformed baby a generation apart. They join in battle over their opposing radical beliefs about how the pregnant daughter should deal with her "fetal issue" should it, too, prove to be deformed. During the course of the story, each woman; first, dilutes her extreme belief; then, unbeknownst to the other, approaches the same moderate belief; and finally, embraces the other's original extreme belief such that both women experience an ironic mutual exchange and reversal of their most-profound moral values.

The Fetal Issue is set in the future; therefore, it requires elements of what is commonly called "science fiction," but, in this book, it is plausible "future technology." However, science and technology are of secondary importance to the story. They are used only to make the action in the future more credible. Based upon the extrapolation of sound physical concepts, the novel contains hard, imaginative technology, but, no fantasy—no magic. The goal is to convince the reader that the future—very well—could be like its description in *The Fetal Issue* ... if the pollution and population of Earth increase at current rates over a long period of time.

The Fetal Issue alerts the entire world to the direction in which our civilization is headed. It caters to mature adults concerned about invoked abortion, overpopulation, environmental degradation, genetic degeneration, and our societal deterioration. Witty dialogue, humorous passages, and logical arguments maintain interest in this controversial, informative, and thought-provoking, yet entertaining, novel.

The Fetal Issue lays out a compelling and convincing possibility for declining genetic health of life on this planet in the future provided that the pollutive quality of human activity of the past century extrapolates out for centuries to come. The dramatic, heart-pounding scenes between head-strong characters, who possess admirable but opposing moral values, will prompt you to grab your own moral values and critically reassess them. Be forewarned—upon starting to read *The Fetal Issue*, you will not be able to set it down until you finish the climactic epilogue, which solves its remaining mysteries in most-plausible and convincing ways.

vi

Prologue—KILLINGS

As for myself, I walk abroad o' nights
And kill sick people groaning under walls.

—Christopher Marlowe

Before dawn, June 10, 2130
Pierre Talon's laboratory
Under the Cascade Mountains

"Only the In-valids must die. Please, Lord, before the hydroxygen detonates, let my robots carry the Valids to safety."

Alone, in the heart of his laboratory, Pierre plunged himself into the whirling holoimages, which mirrored the devastation that he was wreaking miles away. He winced as each explosion rocked yet another building. Fingers of fire curled about his head. He shuddered. Explosions now engulfed the asylum complex in its entirety.

"I had to do it. No other way was possible. They won't listen to me. May God understand … may He forgive me."

Tears blurred the flames, which licked up and enveloped him—like flower petals at dusk curling in to embrace their stamen.

"I will remain. I will endure." Pierre clenched his teeth, squinted his eyes, and screamed his agony.

Later, surrounding embers glowed—a somber end to the morning's deed. Weary, he hung his face into his hands and bleated a wail of anguish. "Computer, stop it … for God's sake, stop the projection."

Instantly, the carnage vanished—no more smoke, flames, ashes … no more bloated corpses, no more holocaustic images … yet, the despair that reigned in the depth of his soul, Pierre could not obliterate.

He felt his feet drag across the floor. He beheld his cot beneath him. He let his body collapse upon it. He heard his lips speak, "May He forgive me for what I have wrought." He allowed his eyes to close.

1—ARSON

Un seul être vous manque,
et tout est dépeuplé.

—Alphonse de Prat de Lamartine

Meanwhile
Andrew Drake's apartment
Seattle, Franklin

Katharine, clad in her nightgown, stood transfixed with horror. Frantically, she scanned one screenframe after another. All confirmed the terrible truth—the destruction of the huge Pineridge Residence for the In-valid had been swift and utter.

Bewildered, she watched the firerobots carry from the smoldering ruins a stream of charred corpses. She shivered and tasted vomit. She whispered a prayer that her son—her beloved Douglas—not be among the dead. "Dear God, please save him ... I beg of You."

Katharine heard a noise and, from the corner of her eye, caught sight of Andy's arm whip around from behind.

As usual, his feigned grab to her crotch preceded his pinch to her rear. Despite flailing elbows, his bear hug enveloped her.

The hollow of her neck recoiled from his attacking mouth. She heard his lips fart against her throat. She felt his spittle dribble between her breasts.

"Gotcha! ... Why up so early, darling?"

Katharine elbowed herself free. "Dammit, Andy, cut it out!" She sobbed and flung her arms toward the wallscreen. "Look! Look! Pineridge is burning, for God's sake."

Andy's head jerked up. His mouth fell agape.

Katharine glimpsed a stalactite of drool rappel from his canine onto his penis.

"Christ Almighty, you're right! That is Pineridge ... burnt to the ground ... shit, not another one!"

Andy's words startled her. "What do you mean 'not another one'?"

"Never mind. ... Computer, get me the fire chief at Pineridge."

Katharine's heart pounded. "Dammit, Andy, answer me. Have other fires like this occurred?"

Before he responded, a new screenframe formed the holoimage of an obviously harried man who, at the sight of Andy, giggled.

That Andy was really nude suddenly dawned on Katharine. Unwittingly, she paused to admire his athletic frame, adorned with just the right amount of muscle. *Jeez, now's not the time.* She shook her head free of sensual thoughts. "For God's sake, you dummy, put something on."

Andy grinned. "Oops, sorry, Sergeant."

Katharine watched Andy lope from the room like a lithe panther, his penis swinging—pendulum-like. Again, she shook her head.

A moment later, he returned clad in his bathrobe.

2

The sergeant chuckled. "Can't say you look any better. ... Look, Andy, the chief's busier 'n hell, but he'll get back to you soon 'cause this looks like another one for you. How many is this now ... seven or eight?"

Andy failed to hide his grimace from Katharine.

"I can't talk now, Sergeant. You'd better get back to duty. See you later."

"Right, Andy." The holoimage collapsed.

"What about Douglas? You didn't ask him about Douglas. You don't care about my son, do you? Say it's true ... you've never cared. All you care about is fucking." She knew that her voice was strident, but, with Andy, it didn't matter.

Andy grabbed her wrists, pulled her toward him, and riveted his gaze onto her eyes. "Darling, calm yourself. The sergeant wouldn't know about Douglas. Besides, this can't be as bad as it seems. On screen, fires always look worse than they really are. I'm sure that your son is unharmed."

"You're hurting me." Katharine gritted her teeth and wrested away from Andy's grip. She felt faint—her mouth, dry. "Christ, Andy, don't treat me as a child. Those holoimages don't lie ... hundreds are dead. How could Douglas survive? ... I'm terribly afraid for him. He's so vulnerable ... can't save himself ... in his condition." Her head spun. Her knees buckled. Her fingers clutched at Andy's robe.

"Darling, why are you looking at the news so early in the morning, anyway?"

Katharine gasped for breath. "Jane called—woke me up—told me to watch—accessed it just now. ... Andy, I'm so worried about Douglas."

The Sun peeked over the horizon, and Katharine saw the holoimages more clearly. Arranged in rows like cord wood, a multitude of carbonized corpses—some, limbless torsos—glistened blackly in the early morning light. They cast grotesque shadows—a sight that made her shudder. She could not tell from the holoimages whether the missing arms and legs were burned off or had been lacking since birth.

"Give a casualty report for the Pineridge fire."

Andy's query seemed to come from afar.

The smooth voice of the computer pounded one statistic after another into Katharine's tormented soul: "Casualties: dead—2231, dying—376, major injured—283, minor injured—134, uninjured—incomplete data, missing—incomplete data—"

"—and the psychiatric wards?" Andy asked.

"—mostly destroyed with high casualties."

Andy groaned. "Oh, those poor people. I hope they didn't suffer. ... What caused the fire?"

The simulated voice continued: "Primary causes: explosions of imported chemicals resulting in fires and fumes; secondary causes: sabotaged computer-surveillance and fire-control systems, immobilization of staff and residents with knockout gas, blocked exits; tertiary causes: fire-code violations in eleven buildings—seven date from the 2070s, slow response from the firerob—"

"Stop!" Andy barked. "Give conclusion."

"Arson."

"No shit!"

Katharine's mind reeled—the evilness of the perpetrators was beyond comprehension. "Andy, how could anyone commit such a wicked deed?"

Andy didn't answer—the wallscreen seemed to mesmerize him. "How was it done?"

The computer droned on. "Corrupted resident robots breached the security system and, to set up the job, let in a dozen foreign robots between one and two in the morning. They placed fire bombs in—"

"Enough! ... How many people escaped unharmed? Were any robots captured?"

"Too early to tell, but those who committed this arson are methodical and consistent. They didn't kill, nor even hurt, one productive person. The robots gassed the occupants into unconsciousness and carried to safety the staff and those in-valids, who, supposedly, were deemed worth saving. Only the insane, terminally ill, and mentally incompetent were left behind to burn. Curiously, those paralyzed or grossly deformed, but whose brains are productive, were spared. Those that died, did so without suffering."

Katharine heard Andy mutter something.

"What did you say?"

"I said, 'Looks like somebody out there is trying to play God.' "

Katharine responded as if she were in a dream. "Yes ... it seems that way."

The computer wouldn't stop talking: "... the robots sealed the exits from the inside and destroyed themselves along with their victims. Some robots were recovered intact, but their memories had been purposely purged beyond retrieval."

Katharine realized that the gruesome holoimages and the computer's droning voice were hypnotizing her. She clapped her hands over her ears. "Stop, dammit, stop!" She leaned against Andy, swallowed hard, and ordered, "Display the casualty names." Before she actually saw her son's name, she knew that it would be there. Tears blurred her vision, yet ... yes, on the fourth screenframe—there it was ... Douglas Howe. Despite the roar in her ears, she heard Andy speak:

"Give a brief bio on Douglas Howe."

Bitterly, Katharine noted that only now had Andy asked about her son. She trembled. She felt her knees give way. She clung to Andy. She barely heard the computer's voice:

"Douglas Lester Howe was born in the city of Seattle in the state of Franklin, as a citizen of The Federated Provinces and States of North America, on September 17, 2118 of Alfred Howe-Carver, aged 28, and of Katharine Carver-Howe, aged 26.

"Douglas possessed a congenitally-damaged brain without the essentials for auto-survival such as retention of memory, control of muscles, and recognition of surroundings."

The computer's summary of her son's life shocked Katharine. To her, he was not a statistic but a child of her flesh. She staggered backward and groped for a chair.

The sound of the artificial voice continued to echo through her skull: "He was placed in the Calvert Home for Retarded Infants in 2123 and transferred to the Pineridge Residence for the In-valid in 2128. Today, on June 10, 2130, in the Pineridge fire, by toxic fume inhalation while unconscious from knockout gas, Douglas Lester Howe, aged eleven, died."

Nauseous, Katharine groaned and slumped into a chair. She felt Andy lift her and carry her to their bed. She let consciousness slip away.

* * *

Andrew knew that he was in a tight spot. Thirty years in the department told him that, if he didn't soon solve this series of crimes, his job as arson chief would be on the line.

Already, the data from the earlier arsons had been correlated for patterns and coincidences. Yet, Andrew wasn't any closer to finding the culprits. This latest one fit the model. That these arsonists were not run-of-the-mill was the only solid information he possessed. They were intelligent, cunning, and purposeful.

"Computer, list the arsons of the last six months that correlate with the subject one."

Instantly, nine entries appeared in a screenframe: three chemical plants, one eugenic laboratory, one plastics factory, and four residences for the in-valid.

"What are the motives for destruction?"

The computer spoke its opinion: "With seventy-three-percent relative correlation, the motive is interdiction of further damage to the human gene pool by reduction of environmental degradation, cessation of eugenic engineering, and ... elimination of in-valids."

"How can these arsons change anything?"

"The three chemical plants had produced insecticides, herbicides, fertilizers, detergents, medicines, and other noxious products—all, of which, enter the food chain and modify chromosomal structures.

"The eugenic laboratory, among the last that still tamper with DNA spirals, had been clandestine since passage of the law that made its activities illegal. Decades of eugenic engineering produced millions of genetically altered persons who mate with normal humans. Their offspring possess serious chromosomal defects, which render them in-valid.

"The plastics factory had produced film for enveloping food. Microscopic plastic particles ingested with food deteriorate the immune system and cause cancer.

"The four residences for the in-valid had harbored thousands of deformed persons, most of whom were damaged either genetically or radioactively. Their deaths help sap the in-valids' political strength, reduce the huge costs for their care, and—most importantly—keep them from begetting more in-valids.

"Eighteen percent of the nation's population and seven percent of Parliament are now in-valid."

Andrew stared at the wallscreen. He could not believe this information. *How is it possible?* "List the sources."

The wallscreen filled with titles of reports and opinions written by some of the world's more prestigious authorities.

Andrew grew alarmed. He could not understand why he hadn't learned of this information before. He feared that, even if only some of it were true, the human race— no, the Earth itself—was in peril.

"Give me an info pellet about this and get me a monocabin."

A pellet dropped into the output cup.

Andrew pocketed it and pivoted to leave his apartment. On the way to the exit, he thought about Douglas and smiled. *So the brat's finally dead. The little shit's better off anyway. Maybe, Kathy will take better care of me from now on.*

Andrew arrived at the door. It refused to slide open. Evidently, the computer had locked it, but Andrew hadn't given the order. "What the hell is going on here?"

The intrusion of a commanding voice startled him. "Mister Drake, the info pellet you just took … please drop it into your eradicator."

Andrew whirled around and stared at the wallscreen. He locked eyes with those of an elderly man's holoimage and recognized Mizuno Yoshimasa, the powerful senior senator from the state of Franklin. "Yes, Sir."

"Thank you. Now then, you are to keep to yourself what you just learned about the so-called motives behind these arsons. Do I make myself clear?"

"Of course, Senator, but why the secrecy?"

"Never you mind. I have corrected the mistake of classifying this information with too low of a security-access code. It will not happen again.

"Now then, when you capture the perpetrators of these crimes, internalize your robots' memories and notify me immediately. I want to filter the data before they stream into Central Database. Access me directly with this pellet—it's priority one for ten days."

"I've got ten days to come up with something?"

"I want this solved before then. Good day, Mister Drake."

The senator's holoimage shrank to nothing, and the door's lock clicked off.

Yoshimasa—talking to me? What a break! Maybe I can get the guy in my corner. Andrew's hand trembled as it pocketed the senator's access pellet. *Wow, priority one— twenty-four-hour access!* Andrew left the apartment just as the monoplace cabin braked to a halt. The cabin hung like a pendulum from the I beam. He climbed aboard, and the cabin accelerated through the pollution barrier to system speed on the spur before re-entering the main line.

Andrew turned and watched the stratoscraper recede into the gray haze, which hovered over Seattle like a smothering hand. His gaze shifted to the surface a thousand feet below. He tried to make out a landmark or two only to see small whirlwinds of dust explore miles of abandoned buildings and weed-clogged streets. *How long ago was I last down to the surface? I forget. How many people still live … no, survive down there? I wonder.*

2—TIDINGS

Though it be honest, it is never good
To bring bad news; give to a gracious message
A host of tongues, but let ill tidings tell
Themselves when they be felt.

—William Shakespeare

Later that morning
Julie Carver-Pavía and Mario Pavía-Carver's apartment
Bellevue, Franklin

Julie Carver felt happy. Rather, Julie Carver-Pavía felt happy. Her husband Mario and she had just returned from their honeymoon. She watched her houserobot unpack their bags.

The computer spoke: "Andrew Drake is at the door."

"Is Mother with him?"

"No—he's alone."

Julie shuddered—the idea of being alone with Andrew chilled her. She wondered why her mother hadn't come along to welcome them home, too. "Unlock."

The computer clicked the door open.

Andrew entered.

Expansive in mood, Julie decided to greet her mother's lover less impassively than usual—but with some aloofness, still. "Hello, Andrew. How have Mother and you been?"

"Fine, Julie. Welcome home. You look wonderful ... so beautiful. My God, Mario is a lucky man ... is he here?"

The trepidation in Andrew's greeting amused her. She was amazed ... no sexual innuendos ... no obscene gestures. He hadn't tried to pinch her behind. Obviously, he felt unsure of the status of their relationship since her marriage to Mario. She hoped that, from now on, Andrew would stop trying to get into bed with her.

Reluctantly, she admitted that she was alone. "No. Poor me! This is our first separation as a married couple ... but one of us must return to work." She feared that he'd recognize her smile for what it was—artificial.

"Sorry I missed him, but ... it's just as well. I need to talk to you alone."

Andrew's seriousness unnerved her. Always he had been jovial—too much so. Apparently, he was preoccupied.

He brightened. "But first, tell me about your honeymoon. Where did you go? What did you do?"

"We went to the Moon."

Andrew chortled. "I knew that Mario couldn't resist. Is lovemaking in one-sixth gravity as exotic as claimed? I would have liked to have been there to watch."

Julie felt herself blush—not of embarrassment, but of ire ... anger toward herself for having mentioned the Moon in the first place. *I should have known.* She turned

7

away. "I'll let Mario answer that one. Knowing you, I'm sure it will be the first question you'll ask him."

Andrew turned her toward him, and his eyes searched her face.

His touch annoyed—no, alarmed—her. She pulled back and—grudgingly—looked squarely at him.

He seemed surprised by her defiance. "Look, Julie, I know you don't like me much ... but I like you a lot and wish you and Mario much happiness."

"Well, what do you expect? For the last three years, you've been sleeping with Mother when it pleased you. When it didn't, you took off for parts unknown. You are nothing but a self-centered egoist."

"And your father? ... He left your mother permanently. Was he an egoist as well?"

Andrew's patronizing irritated Julie. "My father is dead. Let him rest in peace. One reason I married was to find a new life—a beautiful one—away from my martyred mother and her lover. Let her continue to feel sorry for herself. I am free of her. From now on, Andrew, she is yours alone."

"Julie, don't say such things. You don't mean them. Your mother loves you. You can't remove her from your life just because you're married. Who is the egoist now, uh?"

Reluctantly, she accepted his apparent sincerity. "Andrew, I'm going to tell you something I've told only Mario." She hesitated and searched for the best way to express herself.

"... Until I was eight, life with my parents was wonderful. Then, Mother birthed that thing. Against Dad's wishes, she decided to keep it. For five years, she cared for it. I had lost my mother. She was losing Dad. They argued constantly. Finally, he left us and remarried.

"When he was killed, Mom had to go to work and put my dear brother in a foster home. Everything she earned went to quacks promising cures. We lived in poverty—and, at times, went hungry. She spent her weekends at that 'home' staring at it, talking to it ... I was alone ..."

Andrew rushed to her then drew back to lightly touch her arm. "Julie, Julie ... don't punish yourself. I know all this. Kathy never tires talking of it. ... I came here to tell you something, so let me—"

Julie jerked away. "Dammit, Andrew, you've always heard her martyr's version. Hear a victim's version for a change ... while I still have the courage." She fidgeted with her fingernails and paced to and fro while searching for the proper words. "Worst of all, my mother's time, effort, money, and love were wasted. My brother can't know about the sacrifices my family and I have made. He's a vegetable—staring unseeing, unhearing, unfeeling, unknowing ... He never should have been kept alive—never—never—never ... !"

Julie collapsed onto the sofa—face in hands—and cried unabashedly.

After a silence, punctuated only by her sobs, she heard Andrew say, "Julie, I came to tell you something ... Julie, your brother ... Julie, Douglas is dead."

Stunned, Julie ignored Andrew, staggered to the window, and stared across the city far below. With difficulty, she retained her composure although, within, emotions raged—a mixture of sadness, happiness, relief, anger, and ... guilt. She wondered if guilt filled the void because grief did not.

"She is free at last. ... Mother is free at last." Until the whisper left her lips, Julie didn't realize that the words had formed in her throat.

Suddenly, her fury burst forth. She whipped around and glared at Andrew. "You bastard! You let me spill my guts while, all along, you knew ... you knew that he was dead. ... Get out! Go on! Run back to Mother. Her grief is certainly greater than mine, so gloat over her pathetic reactions. I'm sure that she will amuse you much more than I can."

Andrew's expression of disbelief surprised her. Then, she realized that never before had she dared speak to him like this. She felt exhilarated ... she had shed her childhood.

"I'm sorry. I tried to tell you, but, Julie ... you were so wound up."

Andrew's apology left her cold, yet the reality of her new power over him warmed her. "Where's Mother now? Did she go to work?"

"No, Julie, she was in no condition to leave home. I put her to bed. The houserobot is looking after her."

"What caused my brother's death?"

Andrew ordered, "Computer, give news of the Pineridge fire."

Julie listened to the computer until she felt its voice would drive her crazy. She yelled, "Stop!" then, whispered, "At least it didn't suffer—even if it had been capable."

"Why do you keep calling your brother 'it,' Julie? ... We even call our pets 'he' or 'she.' "

Julie didn't even try to suppress a smile. She felt relief ... relief for her mother—and for herself, too. She looked at Andrew—and, for the first time—through adult eyes. No longer was he the handsome arson chief who had awed her with his muscles. He seemed pathetic. To think that she almost had let him get into her pants made her want to puke. Indeed, Mario entered her life at the right moment. She answered Andrew calmly, yet firmly—as if lecturing a little boy:

"Pets are viable beings, useful to their environment. They relate with humans and with themselves. They recognize you, love you ... make your days happier. If alone or unloved, they suffer. Except for lack of speech and advanced thought, these animals are like ourselves—with similar needs and emotions. Yet ... they are unprotected by law.

"If I should choose to kill my cat, I could lawfully do so—provided that the act be performed humanely. But, 'it'—who never possessed any of these qualities—was kept alive. 'It'—could not have been legally euthanized, even if 'it' had been capable of asking. Such are the quirks of laws based upon contemporary misinterpretations of old Judeo-Christian sentiments.

"I never had a brother; my mother—no son. I call it 'it' because that is what 'it' was—a thing ... not a person."

Julie shuddered—a spasm raced down her spine. "I would never birth anything like that. I'd rather kill it ... or myself, first.

"... Andrew! Leave! ... Please!"

3—MEDITATION

> A man, doubtful of his dinner, is not
> much disposed to abstract meditation.
>
> —Samuel Johnson

That evening
Andrew's apartment
Seattle, Franklin

Andrew arrived home and found Kathy in bed—prostrate with grief. He tried caressing her to sexual arousal, but she screamed to be left alone. He retreated to the kitchen.

The houserobot prepared dinner. Andrew ate and, to mask Kathy's distant sobs, submerged himself in thought. A life shared with her had given him some insight into how she must now be dealing with the shock of losing her son.

He imagined that her first reaction to the news of her son's death might have been what she believed to be grief. However, Andrew realized that her feelings were, in reality, self pity. Most grieve, he thought, not for the departed beloved, but for the departed beloved portion of their own life style.

He believed that Kathy must be aware of how greatly her reaction to her son's affliction had adversely affected her life and that of her family: a lost husband, an alienated daughter, wasted time in the flower of her life ...

Andrew felt that, surely, she must now be seeing her own life as squandered—sacrificed for her womb's issue, an issue that had been forever oblivious of all things ... including life itself.

He was convinced that Kathy's final analysis would be objective and that, eventually, she would see her life in proper perspective.

Long ago, he had decided that, when that day should arrive, he would marry her. On several occasions, though, he had left Kathy because, like her husband, he found himself isolated from her love. Yet, never was he able to resist her deep and volatile emotions. Always, he was drawn back to her. The intensity and profoundness of her sexual prowess gave him orgasmic ecstasies that he never before had experienced.

Andrew had been distressed by Kathy's obsession with her in-valid child. It had driven a wedge between them in every aspect of their lives—except sexual. At times, he had felt that all Kathy wanted of him was strength from his maleness—sufficient enough to help her cope with her problems.

The realization that Kathy's only interest was her son, Douglas, had left him emotionally drained. He knew that, had he married her, he would have been drawn into caring for her son. He hadn't had enough courage—maybe not enough maturity—to have taken on that burden.

Perhaps that is why Julie dislikes me ... but, if Douglas's own father hadn't been able to handle Kathy's obsession, why should I have been expected to?

Andrew thought about Mario—that lucky dog. The mental image of Mario in bed with Julie aroused him. Often, he had tried to make it with Kathy's daughter, but she'd always resisted. Now, it was too late. He knew that Kathy must have been as voluptuous as Julie at the same age, and she was still a handsome woman, yet when they made love, he imagined that he was with Julie. It was easy—mother and daughter were so much alike.

Yet, he was sure that Julie's flesh was more pliant and supple; her breasts, more erect and firm; her belly, more tight and flat; her lips, more fresh and eager... . He felt the rising bulge between his legs. *God, I know that Kathy must be more adept sexually, but half the fun is in the teaching.*

The computer interrupted Andrew's thoughts: "Julie wishes to speak with you."

"Julie?"

"Yes, Andrew. I tried calling Mother. She doesn't respond. I hope she hasn't done anything foolish."

"She's okay ... just exhausted. She won't talk to me, either. Don't worry, Julie, I'll look in on her during the night. I'll call you in the morning before leaving for work ... okay?"

"Sure, Andrew. ... and, Andrew? ..."

"Yeah?"

"I'm sorry about what I said. ... We're still friends?"

"Sure. ... I understand."

" 'Bye."

"Good-bye, Julie."

After the connection clicked off, Andrew grabbed his crotch and groaned, "Oh, Julie—BABY!"

4—HYDROXYGEN

Energy is Eternal Delight.

—William Blake

The next morning, June 11, 2130

Andrew finished breakfast. He was glad Kathy still slept. He had neither the time nor the desire to talk to her now—the monocabin had braked to a halt at his front door—right on schedule.

While riding to work, he called Julie to ease her fears and, then, her husband. "Computer, get me Mario Pavía at Fuerza Cortés in La Paz, Baja California."

After a banal exchange of news, Andrew got to the point. "Mario, hydroxygen fueled the Pineridge fire. Fuerza Cortés makes the stuff, so maybe you can find out how the arsonists are getting it."

"Andy, you've never been down to our production plant, have you?" Before Andrew could answer, Mario continued, "Take one of our sub-orbital shuttles from the Bellevue Spaceport. Can you come now? ... this morning?"

"I don't have time, Mario. I'm in the middle of this hot case. Can you just give me some information, now?"

"No ... too busy myself, but I've got you authorized to take the shuttle. It's only 2,000 miles and fifteen minutes—port to port. I'll meet you at the La Paz Spaceport, okay? I've got to go now, Andy."

The screen blanked out.

Andrew was perplexed—Mario had seemed wary. Then, he understood. "Computer, change my destination to La Paz, Baja California."

At the next wye switch, the cabin shunted to another line and, at a constant eighty-mile-per-hour system speed, arrived at the spaceport half an hour later.

Andrew was the only passenger on Fuerza Cortés's little corporate shuttle. Powered by hydroxygen, it depadded in a cloud of steam and, for five minutes, accelerated at a comfortable two 'g's' to 13,000 miles per hour. It coasted—weightless—for another five and passed the half-way point 300 miles above Las Vegas, Alta California. Before re-entering the atmosphere, the shuttle pivoted to point itself in the opposite direction. After a last five minutes of deceleration, the craft backed down its rocket plume and empadded at La Paz.

Seeing Mario again reminded Andrew of how handsome the young man was. He possessed the straight black hair and bronze skin of a typical Mexican, and his body exuded an aura of athleticism. *No doubt, the sensuousness of his body pleases Julie the most*, he thought.

Mario prolonged a banal greeting until the car was on the coastal road to La Paz. "I think it's safe to talk now. Satellite surveillance can't eavesdrop while the solar cells on the roof are recharging the batteries—an unplanned side effect, which I have covertly enhanced."

"You mean, you're being monitored?"

"Yeah, Fuerza Cortés—the whole company—is being investigated by both México and North America. That's why I didn't want to say anything over the computer channel. The two governments have sent investigative teams—from San Francisco and from Winnipeg. They're trying to find out how the arsonists are getting their hydroxygen and, more importantly, how they are igniting it."

"So … this investigation has gone international—"

"—at the request of México's president, no less. … Let's see what you've got, Andy."

Andrew slipped his info pellet into the car's input tube. "Computer, display hydroxygen-canister identity info from the Pineridge fire."

Mario scanned the information as it scrolled up the screen. Charred remains of canisters appeared on several videographs.

"Amazing! These canisters appear to have come from a batch that's supposed to be still here in La Paz. I guess they're right—our security is the one that's fouling up. Stealing hydroxygen is easier than before—now that it no longer needs supercooling. What's really giving México the shivers, though, is that the arsonists have perfected a catalyst."

In the distance, a huge domed centrifuge loomed offshore. Andrew was excited—he had never seen one before. As the car drew closer, the centrifuge resembled an enormous waterbug poised over the sea. For the past four decades, these hydrogen-oxygen separators had been considered one of the marvels of the modern world. The hydroxygen technology maintained México's wealth and power.

"Mario, what do you mean … catalyst?"

"Well, assuming you don't know the process: A powerful laser beam from one of our solar-energy collection satellites enters through the top of the dome. When it hits the surface of the sea, each photon in the beam transfers its energy to a water molecule and separates it into hydrogen and oxygen gas."

"Why can't you just focus a big lens on the water instead of using all this expensive high-tech?"

Mario laughed. "That would just separate the molecules … make water vapor. The energy beam must contain only photons possessing a particularly high energy called the disassociation energy of a water molecule.

"Forty years ago, the domed centrifuges separated the gaseous hydrogen and oxygen rising from the sea and individually cooled them into liquid states. The process was dangerous. Static electricity and lightning were a problem. Several domes blew up. The volatility of hydrogen and oxygen limited their use as a fuel to rockets, generating plants, and large aircraft. Recombining the two elements at the point of combustion was always tricky."

"The technology doesn't seem dangerous now."

"No, but to make it safe required much time and money. The result is hydroxygen—the wonder fuel. By adding a stabilizer that raised the vapor points, liquid hydrogen and oxygen could be mixed together safely—like being homogenized. Now, hydroxygen remains liquid and stable even at room temperature."

"It seems like it would be back in the water state."

"Not at all. Sure, the two elements are mixed together, but as individual hydrogen and oxygen molecules—not water molecules. At combustion time, a catalyst added to the hydroxygen counteracts the effect of the stabilizer. The stabilizer-production process is well known—it is no secret. But, the opposite is true for the catalyst.

"Now, Andy, here's the paradox—there is no way the arsonists could have stolen the catalyst."

"Ah, come on, Mario, they stole the hydroxygen, didn't they? Couldn't they get the catalyst the same way?"

"The catalyst doesn't exist ... not anywhere. It is too volatile for safe storage—even at low temperatures. It is produced and injected into the hydroxygen jet at combustion time—as needed. Computers, only here in La Paz, control the process."

"You mean my shuttle's rocket engine would have shut down if your computer link with it had failed?"

"Absolutely ... but such failure is unlikely. Every day, our computers control the combustion in thousands of power plants and transport craft throughout the solar system—without mishap."

"Maybe a disgruntled employee or corrupted robot could have—"

"No way! No one knows the secret. Computers created the process, and bits and pieces of it are stored in various data banks around the world. These small algorithmic segments must come together under the control of a foolproof encrypted program every time the catalyst is produced. To maintain our monopoly of this process requires stringent precautions. Fuerza Cortés's and México's economic survival depend upon keeping the catalyst production process a secret. Now you know why they are so anxious to catch the perpetrators. Of course, because of terrorist consequences, the whole world is concerned."

The car drew abreast of the centrifuge, which stood five hundred yards offshore.

Andrew felt a sense of awe. "I never before realized the immensity of these structures. Is this one operating? I don't see any energy beam."

"You bet it's operating. The frequency of the laser beam is far above that of visible light. One of six solar-energy collection satellites in a near-polar orbit transmit the beam."

"Why polar?"

Mario laughed. "So that the satellites can stay out of the Earth's shadow—no Sun, no hydroxygen."

The car left the centrifuge behind and approached company headquarters.

Mario said, "Andy, my father is here on an inspection tour, so I suppose we'll be forced to see him."

"He's not as bad as all that, is he?"

"You haven't met him yet. My father is the genius behind the catalyst breakthrough and became executive vice-president of Fuerza Cortés instead of president only because he lacked money. Maybe that's why he's so overbearing with everybody.

"Andy, you know I love Julie very much. Yet, perhaps, subconsciously, one reason I married her, took North-American citizenship, and now live outside of México was to frustrate my father. I wanted him to realize that he could no longer run my life. He's made my mother's, a living hell. I can't forgive him for that."

"Is that why you chose to attend the University of Franklin?"

"To get far away from my father? ... Yes, that's part of it, I guess."

"Then, your real reason for marrying Julie was not love … it was for her North-American citizenship."

"You misunderstand, Andy. The truth is, I fell in love with Julie and wanted to marry her before any idea to thwart my father came to mind. My break with him occurred after he disapproved of our marriage."

"I notice you're still working for him."

"Do you know how much he's paying me? I couldn't get half that anywhere else. He thinks he's buying my love—so, I let him."

Upon arrival at Fuerza Cortés headquarters, Mario led Andrew on a tour of the facilities, interrupted by an interesting lunch with Mario's father and his entourage. In the late afternoon, they headed back to the spaceport.

After they depadded and were in weightlessness, Mario finally spoke, "Well, how did you like my father?"

"He sure bats down opposing opinions—I'll say that much, but … he's forthright and sincere. … I like him."

"Well, you don't work under him. You're not in his family."

"That's true."

Silently, the shuttle arched over the top of its trajectory.

Andrew decided to confide in Mario about his forebodings concerning the aftermath of Douglas's demise. "You know, Mario … Kathy is taking Douglas's death pretty hard. I dread facing her tonight."

"Well, I'd expect her to be upset. Her whole life was wrapped up in that poor son of hers … but, I guess, in the long run, it's for the best. Maybe—eventually—I'll have a normal, cheerful mother-in-law."

"I'm glad we see eye-to-eye about this because I'm planning on making you my step son-in-law … if Kathy accepts, naturally."

Mario was slow to respond.

Andrew bit his lip. *Damn! Me and my flapping mouth—it's too soon, … and it may never happen.*

Finally, Mario looked at Andrew and said bluntly, "Had you cared enough for her, you could have married her before Douglas's death. She really needed your support then."

Mario must think me a real son of a bitch. "Look, I never claimed to be a self-flagellating saint, but I feel I'm holier than her old man was. … It's just that, after a disastrous first marriage, you're more cautious the second time 'round. … Dammit Mario, I've the right to crave the good life just like everyone else."

"I'm sorry, Andy. Criticism comes easy. I'd probably have done the same in your situation."

Andrew smiled. *The fool believes me.*

The computer interrupted: "Gentlemen, prepare for deceleration. …"

Upon arrival at the Bellevue Spaceport, Andrew went his separate way … home to Kathy.

5—GRIEF

For the born, death is certain.
For the dead, birth is certain.
Grieve not for the unavoidable.

—The Bhagavadgita of the Mahabharata

The next morning, June 12, 2130

Again, Katharine awoke—not remembering how many times during the last two days she had done so. Again, she stared at the ceiling—no longer could she force sleep to shield herself from despondency. Again, she tried to convince herself that she had dreamt it all—that her son must still be alive. Yet, emptiness and hopelessness prevailed.

Although time spent with Andy and with her job had been satisfying, Katharine had especially looked forward to her daily visits to her son—not that she had enjoyed any real rapport with him. On the contrary, always he had continued to stare into infinity, oblivious of everything and, most important of all, oblivious of her—his loving mother.

Whenever she had been near him—feeding him, caressing him, washing him—he never had acknowledged her presence, yet never had she lost hope. Her greatest satisfaction of each day had occurred, upon leaving Douglas, with the realization that, once again, she had done her motherly best for her son.

With a rush, the real world invaded Katharine. Quite suddenly, she understood that her son's death was no nightmare. She realized that Douglas actually was gone—forever gone—no more daily visits, no more caresses, no more talking to him. Deep, everlasting despair triumphed. Her life was devoid of happiness ... of purpose ... of goals. Thoughts of Andy and of her job no longer appealed to her. Life seemed empty. She wondered, *What do I do, now?*

Again, Katharine closed her eyes and tried to escape into sleep, but her body accepted it no longer. After what seemed an eternity, she felt a certain warmth invade her—or did she imagine it? Was courage being rekindled? If so—why? Was it to face reality—to face the world? ... but, toward what end? ... Is the effort really worth it?

The image of her beautiful daughter came to mind. She was surprised ... why hadn't she realized sooner that she still possessed a daughter—a healthy young girl, who had blossomed into an enchanting woman and was now married. *Yes ... my daughter, I still have my Julie.* Katharine felt better.

She arose from bed and crossed the room to her vanity. A glance into the mirror stunned her. A slouched, disheveled woman peered back from puffy eyes. *That's me? ... Katharine Carver?* She was shocked by how greatly grief had changed her. *Can these signs of middle age be reversed?* She thrust herself forward until her nose nearly touched its image. *My God, I'll be forty in two years! What have I done with my life? My family is gone. I'm broke—living in the bed of my lover—and working for a woman who wants to steal him from me.*

Thoughts of her daughter turned sad. That Julie was no longer hers had finally dawned on her. Now, her little girl belonged to Mario. *I am alone—so very alone.* Listlessly, she tried to brush her hair into some semblance of neatness.

She wondered what the reaction by Julie and Andy to her son's death had been. In the past, each had offered unsolicited advice about how she should deal with her "obsession." She knew that her fear of ridicule was unfounded, still, she was reluctant to face them. She felt that her grief over the loss of Douglas was enough to contend with.

Katharine had asked herself over and over—Had she been right? ... right to protect her son? ... right to try having him cured? Each time, her answer had been ... yes, yes, and yes, again.

As his mother, I was my son's shield. I was right to do my duty. Yes, it was a duty—a sacred duty—a duty entrusted to me by God. From the moment of conception, a mother's duty is to safeguard the new life until it can fend for itself. Parents cannot have the right to reject a child simply because he is not to their liking—no matter the reason. ... Only God can.

Katharine's reminiscences turned to her childhood, when a great aunt had abandoned her baby—an armless son—soon after birth. From time to time, Katharine had heard about this cousin. She remembered having listened to self-righteous criticisms in snatches of conversation between her mother and grandmother.

Both fanatically religious, they had condemned her great aunt's cowardly action. "... selfish woman ... unworthy to be my brother's wife ... un-Christian-like act ... unfit mother ... hedonistic character ..."

The family's condemnation peaked when the rejected child, as a grown man, searched for and located his natural parents. Katharine would always remember the day she met her cousin. She, an impressionable girl of thirteen, had expected to see a wretched cripple, but he was handsome, distinguished, and making a name for himself as a budding scholar. His prosthetic arms seemed natural—as if they had come at birth.

Katharine was sure that family pressure hadn't caused her to loath her great aunt's act of cowardice. Had her mother and grandmother not condemned the irresponsibility, Katharine was confident that, on her own, she would have done so—as God, Himself, must have done. She knew that all mothers guard and nurture their babies—even terribly-malformed or mentally-retarded ones. Certainly, her great aunt was a freak of nature, devoid of all motherly instinct—of any sense of human decency.

She wondered what her family would have thought had she followed her great aunt's example. Could she even have lived with herself? Would God have condemned her for such a sin?

At Douglas's birth, her husband's reaction had surprised her. Instead of supporting her resolve to care for the baby—come what may—he rejected their son and criticized his wife's decision to keep him. Over time, their positions became adamant, their relationship—bitter. She felt trapped between two painful alternatives—the loss of husband or, of son.

Katharine was sure that Douglas, in time, could have been partially cured. Perhaps, he might not have been like her cousin, but, eventually, he might have led a meaningful life.

She wondered what monster could kill defenseless children. She struck the dresser with her hairbrush and yelled at the mirror, "They'll pay for this. I'll find out who killed my son ... and they'll pay dearly."

"Your daughter arrives in five minutes. Do you wish the door unlocked for her?" The computer paused for an answer.

Katharine felt panicked. "Oh, God ... ! No, absolutely not. I can't see her now. Tell her to go back home."

"Very well."

Katharine always assumed that Julie, out of a sense of duty as a loving sister, had accepted the sacrifices made for her brother. The girl never complained. Since, to Katharine, any other choice was unthinkable, she believed that Julie had felt the same.

Katharine thought back to when Julie was eight. She realized that her daughter had been greatly harmed by the consequences of her brother's birth. She knew that her daughter was especially hurt when her husband—Julie's adored father—abandoned the family and eventually was killed in an accident.

On the few occasions that Julie appeared resentful, Katharine would say, "Life, as it is dealt out, must be lived without complaint." The reply always seemed to mollify her daughter. However, after Julie's engagement to Mario, Katharine noticed that her daughter had become more willful and outspoken. At first, Katharine believed that Mario had turned Julie against her, but, later, upon learning that Julie had harbored ill feelings all along, she felt greatly distressed.

Katharine thought it indeed ironic that she be condemned for those acts whose opposites had condemned her great aunt half a century before.

More and more, a feeling of panic and impending doom replaced her grief. Why? Was it loneliness? ... or, perhaps, the realization that she no longer was needed or wanted ... or loved?

How could I have neglected my daughter for so many years? ... but I had to sacrifice her—for Douglas's sake. Oh, God, I did have to, didn't I? ... Now that Douglas is gone, I must win here back—I must!

"Your daughter is here. She insists upon seeing you."

6—FACE-TO-FACE

For now we see through a glass, darkly;
but then face to face: now I know in part;
but then shall I know even as also I am known.

—1 Corinthians 13:12

A moment later

Julie felt uneasy about confronting her mother. However, as a newlywed, new-found independence gave courage she'd always thought she never would muster. Therefore, she erected a façade of confidence and strode boldly across the threshold.

She burst into Andrew's apartment, talking as she went. "Mother, I've tried for hours to contact you. Why are you refusing calls? Shutting the world out like this doesn't do anybody any good. What's done is done, and, believe me, we're all the better for it—especially you, Mother. From now on, your life will be—"

"Oh, shut up, Julie. Don't you have any feeling for him—your own brother ... or for me, either?

"Oh, yes! Yes, I do have feelings. I'm glad you asked, Mother ... finally. In my childhood, I often had feelings. You chose to ignore them because of my so-called brother, who had none ... and never would've had any—"

Her mother held up a hand. "Please, child ... no melodrama—it is unbecoming. ... Julie, I've always done what I thought was right. You always have been strong—right from birth. Douglas needed my love more than you ... but, you never understood—neither did your father."

Julie forced a thin smile. "Well, Mother, add more misunderstanding persons to your list—Andrew and Jane, for instance."

"Jane Stevens? My boss? What makes you think that? When did she confide in you?"

"This morning. When you wouldn't return her calls, she contacted me. We had a nice long talk."

"What about?"

"—about Douglas's death and the future of your job. Jane is ready to fire you, Mother. Your fellow reporters have been covering for you so far, but, if you continue to ignore Jane, she'll have you replaced."

"Never! She knows I'm the best reporter—and interviewer—she's got."

"Maybe so, Mother, but are you aware of her feeling toward Andrew? She's more envious of you than you realize. I'm sure she'd fire you just for the pleasure."

"Hardly. Why do you think she invites me to all her parties? I bring Andy for her to drool over, that's why. If she fires me ... there's no more Andy."

"Maybe she'll invite him without you. Aren't you afraid she might eventually steal him?"

"Not really. If Andy were infatuated with her, I wouldn't want him. He'd be no great loss—my attraction to him is strictly sexual."

"Oh, come now, Mother. I remember our lifestyle took a big jump for the better when we moved in with him. After the hovel we existed in, this place is a palace. I don't see what Andrew gets for his money, though … unless, of course, you're a hel-lava good lay."

"Don't you dare talk to me like that! I won't—"

Julie spread her arms. "Well, you're the one who said that the attraction is 'strictly sexual.' I'm just being more blunt. Perhaps, the real truth is, you already feel that you don't need his money any more—now that the Pineridge rat hole is plugged."

"Julie! Stop it! I won't listen to your insults another instant."

"Don't worry, Mother, I'm on my way out. I came only to inform you about Jane's intentions."

Julie spun around and walked out. The door slid shut behind her. She leaned against it, bit her lip, and tried to blink away the tears.

Why did I do it? Why do I say such things?

7—SUCCESS

If at first you don't succeed,
Try, try, again.

—W. E. Hickson

Three weeks later, July 4, 2130
Pierre Talon's laboratory
Under the Cascade mountains

An elated Andrew stood among the ruins of what he hoped was the laboratory of the arsonist for whom he had searched so long. The battle had been ferocious, but at no time did Andrew doubt that his people would prevail.

* * *

Andrew realized that the arsonist's weakness was his continual need for more robots. Because the robots used in each arson were destroyed, the perpetrator was forced to obtain more robots for future raids.

Andrew put the robot outlets under surveillance. At first, the effort proved fruitless—all of the large purchases seemed legitimate. Then, his people tracked the single-robot purchases. Many of them led to one place—an eastern suburb of Bellevue among the foothills of the Cascade Mountains. And what a place it was … mostly underground, protected by state-of-the-art electronic barriers and armed robots. Initial attempts to overcome the complex failed, but superior firepower triumphed over ferocious resistance, and, finally, it was secured.

Upon entering the heart of the premises, which was deep in an abandoned mine, Andrew and his people discovered a sophisticated laboratory containing computers, robots, hydroxygen canisters, and much, advanced paraphernalia of bewildering design. They found one arson suspect—a wounded man, who was unconscious or perhaps comatose.

The equipment baffled the experts. The most intriguing apparatus was destroyed, not accidentally as a result of the assault but, on purpose. Evidently, before the man lost consciousness, he demolished it. Possibly, it produced the elusive catalyst that Fuerza Cortés—and México—believed was their monopoly.

* * *

Andrew watched Senator Mizuno Yoshimasa approach. Surprisingly, he was alone. He had left his usual retinue of aides and bodyguards outside. Andrew admired the man's agility as—despite advanced age—he wove adroitly through the debris of the laboratory. His ninja training, no doubt.

"Mister Drake," Senator Yoshimasa barked, "why did you delay notifying me of this seizure?"

"I'm sorry, Senator. At the time of the assault, I hadn't realized we had your man … and I've been quite busy."

21

"Who is he? Are there others?"

"No others, Senator. ... We don't know who the man is. He draws a blank: DNA match, brain scan, heartbeat patterns ... even fingerprints. It's as if he'd never been born. We're waiting for him to regain consciousness for interrogation. It may take some time—he appears to be comatose."

"How far back did you search?" The senator smirked.

"Sixty years—almost to the Wall. A tooth and bone analysis puts him at not over forty-five."

The senator simpered outrightly. "Where is he?"

"To be safe, we've put him in Franklin State Asylum Number Fifteen, Building 23A. It's maximum security and holds only 1,100 inmates."

"Go there with me. On the way, we need a serious tête-à-tête."

"Very well, Sir."

The senator's cabin could seat eight persons and was suspended from the I beam by three arms. *Very plush,* Andrew thought, *perhaps I'll have one someday.* He boarded before the senator, and the cabin headed for the asylum.

"Mister Drake, would you care for a glass of Peshastin Extra Old? It can stand up to any Calvados. My grandfather casked it a century ago."

"Why thank you, Sir. I'm greatly honored." *What does he want from me—this powerful man? More importantly, what can he give me? Why did he leave his retinue behind?*

"Honored you are, my good man, honored you are—only a few irreplaceable cases remain. Some decades ago, my great grandfather's apple orchards in the Wenatchee Valley joined the Grand Coulee Desert. ... He was an issei, you know."

Then, you'd be a yonsei ... right?"

For an instant, the senator's frown vanished. "Fourth generation—yes ... so, you know some Japanese, Mister Drake."

"Yes, a little."

Apparently unimpressed, the grizzled senator simply grunted. Hunched over, he sighed and muttered, "I am barely old enough to remember what the orchards were like back then—only videographs and old memories remain ... and sand—lots of sand."

The old man stared off into infinity for awhile before suddenly coming back to life. He sat bolt upright and slapped his knee. "Mister Drake, you are privy to knowledge whose integrity is vital to the security of The Federated Provinces and States of North America. Your people must not divulge what they have learned so far. In a few hours, my own investigative team from Winnipeg replaces them at the site."

"But, Sir, I have the authority here to—"

"Not any longer. As the parliamentary majority leader and senator from Franklin, I appointed myself to head this investigation. Franklin's governor and the President gave their blessings."

"Okay, okay!" Andrew raised his hands in submission. "Then, what's at stake here?"

"The very survival of our country ..." Senator Yoshimasa examined his snifter of Peshastin. Finally, he looked up, riveted a steady gaze upon Andrew, and blurted, "How good a friend of Mario Pavía are you?"

"Just a casual acquaintance—"

The senator snorted. "Look, every time you take a piss, I know by how much, so don't you shit me. Don't you ever shit me."

Surprised, Andrew found a wrinkled finger wagging in his face, backed by an angry Samurai-like scowl.

"He's your mistress's son-in-law and a native mejicano ... right?"

Andrew felt blood throb in his neck. With difficulty, he controlled himself. "Yes, Sir. ... I apologize, Sir."

"That's better."

"Sir, Mario is a naturalized North-American citizen and loves his adopted country."

The senator dismissed Andrew's response with an impatient wave of a hand. "Whatever! ... I'm interested in Mister Pavía's loyalty only if it affects your own."

"Look, Senator Yoshimasa, I am a loyal North-American citizen too, and, certainly, if Mario had a conflict of interest between Fuerza Cortés and this country, he'd opt for the latter. What are you driving at, anyway?"

The senator leaned forward and fixed piercing black eyes upon Andrew. "Mister Drake, we have an opportunity here to break México's monopoly in our energy war with each other. You've investigated these arsons from the beginning and have demonstrated great capabilities. You passed a security check; therefore, I have decided that I want you as my liaison here in Franklin. ... What about it?"

Andrew paused to think over his options. "How would that position change my current job?"

"Not much ... your authority in this particular investigation would be a bit more. However, if you don't accept my offer, you'll be out of it all together."

Andrew thought, ... *and I'd lose access to you, old man.* He took his time emptying his glass. Then, he extended it toward the senator. "Could I have more Peshastin, Senator?"

"Only if you are working for me," the senator said with a rare show of humor.

Andrew forced a laugh and kept his arm outstretched.

The senator doled out a small amount of his liquid gold. "It's agreed then, Mister Drake."

Andrew smiled and clinked his glass against the senator's.

"I must say that, were I not of Japanese descent, possibly I would not have offered you this position ... but, I refuse to repeat what the government of the United States did during World War II to citizens of Japanese blood."

Andrew was dumbstruck. "Sir, do you know about the War of the World Two? It occurred before the Wall, didn't it?"

The senator laughed derisively. "My boy, it was called World War II—World War II. ... Yes—over a century before. My grandfather told me about it when I was little."

"He wasn't afraid? ... afraid to tell you about events that happened before the Wall, I mean."

"No, I was mature for my age. I'd already learned to keep my mouth shut. Besides, my grandfather only spoke of history that pertained to our Japanese heritage."

"As a powerful senator, don't you have access to the archives that were sealed during the Wall?"

The Senator laughed. "Mister Drake, the revisionists of the Wall destroyed almost all historical records before saner minds could prevail and save them. Yet, the revisionists did succeed in isolating the remaining information from the public. Even I cannot access them."

"Sir, could you tell me about the War of ah … World War II? I cannot believe that Japan was ever our enemy. Was it really true?"

"Enough! I've told you too much as it is. … Mister Drake, under the circumstances, we had better not tempt Mister Pavía. You will no longer confide in him. … Yes, I know about your little trip to La Paz and your meeting with Señor Pavía … the father, that is."

"Sir, I already have Mario investigating how the arsonist got his hydroxygen. I can't just cut him off now—he'd be suspicious."

The senator paused and pursed his lips. "Very well, continue to work with him— but only in that aspect of the investigation. After all, Winnipeg and San Francisco are cooperating in that area also.

"Mister Drake, remember … what's important here—is the bottom line. We must discover for North America, the secret of hydroxygen ignition. Your suspected arsonist knows that secret, and we've just got to get it out of him."

"First, Senator, 'we've just got to get' him out of his coma."

* * *

The doctor ushered the senator and Andrew into the patient's room. "Gentlemen, your man will survive. He is still in a coma, but a brain scan suggests that, with time, he will regain consciousness."

"When? How soon? I want him awake now."

Andrew stifled a smile at the doctor's obvious irritation with the senator's overbearing manner.

"Medicine isn't like politics, Senator Yoshimasa. We can't get what we want just by snapping our fingers. We can do nothing more than let nature take its course. We might wait from a few hours to many days."

"Can't you infuse oxygen to the damaged area of the brain."

The doctor snorted. "Of course, but the procedure is risky."

The senator approached the patient and scrutinized his face from many angles. "Very well. … When he awakens, notify me immediately. No one is to speak with him before I. If the media discover that he is here, keep them away and don't answer their questions. If you have nothing else for us, Doctor, we must be going."

"One thing more. … He possesses a prosthetic knee."

"So? … Thousands of people have them."

"Not this model. They stopped putting it in people long before the Wall."

Andrew gasped.

Apparently unimpressed, the senator said, "Let us be on our way, Mister Drake. … Good day, Doctor."

8—HARBINGER

I'm the Prophet of the Utterly Absurd,
of the Patently Impossible and Vain.

—Rudyard Kipling

A few minutes later

Back in the security of the senator's cabin, Andrew let his curiosity surface. "Senator, I believe that you know this man. When told about his knee, you weren't even surprised. When I told you that we couldn't identify him, you mocked me. You do know him, don't you?"

"Possibly." The senator remained impassive and seemed reluctant to respond further. After a long while, he continued:

"Seven years ago, seemingly from nowhere, a Pierre Talon appeared in political circles and promptly made trouble. He railed about the world's overpopulation, the ravaged environment, and our declining geneticism (sic). As a self-proclaimed harbinger of the decadence of the human race, he preached that certain measures should be taken, which would forestall this downfall of our species."

Andrew thought for a moment. "I don't remember any news about him ... and what's he got to do with the arsons?"

"Listen to me, Mister Drake. Be quiet and listen. ... You don't know of him because he was deemed a charlatan and mentally unbalanced, so, before he reached the masses, he was secretly incarcerated."

"Why?"

"Mister Drake, I'm surprised at you. Obviously, the man was a danger to society. However, he was not taken seriously because of what he preached—but of how. By ruffling the feathers of powerful vested interests, he caused his own downfall."

"Were you, Senator, partly responsible for his eclipse?"

"In a small way, yes, but my job is to protect the constituency from crackpots."

"You mean—protect the paying lobbyists—don't you?"

A flare of anger in the senator's eyes made Andrew regret his brashness. *Oh, shit! Why do I open my mouth before I think?*

"In my youth, your remark would have offended me, but age makes one more practical. ... Yes, I protect the power brokers—they put me where I am. I shan't apologize for it."

"Your family's apple orchards are nothing but sand because of the greed of the Establishment. Doesn't that disturb you? After all, you are in an enviable position of power. You could have made happen the changes that this Pierre Talon professed."

The senator chuckled. "Despite your graying sideburns, Mister Drake, you are still a typical grassroots—novice—no ... dreamer."

Andrew felt his face flush. *He's mocking my political naïveté ...*

"Do you really believe that an honest and capable politician can make the right things happen, Mister Drake? ... Never! Do you think that parliament—or even the

25

president—can succeed? ... Never! Only an aroused and determined body of constitu-
ents can, and how many of those have you seen lately? ... None! No, my friend, your
mind wanders in the clouds.

"Had I supported this Pierre Talon's views—by now, I would have been turned out
to pasture ... or possibly even lynched. You are partially right though—my family's
orchards did succumb—but, to the inevitable—not, the preventable. No power on
Earth can prevent the fall of the human race. We are condemned by our collective
greed to destroy ourselves. I may be selfish, but, at my age, I am resigned to our fate.
For all the good it will do them, let the young be the martyrs."

Silently, the senator's cabin continued on its way to Andrew's apartment. Andrew
wondered what the senator was thinking.

He was startled when Senator Yoshimasa dropped an info pellet into the computer's input tube. The cabin's screen filled with data, and a voice spoke of Pierre
Talon. At first mildly curious, eventually, Andrew sat entranced as he watched and listened to the computer's output:

"Be aware that the following information is classified A7 security. ... Over seven
years ago, in February 2123, a man calling himself Pierre Talon began a personal cam-
paign to warn the world of the devastating effects of modern civilization and of the
huge human population—over fifteen billion souls—upon life on this planet and in this
star system. He brutally attacked our society for its long-term pollution of Earth's environment and the resultant degradation of our genetic heritage. He accused individuals
of negligence in maintaining the health of their living spaces.

"This Pierre Talon criticized governments and businesses for their failure to safeguard the ecosystem. He scribbled damaging articles, ranted accusatory speeches, but-
tonholed powerful politicians, and, in the end, alienated himself from the most
influential persons in the world. In his feverish effort to force his message upon them,
he only offended them."

A series of holographs of the man called Pierre Talon flashed on the screen.

Andrew gasped. "Oh, my God, he is the arsonist. This Pierre Talon and the man in
a coma are one and the same."

The senator grunted in agreement, and the computer continued:

"The alleged Pierre Talon finally realized that he was losing his battle of words.
He believed that he could make a comeback by making himself more credible through
the perpetration of a hoax. Its disclosure proved him to be insane.

"He claimed that he was born on April twenty-fifth 2012, but that was absurd
because he was obviously in his middle thirties—not an old man of over a hundred
years of age. However, medical archives, exempt from the Wall purge, prove that a certain Pierre Talon actually existed—born in that same year—2012, and on April
twenty-fifth. A brilliant theoretical physicist, he disappeared at age thirty-three along
with his fellow crew members in a spaceship powered by an experimental, matter-antimatter thruster. The spaceship was lost in the year 2045 ... eighty-five years ago.

"To resolve this paradox, a theory was proposed by the media: Perhaps, before the
pretender started his crusade, he discovered his resemblance to the real Pierre Talon.
Then, in the belief that he might eventually need this ruse to succeed in his mission, the
pretender took his identity. Note that this was only a theory concocted by someone in
the media."

Images of both men in similar poses appeared on the screen.

"Amazing!"

The senator responded, "There's even more 'amazing' to come, Mister Drake."

The computer continued: "The pretender offered to undergo a medical examination. He claimed that at age 18, after a football injury, his right knee was replaced. Miraculously, the record of this operation, performed in 2030, was found in an archival data vault."

Andrew's jaw dropped. He muttered, "The doctor said 'before the Wall.' "

The senator nodded knowingly. "The contents of the medical record proved that the two individuals were one and the same. All of their biopatterns matched—including DNA."

"But, that's impossible. How can—"

"We thought so, too," the senator interrupted, "but Einstein's Special Theory of Relativity came to the rescue. ... At this point in the investigation, Pierre Talon was sequestered from the public and the media, and all data were classified top secret. That's why you couldn't discover his identity. ... Ssh! Let's be quiet, it's coming up on the screen, now."

"—Pierre Talon claimed that they had underestimated their acceleration and velocity calculations. For weeks, the thruster accelerated them more than they had calculated for until they approached the full velocity of light rather than the planned quarter velocity. Thus, time, in the spaceship, passed much slower than back on Earth. The end result was that he—relatively unaged—returned to a future earth.

"The media accepted this part of his story after physicists convinced them of its possibility. Had Pierre Talon stopped there, perhaps he would have been believed, and his crusade could have partially succeeded.

"Obviously, Pierre Talon, returning to Earth 78 years later, was shocked by the declined state of the quality of life. He felt forced to do something to redress it. He needed to shock the world, so he gambled. He claimed that the spaceship came down, not in 2123, but to a ravaged earth in the far future—in the year 2786. Supposedly, the remains of the human race consisted of high-tech in-valids living in cities 'floating' five miles above the poles in order to escape surface temperatures of 180 degrees Fahrenheit. He insisted that he returned to 2123 after a three-year stay in the future.

"Experts agree that time travel into the past is impossible. Repeated, unsuccessful attempts to make him recant his claim led to his permanent incarceration. In 2127, Pierre Talon escaped from the insane asylum and was not seen since ... until today."

After the screen blanked out, Andrew continued to stare at it. He shook his head. "Wow! This Pierre Talon really took his mission in life seriously, didn't he. Will he be returned to the asylum, Senator?"

"If he is proved to be the arsonist, he may be executed. After all, those fires killed many people."

Andrew pooh poohed the senator. "All deadwood! They had already expired. The arsons just made their deaths official."

"Agreed. But, under the law, they were still human beings—and murdered."

"Yes, I guess you're right."

The cabin glided to a stop.

Andrew descended, bid the senator good-bye, and entered his apartment.

9—SEDUCTRESS

She did not seduce, she ravished.

—George Meredith

A moment later
Andrew's apartment
Seattle, Franklin

"Andy, where have you been?" Kathy whispered. "The computer couldn't locate you. Jane Stevens is here. She's in the kitchen now, but she wanders around your place as if she owns it."

"Did you invite her?"

"Ssh! Be quiet. ... No, of course not. She's waiting to see you, you dummy ... says you've captured my son's murderer. Is that true, Andy? I want him dead—do you hear? ... dead."

"Hold it, Kathy. First, he has to be charged, tried, convicted, and sentenced ... but you just can't wait, can you?"

"He ruined my life, Andy. Can't you see that?"

"So, it's finally boiled down to that—your life—not Douglas's."

"You bastard," she whispered, "you always twist everything I say."

"Ssh, let's go see Jane."

Andrew entered the kitchen, and there she was. He could not help but gawk. Jane faced the window and looked down upon Seattle like some svelte Tutsi lord. He had never seen her looking better—even from behind. He noticed the two firm mounds of her buttocks and felt blood rush to his crotch. The rays from the setting sun pierced her outfit and outlined her tall, supple body—especially her thighs—nice and long and hard ... rock-hard. He knew that they had to be—Jane took good care of her body. After all, she established her college's record in the 400-meter hurdles back in aught eight. To Andrew, she looked younger than Kathy, although he knew her to be seven years older ... but she was his junior.

"Hi, Jane. You're lookin' real good today."

Instantly, Jane spun around, and her long, black hair whirled straight out for the briefest moment before settling to her shoulders. A rebel strand found its way between her breasts, which strained to erupt from her bodice. At Andrew's compliment, she broke into a proud, toothy smile. Her beauty—the whiteness of her teeth in contrast to her dark skin—took Andrew's breath away.

She seems so vivacious and tantalizing ... more than Kathy, he thought.

"Thanks, Andy, you look great to me, too." She moved close, put her arms around his chest, and kissed him on the neck.

Impulsively, Andrew thrust his hips forward. Jane's response in kind made his temples throb. He knew that they remained pressed together for only an instant, but it seemed longer.

28

He wondered if Kathy entered the kitchen in time to witness their warm greeting. Actually, he didn't care, yet he made a half-hearted effort to hide his agitation from her.

"Well, Jane, so you've heard—"

"—about the arsonist's capture? ... Yes—and the asylum people refuse interviews and won't let my people near him for one, either."

"Well, you wouldn't get anything out of him anyway. He's still in a coma."

" 'Still in a coma' is news in itself, but we need more than that. This is big news. Come on, Andy, what gives?"

"Top secret ... they even hesitated to give me a security clearance. I guess they figured I already knew so much, they'd have to let me in on it just to shut me up."

"They, they, they! It's Senator Yoshimasa—pure and simple—isn't it?"

"Yeah, and, if you want anything, it has to come from him."

"But, Andy, I would prefer something from you," Jane said, as she rolled her large, brown eyes.

"What's that supposed to mean?" interrupted Kathy.

"Whatever you want it to mean, Kathy dear. ... I don't trust the darling senator, so I'd rather have Andy inform me. ... Anything wrong in that?"

Andrew was amused by Jane's affected innocence and glanced at Kathy to catch her response. He saw none. Apparently, she thought the incident too juvenile to merit one.

Jane continued. "The public wants and needs to know what's going on. If you deny the media access to your prisoner and his capture site much longer, they'll just have to fill in with rumors and hearsay. Biased or distorted news will result. You don't want that, do you, Andy?"

Andrew knew that he had already succumbed to Jane's insistence ... and charm. "No, of course not. ... I'll see what I can do."

"Thanks, Andy. ... Well, I must be going. I'll talk to—"

On a whim, Andrew blurted, "Jane, why not stay for dinner." He turned toward Kathy. "We'd enjoy her company, wouldn't we?"

Andrew noticed that Kathy's scorching look—targeted for him—was intercepted by Jane.

"I'd love to, but I've got a dinner date with an absolutely charming man. Good-bye, Andy, I'll talk to you in the morning." She cupped his head in her hands and kissed both cheeks—French style. Then, with a backward " 'Bye, Kathy," she left.

During dinner, Andrew dared not speak to or even glance toward Kathy. She responded in kind, then arose and muttered—as if to no one in particular, "I'm going to bed ... see you tomorrow."

10—ENIGMA

It is a riddle wrapped in a
mystery inside an enigma.

—Winston Churchill

Two days later, July 6, 2130
Andrew's Arson Control Center
Bellevue, Franklin

Andrew was perplexed. He knew that he must solve four questions whose answers must lie in the ruins of Pierre Talon's laboratory. What was the origin of the hydroxygen? How was the catalyst produced? Where was the data stored? How was the operation financed?

He was elated when, despite sifting through much incomprehensible data, the investigation solved the first question quickly. He was amazed when he learned that the hydroxygen was produced on the premises by an unknown process beyond the capability of current technology.

Andrew—with Senator Yoshimasa's approval, of course—relayed a limited amount of findings to Mario Pavía.

"Mario, tell me what you think of this. It should be coming up on your screen now."

The computer started its transmission to La Paz:

"Hidden by a sophisticated, surveillance-jamming system, an unusually-efficient solarcell array blanketed the hillside that covered the laboratory's roof. The generated energy disassociated water from nearby springs into hydrogen and oxygen. How the two gases were fused into room-temperature liquid hydroxygen is still a mystery.

"Used canisters, easily purchased at any recyclation (sic) depot, stored the hydroxygen. Supposedly to confuse investigation, the canisters' labels were counterfeit. A robotic retinal pattern of pixels made up their master image."

The computer's output came to a halt.

"Is that all? You didn't discover the stabilizer-fusing process or anything about catalytic production?"

Andrew winced at Mario's disappointed voice and groped for a plausible answer. "Well, ah ... no, Mario ... the technology is beyond us, but we're working on it."

"Andy, you make it sound downright futuristic. We'd send up a team to help you, but the Mexican government is having trouble getting approval from Winnipeg.

"Anyway, I believe we can solve the label mystery. A robosentry at our canister warehouse here in La Paz illegally transmitted some of its retinal images about two months ago. At the time, we didn't know the answers to how, what, and to whom. But, now, some futuristic, telecommunication technology, seemingly, corrupted the robot's mission into transmitting label images to Pierre Talon. Also, some of our nanotech robots have stopped transmitting. Possibly, they were destroyed. I hope that our nano-security network hasn't been breached."

"Mario, you've used the term futuristic twice—"

"Well, how else can you describe what's going on? You have investigated this from the start and, certainly, are aware that we are confronting a very advanced technology here. How could this Pierre Talon have come up with it?"

"I don't know, Mario," Andrew lied, "I really don't know. ... I've got to go, now."

"Sure, Andy. By the way, how's it going with Kathy?"

"Not too good. At home, she hardly speaks ... contemplates imagined problems, I guess. However, Jane says she's a terror on the job—always work, work, work at a feverish pitch. Perhaps, she hopes to escape her gloomy thoughts by focusing all of her attention on her career. ... Well, 'bye, Mario."

"Good-bye, Andy."

Andrew felt bad about deceiving Mario, but the senator was just too powerful to cross. He was sorely tempted though. *This Pierre Talon, if he survives, is a man whose friendship I definitely intend to cultivate.*

Andrew knew that the answer to the second question—about catalyst production—would come with difficulty. He suspected that the apparatus that Pierre Talon destroyed had created the catalyst, but, because so little of the equipment was intact, the scientists could not reconstruct the process.

He hated to admit that this failure probably resided in the incompetence of the investigating scientists. Although they were the world's best, the fault was not theirs. This advanced technology—so far above anything yet known—just overwhelmed them.

Andrew was sure that the answers to questions three and four, if found at all, would surface together.

He was unable to discover Pierre Talon's database. Perhaps, the man had time enough to destroy it—there was no trace of its remains. Yet, the purpose of much of the equipment remained to be discovered. Possibly, the answers lay there.

Helter skelter, questions and answers came to Andrew's mind in sharp staccatos: Who backed the operation? Could one man alone—Pierre Talon—be behind those arsons? That seemed unlikely. The laboratory must have cost hundreds of millions of dollars to build. Certainly, the advanced technology was developed elsewhere.

Was the laboratory a secret project of the North-American government? Was Andrew's little military operation against it just one, humongous blunder? He shuddered at the thought, although he doubted that the government was involved. If it were, Senator Yoshimasa would know. Maybe, he does know but hasn't told me.

Andrew's fears subsided when he remembered that the laboratory did, indeed, contain a fugitive from justice—Pierre Talon. Finally, he was reassured when he recalled that the hydroxygen in the arson jobs definitely did come from that laboratory—no government could be behind those criminal acts ... or could it? All was an enigma.

Andrew's reveries ended with the computer's summons: "Pierre Talon is conscious. Your presence is requested at the asyl—"

"I'm on my way."

11—SKULLDUGGERY

'Tis the talk, and not the
intrigue, that's the crime.
—George Granville, Baron Lansdowne

Later that day
Franklin State Asylum Number Fifteen, Building 23A
Bellevue, Franklin

Pierre Talon sat up in bed. He watched holovision of himself while a nurse shaved him and combed his hair. A final glance confirmed that he was presentable to whomever he must face. The nurse commented on his youthful good looks, although Pierre noticed only his uncommon pallor. He came out of his coma a few hours before and found an aching left shoulder and arm in a restrainer.

He wanted news about the seizure of his laboratory, but those around him would answer only questions of a medical nature. The computer wouldn't respond to him either. He wondered if some of his picogremlins still resided in his body. Even if they did, he had no way of commanding them to help him escape. Besides, in his condition, he knew escape was impossible—even without bars on the window and guards at the door.

Pierre saw a robosentry enter and heard it announce, "You have a visitor."

A short, wiry man of asian face strode in. Pierre shuddered in recognition … his old enemy, Mizuno Yoshimasa.

"Good day, Mister Talon. You seem to be in good shape … considering."

"Good day to you, Senator. Yes, I need to be in condition to continue my mission."

The senator snorted. "Sir, your missionary days are over. These arson jobs of yours promise you either another asylum internment or an interment two meters under."

"Very cute. Then, I assume criminal charges will be brought against me. I'll have a trial, won't I? … a public trial." Pierre felt excited. "That's it! A widely publicized trial—to scatter my message across the nation, no … around the world."

"Mister Talon, I can put you back in the asylum whence you escaped—without fanfare—without publicity."

"—an empty threat. … You desperately want something only I can give … but I won't … without something in return."

"Ha! You flatter yourself. You can give me nothing."

The senator's laugh sounded forced. "Ah, but you know that is untrue. You want the secret of the hydroxygen catalyst."

He caught the senator's wince. In that instant, Pierre knew that he would eventually win.

"What you don't know, Senator, is that … not only can I give you the secret you seek, but, to this country, to the human race, and to this entire planet, I can give—I must give—infinitely more … something more vital than anything any person has offered humankind since the dawn of our species.

"Conversely, my isolation in an asylum for the rest of my days would allow life on this planet to continue its decline until, in the year 2789, the human species will have become extinct. No matter what you may wish to believe, my dear Senator, I did live on this dying planet over 650 years into the future, and I did witness the extinction of our species. What I learned in that time—"

"You are insane; you will be put—"

The senator's rude interruption irritated Pierre. He cut the little man off with an accusing finger and a bellow. "Be quiet! I am more sane than any person in the Solar System. You, Senator, are the insane one … you and your cronies. You protect the huge corporations that wreak havoc on life's habitat—all in the name of profit."

The senator turned speechless. He seemed suddenly introspective.

Pierre decided to push his advantage. "Let us cease parrying, Senator Yoshimasa. If you support my cause and allow me access to the media, I will give you the secret of the hydroxygen catalyst."

The senator appeared to be taken aback, but he recovered quickly. His eyes narrowed. "We'll obtain the secret anyway, Mister Talon. My scientists are sifting through every speck of evidence in that laboratory. We will find your partners in crime and make them talk."

This man is exasperating, Pierre thought. "Your people will discover nothing. First, I alone possess the secret. I destroyed the apparatus beyond anyone's comprehension. Second, I have no 'partners in crime.' Third, you misunderstand my proposal.

"I propose to give you the secret of the catalyst … not to your scientists, but to you … not to the North-American government, but to you … to you alone … only you." Pierre pointed at the senator each time he uttered the word "you."

He paused to let the significance of his proposal seep into the senator's soul, which he judged to be a greedy one. He knew that time was his ally. He knew they would find nothing of use in the laboratory. He knew that the senator would return—eventually—and bow to his demands. … Of this, he was certain.

Pierre could prove that he visited the future but preferred that the fact be accepted through his powers of persuasion. He remembered the warning of Boniface the Valid about the consequences of revealing to the past, too many secrets of the future. Yes, he must hold these proofs in reserve and dole them out sparingly.

However, revealing the secret of the catalyst, in return for being allowed to alert humankind of its peril, was justified. After all, México already possessed the secret. Not only could Pierre more easily create a better catalyst but better hydroxygen and a better stabilizer, as well. His willingness to break México's energy monopoly was tempered not by compassion or patriotism but by his unique awareness of future history.

The door slid open, and a man of Pierre's own age entered.

"Ah, Mister Drake, there you are." The senator laid his hand on the man's shoulder and said, "This is Andrew Drake, Mister Talon. He is responsible for your presence here. … He is your captor."

Pierre nodded warily at the staring man. "Please excuse my coolness toward you, Mister Drake, but everyone condemns me. … You see, historically, the bearer of sad tidings is put to death ... and, now, I am accused of murder. ... What is your opinion of me, Mister Drake? Do you see a monster before you, too?"

As the moment passed, Pierre realized that the silent stare was of awe rather than of revulsion. He saw Mister Drake gulp and glance sideways at the senator before he heard the man say, "Even monsters are innocent before proven guilty."

The senator snorted and turned toward the exit. "You need your rest, and we have other duties. Mister Drake ... Come!"

"Sir, I—aah ... I'd like to stay awhile, if I may."

"If you wish, but remember, the room is monitored, so don't you two talk about anything stupid."

The door slid open and shut, and, in between, the senator vanished.

12—REMINISCENCES

Reminiscences make one feel
so deliciously aged and sad.

—George Bernard Shaw

A moment later

Pierre felt uneasy under Mister Drake's silent stare. "Please believe me—I am no monster. Come. Sit down. Perhaps we can talk despite the monitor."

Almost reverently, the man blurted, "You were an adult before the Wall, weren't you. You know history, don't you?"

"Yes, and those ignorant of it repeat it. Yet, I'm kept from revealing it to the world."

"Then, reveal it to me."

Pierre smiled. "If I do, will you believe me?"

"Yes ... Oh yes, I want to believe. I need to know what happened before the Wall."

Pierre sighed and waited a moment before he spoke. "Well, I left for the future in 2045, only 16 years before the Wall occurred, but I'll do my best.

"When I left, the United States was still an intact country. The southwestern states of the United States were yet to be absorbed into México—with San Francisco as its new capitol. The high Mexican birth rate and migration away from the rising temperatures of equatorial Earth were yet to maximize their impact. The Great Amazonian Desert was yet to rival the size of the Sahara. Earth's atmosphere was yet to lose more oxygen. The corn belt was yet to shift into the poorer soil of Canada. Finally, Americans seeking cooler climes were yet to inundate that country. The causes of the North American Revolution of 2094 were only beginning when I left for the Earth of the future."

"All these changes certainly must have shocked you."

"Yes, indeed. Upon returning from 2789 to 2123, rather than to the year of my departure, the condition of Earth really did shock me. Certainly, 2789 was horrible, but the earth of 2123 was further along in its demise than I had thought was possible during the 78 years that I had missed."

"What shocked you the most?"

"The deterioration of Earth's atmosphere. Farming, deforestation, and the burning of fossil fuels had altered the composition of Earth's atmosphere. Carbon-dioxide and methane replacement of oxygen caused an emphysemic pandemic of monstrous proportions. Millions suffered lung damage. Tens of thousands suffocated. Riots spread. The clamor to cleanse the atmosphere threatened entire industries. However, their deep-pocketed lobbyists countered the pressures of a disorganized constituency preaching reform. Environmental concerns failed.

"Economic realities succeeded. In low-power applications, solarcell technology already usurped the place of fossil fuels. However, a practical replacement for transportable concentrated energy was yet to be found. Fossil-fuel depletion resulted in economic depression and fostered worldwide competition in energy research.

"When hydroxygen was invented, it proved more expensive than fossil fuels. Of course, the environmentalists wholeheartedly embraced the new technology—it was pollutant-free. Water vapor was its sole by-product, which produced much-needed rain. Gone would be increasing smog, acid rain, and carbon and nitrogen oxides.

"Of course, you know that, in 2090, long after the Wall occurred, the Fuerza Cortés company in México mastered the process of cheaply producing mass quantities of hydroxygen and of safely utilizing its energy. México became one of the world's economic powers. Thus, the consequences of the energy crisis were resolved in México's favor."

"Yes, I know vaguely about it, but, even after the Wall, the National Censorship Board has always tried to squash memories of incidences that are embarrassments to the government."

They're not even taught in school?"

"Nope. Please, continue. Over the years, I've only heard bits and pieces of what you're saying. You put it all in context. It's wonderful."

"Well, in return for advantageous terms in acquiring hydroxygen from México, the United States allowed a secession referendum to transpire in the nine states of Mexican majority. To Washington's surprise, every state except Kansas passed the initiative. The United States renounced the results of the vote, and the consequent alienation of México began the country's most serious energy crisis—the North American Revolution of 2094.

"Due to the climatic shift toward Earth's poles, Canada approached the United States in population and economic production. Even so, together, they still lagged far behind the world's superpowers—the Republic of Europe and Northern Asia (RENA) whose capital was Monnetville (formerly Gdansk) and the Confederation of Asiatic States of the Orient (CASO) headquartered at Tientsen.

"México's energy hegemony gave it leverage enough to demand incorporation of those areas of the United States with over a two-thirds Mexican population—from Mount Shasta to the Rio Grande and from the Pacific to the Brazos. Already, México had swallowed Central and South America down to the middle of the Great Amazonian Desert. Of course, Argentina continued to dominate the subcontinent since the breakup of Brazil following the deforestation and desertation (sic) of that former country's territory.

"Establishment of this larger and more powerful Mexican nation prompted the union of Canada and the United States into the Federated Provinces and States of North America headquartered in Winnipeg.

"These boundary changes were the most visible indications of a new order in the Western Hemisphere—an order that had arrived during my absence. Although these geopolitical events disturbed me, my main concern was the worsening of the world's genetic and environmental health."

Pierre felt tired but continued. "How can I—only one man—alert the entire world to a peril of such magnitude? Even if my efforts spur universal recognition of the peril, how can I—only one man—force society to apply corrective measures while special-interest groups continue to oppose me?"

Pierre stopped and looked at Mister Drake, thinking that, perhaps, by some miracle, the man might offer some answers, but he only stared silently, in apparent awe.

Pierre tried again. "If my arson trial is publicized, how can I—only one man—make an impact enough to save the world? What else can I do to help win this war of survival?"

Finally, Mister Drake answered. "I don't know. I really don't know."

The door slid open, and the robosentry entered. "Mister Drake, you must leave now."

* * *

Pierre needed rest. He knew that he must be ready to engage the enemy again tomorrow. He snuggled deeper into his hospital bed. His eyes closed … Before he slept, the specter of failure returned to haunt him … a vision of Earth … devoid of human life … devoid of any life.

13—LUNCH

So munch on, crunch on, take your nuncheon,
Breakfast, supper, dinner, luncheon.

—Robert Browning

A month later, August 6, 2130
Jane Stevens' Informational News Agency
Bellevue, Franklin

Andrew was proud of himself. Finally, he had his way with a stubborn Senator Yoshimasa.

The many weeks of sifting through the wreckage of Pierre Talon's laboratory revealed precious little more than what was discovered during the first few days after its seizure. The catalyst mystery remained no closer to a solution than before. Also, further attempts to locate possible accomplices for questioning were fruitless.

Andrew realized that Senator Yoshimasa was more than disappointed by these failures. The senator's fury was awesome. Andrew witnessed his mimicry of an embattled Samurai in accompaniment to unintelligible screams of guttural Japanese. He wondered if the senator's utterances were punctuated with an English accent or if—perhaps—his gibberish wasn't even genuine Japanese.

Many times, he heard the senator attempt offhandedly to question Pierre for information. Each time, Pierre gave the senator nothing but increased demands. Andrew admired Pierre's seemingly indifferent attitude about the whole affair.

At some point, the senator seemed to realize that diplomacy—or guile—was better than intimidation. The time was ripe for Andrew's plan—a plan that, after a few changes, was acceptable to both Messieurs Talon and Yoshimasa. However, the senator made two points clear: He refused his presence at any of the interview sessions, and the computer must monitor every instant of the sessions—no secret communications.

* * *

Andrew arrived to meet Jane Stevens at her information control center. Lunchtime approached. He could have conducted his business with her over the computer or arrived at a different time, but he failed to suppress the urge to have lunch with that sleek lady. As soon as he entered, he noticed that she caught sight of him from across the room.

Jane smiled broadly, grabbed her jacket, and strode briskly toward him—hips undulating elegantly at every step.

His pulse quickened. Oh, my God! … that gliding walk—like a queen's.

She greeted him politely with light kisses on the cheeks. "I'm ready to go, Andrew dear."

Deeply, he inhaled her scent. His temples pounded. "Go where?" he teased. "I'm here only to say you've got your interview with Pierre Talon … and I'm in charge of access to him. What do you say to that, uh?"

"That's great news, Andy, but you do want to talk about it over lunch, don't you?" She grabbed his arm and cheerfully propelled him toward the exit.

"Think you can read my mind?"

"You bet ... when you arrive at this time of day."

"Well, let's go then." He followed her out.

Jane took him to one of her favorite restaurants—one that employed retardic service. Andrew preferred the more-precise robots. Evidently, Jane liked the human aspect of retards, even if the service was sometimes pretty bad. Andrew had to admit that retards were often quite comical. When they made their silly mistakes, Andrew could barely refrain from laughing. So long as they didn't become violent, he could tolerate them.

Over martinis, Andrew explained the terms of the interviews, but Jane was outraged.

"Dammit, Andy, if he's guilty, it's my job to expose him for what he really is."

"I admit you'd be quite the celebrity if you could, Jane, but that won't happen."

Her brown eyes sparkled daggers. "And why not?"

"Pierre won't let you. If you slant the story against him—make him look like a cold-blooded killer, he'd cut you off, and we'd be forced to get someone else. ... Jane, just let him tell his story."

"But I'm the one that's supposed to decide what's newsworthy here. I'm the one that's doing the interview, for Christ' sake."

"Look, this is not an interrogation. ... Okay? Pierre is going to give a monologue, and you are simply the medium through which it's piped to the public."

Jane was really hyper, now. She gestured with huge loops of her long, spider-like arms. "Andy, why is that guy getting all this consideration? He's just a lousy murderer—right?" She turned her head and suddenly burst out laughing.

He followed her lead and saw, at a discreet distance, their retardic waiter, mouth agape, eyes wide in fear. The poor fellow, drooling at a corner of his mouth, stared at Jane as one would at a frenzied dervish.

The incident seemed to clear away the tension.

"Jane, listen to me very carefully." Andrew ticked off facts finger by finger. "We possess absolute proof that he is a theoretical physicist, was born in the year 2012, was lost in space in 2045, returned in 2123, and accessed technology that is centuries ahead of what we've got now. When you consider everything—even though it boggles you—all of Pierre's claims make sense."

Lunch arrived, and, while they feasted on it, Andrew's eyes did likewise on Jane. Obviously, she relished his attention.

Andrew continued. "I've finally convinced Senator Yoshimasa to accept Pierre's demands. What if Pierre is right? What if he really did spend three years on a devastated, future earth—no matter how farfetched that may seem? It sure explains why he's done what he's done over the past few years. No doubt his frustrations finally culminated in these, finely-targeted acts of arson. ... No, Jane, the man needs to be heard. If he's a crackpot, there's little lost. But, if he isn't, well ... he might just save the world."

"Andy, you act as if Talon's murders are unimportant. They are not—they are terrible crimes. He has killed thousands. I can't just sit and dispassionately listen to his 'monologue,' as you call it. I've got to make him admit before my audience, that he is a murderer."

"Fine! Try it! He'll love it. He'll exploit you to his advantage. Even if he's guilty—which has yet to be proven—whom has he killed? In-valids—that's who—only in-valids."

"Christ, Andy, in-valids are people, too."

"Jane, I don't believe you realize how many in-valids exist in the world—tens of millions—maybe hundreds of millions. Many are unaware that they are even alive. Those that are aware, exist in a living hell. The cost of their care is an ever-increasing burden for the rest of us.

"The person in the street is oblivious of the problem because robots perform the actual care. The disguised institutions that contain and hide these in-valids are them-selves hidden from public view—down dead-end roads labeled 'private—no entry.'

"Most in-valids exist in squalor. In the more notorious places, they torture and kill each other. They die young and are thrown into mass graves if not dissected into spare parts or ground into pet food."

"My God, Andy, that is disgusting. Where do you hear such trash ... from Talon?"

"Yes, and I've checked some of it out ... and it's true. But, I've also found out something else."

"What's that?"

"Any attempt to investigate is fiercely resisted. Pierre warned me that even my life might be in danger. He said that many of those, who, seven years ago, publicly expressed support for him, have disappeared. While he was in the asylum, he thwarted the attempts on his own life only because of his advanced knowledge of robotics. When he finally escaped, he took a slew of robotic bodyguards with him."

"Andy, I admit that many in-valids exist in the world. Every family seems to have one or two. Why, so many?"

"Jane, everything is out of kilter and getting worse. The degraded environment creates in-valids. Laws protect them. Money and technology keep them alive.

"Nature destroys in-valids the moment they no longer can cope with the ecosys-tem. Just as the immune system protects the body from invaders, the harshness of the environment protects a species from degeneration.

"We 'civilized animals,' in our 'improvement' upon nature, try to modify this pro-cess of natural selection. The culprit is centuries of ingrained religious dogma. From childhood, we are taught that every living entity is God's creation, and to kill His cre-ation is a sin.

"First, we learned to pity and protect the weak, the poor, and the underprivileged. When modern medicine began to save the deformed and the insane, and, ultimately, to create monstrosities through in-vitro eugenics, we extended this misplaced compassion to them, also. These sentiments produced laws that protect life from the moment of conception. We have halted the natural 'weeding' process, which is so vital to the long-term vitality of a species. We are self-destructing for Christ' sake."

"... Well, Andrew Drake, after that speech, I'd guess that you've been taking les-sons from Talon. He must be quite a guy."

"Yes, Jane, he is. He possesses the vision to cut to the heart of the problem and the guts to try to solve it." He thought, ... *and the knowledge to make me rich.*

Andrew decided to broach a subject that he had wanted for some time to discuss with Jane. "Are you going to conduct the interviews by yourself? Won't some of your reporters help—such as your star repor—?"

"You mean Kathy? ... Well, I'd rather do these myself—at first. Talon is big news, you know. But, sure—once the interviews fall into a routine—why not ... if she'll do them."

"Thanks, Jane. In the long run, interviewing Pierre just might be good therapy for her."

"You mean once she no longer wants him dead."

"Yes, and I've made a point not to talk to her about him. She doesn't even know his name. To her, he's still a nameless, faceless entity. Of course, that'll change once the interviews begin. She's stubborn, but maybe, after you've had a few sessions with Pierre, you could try to mollify her—change her prejudiced opinion of him."

Jane reached across the table and, with her slender fingers, softly touched Andrew's cheek. "Andy, before I try to change hers, I'll need to change mine. You've already told me things that make me consider Talon less harshly. Maybe, he can win me over, even more. I am trying to be open-minded. I'm doing this because of you, Andy."

"I appreciate it, Jane." Andrew felt her warmth as he took her hand in his and planted a long kiss in its palm. He glanced over at their waiter.

The retard's face was plastered with a stupid, ear-to-ear grin of approval.

14—LIGHTSPEED

Puro e disposto a salire alle stelle.

—Dante Alighieri

A week later, August 13, 2130
Franklin State Asylum Number Fifteen, Building 10D
Bellevue, Franklin

Jane entered the isolation block. She was apprehensive. She was to meet the man about whom she had been hearing so much—Pierre Talon. He had recovered from his wounds and had been moved out of the hospital wing into a special isolation cell in the asylum's old administration building.

Normally, a computer terminal already built into the cell would record interviews and send the recordings to Central Databank for censorship. After being edited, they'd pass to Public Database for viewing by anyone interested. However, Talon had insisted that the interviews be piped directly to Public Database—without censorship. In addition, he demanded live transmissions by the worldwide news networks by way of Jane's own holocameras. Jane was rankled by Talon's success in getting his demands met. She wondered what hold he had over Senator Yoshimasa to win his support.

Jane followed two robosentries down the long, gloomy corridor, which was flanked by the cells of the asylum's more infamous inmates. Her two, camera-transmitter robots walked behind. She felt as though she were being escorted to the gallows—two in front, two behind. She shivered.

They stopped before a solid door through which one of the robosentries apparently scanned the interior of the isolation cell before transmitting the unlock code. The latch clanked. With a rumble, the heavy door slid open.

Jane stepped into a sparse cell—in one corner, a cot; in another, a seatless toilet; and in the middle, securely attached to the floor, a small table and two chairs. She saw Andy. No doubt, he had arrived early to prime Talon for their meeting.

"Jane, may I present Pierre Talon." Andy gestured toward Talon with an elegant sweep of his arm.

Jane felt as if she were being introduced to some royal personage. He was a handsome man, rather slim—younger than she had presumed. His eyes drew her attention—they seemed to probe her very soul and made her feel spiritually naked.

"Pierre, ... Jane Stevens, director of INS—the Informational News Agency."

Talon stepped forward, grasped her hand, and shook it warmly. His eyes never left hers. "I am delighted to meet you ... such a charming lady."

Confused, Jane said, "Thank you, Sir." ... *Why am I saying "sir" to a murderer? ... but he's not at all like I'd imagined. An aura of sanctity appears to surround him.*

"Pierre," Andy said, "I must remind you that the interview is transmitted live ... to the whole world. I may get in trouble for warning you, but watch what you say."

"Andy, I insisted upon these conditions—remember? ... Thanks, anyway."

Andy left, and Jane found herself alone with Talon.

42

She ignored his presence and quietly went about her business of setting up the interview. She ordered the robots into position—one to train its holocamera on Talon, the other, on herself. She felt self-conscious—not just about being alone with Talon—but because she knew that Andy, Senator Yoshimasa, and God-knows-who-else were already monitoring their every gesture and utterance. She sensed the scrutiny of the computer's eyes and ears hidden behind the ceiling and walls. She doubted that there was even one cubic inch of unmonitored space in the room—including the toilet. After all, she was in an asylum.

"Are you ready, Mister Talon?"

"Anytime, Jane."

She bristled at his first-name intimacy yet remained impassive. "Cameras on. Transmit—three—two—one—now." She smiled into the camera, knowing that her sparkling teeth flashed white in striking contrast to her dark, African skin. Those teeth were her trademark. They had helped her obtain her first, news-anchor position. She was proud of them.

"Good evening, ladies and gentlemen. My name is Jane Stevens. Tonight, the Informational News Agency begins a series of interview sessions with a Mister Pierre Talon. I am reporting to you live from the man's isolation cell deep in a complex that is part of the Franklin State Asylums.

"First, let me bring you up to date on the news of the recent series of arsons that have occurred throughout the State of Franklin and the nation."

Jane recounted highlights of the arsons including descriptions of the targets and the destruction at each. At appropriate times, file holovideos displayed automatically in the transmission. She described the hunt for the arsonists, which culminated in Talon's capture in a laboratory proven to have produced the hydroxygen that caused the arson fires. She forced herself not to speculate and to present only the facts, yet she succeeded in making clear whom she thought the perpetrator might be.

Jane decided that a frontal attack was best. "Mister Talon, you were the only person found in that laboratory, and, by your own admission, you had no accomplices. ... I must ask you ... Are you the arsonist?"

Talon frowned. "Ms. Stevens, at this time, an answer to that question is inappropriate."

She forced a snort. "Obviously, if you are not the arsonist, you would say so—emphatically. Your response can only be construed to mean that you are the arsonist."

"Not at all. If I were not considered to be a suspect, would I get this interview? ... I think not. The world can believe what it wants. I need this interview—I have important things to tell the world. Besides, if I'm to be tried in court, I certainly wouldn't confess beforehand—even if I were guilty.

"Ms. Stevens, I am unhappy with the vein of your presentation. I assume that you are aware of the tack I wish to take, so let's take it, okay?"

Jane felt hot. She knew that Andy was having a good laugh at her expense. She ignored Talon's brashness and inserted into the transmission a heretofore top-secret file that Senator Yoshimasa had given her. It contained information about Talon's origins and his trip through time from 2045 to 2123. When she first read it, she didn't believe its contents; however, after a session with a renowned physicist, she became less skeptical.

While the contents of the file played out, Jane watched Talon intently. *He doesn't look dangerous, but, in this business, I've learned that looks means nothing. I cannot let his handsomeness sway me.* The file's transmission came to an end. *Boy, that stuff will really get everybody glued to holoscreens tomorrow night.*

"Mister Talon, why were you put in an insane asylum seven years ago?"

"Evidently, they thought I was crazy."

"How is that?"

"I told them I had arrived in 2123 from the future—not from the past."

Jane feigned an expression of confusion. "But, you are from the past—that is a well-established fact. How can you come from both the past and the future? ... and, isn't travel backward in time impossible?"

"I traveled from 2045 to the year 2786, but they wouldn't believe me."

She tried to appear incredulous. "I don't blame them. You go from barely conceivable to absolutely unbelievable, so—."

Talon interrupted. "Time travel can be either forward or backward. Up to the twentieth century, time travel in either direction was considered impossible—period. Then, Albert Einstein suggested the possibility of travel into the future in his Special Theory of Relativity. In subsequent decades, he was proven correct.

"In the twenty-third century, just a hundred years from now, the Theory of Universal Duality will be proposed, which will be the basis for the development of time travel into the past. Of course, time travel into the past will not become a reality for 550 years. I am the first person who will have used that technology."

Jane didn't even try to suppress a smirk. "So you used it in 2786?"

Straight-faced, Talon answered, "No, I will have remained in the future for three years, so it will have been in 2789 that I will have left the future for my time of original departure—2045. A miscalculation will have brought me back to 2123 instead."

Jane smiled as sweetly as she could. "For the moment, let's forget about how you returned from the future. Concentrate on how you got there in the first place. Why, in particular, was it you and not someone else?"

"Ms. Stevens, why, in particular, did humans evolve on Earth rather than on some other planet in the Universe?"

"Well, I ... uh—"

"Because, if they had, that other planet would be called Earth and we'd be on it. So, your question is rather foolish, don't you think?"

"No, I—"

"Ms. Stevens, let me tell you something that may sound fantastic and unbelievable, but it is the truth. Several years ago, I tried to convince others but was locked away for my efforts. Perhaps, with your help, this time, I will be believed and understood."

"Please ... go on. I'll try not to interrupt." Jane smiled as hypocritically as she could.

"Thank you. ... After the Drug War of 2035, I acquired my doctorate in astrophysics and started postdoctoral research—specializing in antimatter. The Lee-Yang Institute in Hofei, west of Shanghai, invited me to join a group, which already had made a greatly improved antiproton trap—an electromagnetic chamber that holds charged antimatter in isolation from matter. I needed to remain near my ailing mother, so, I accepted the position only after her death in 2037.

"I felt honored to be at the Lee-Yang Institute because its research had yielded many recent discoveries. One of the more important was proof that an energy beam of photons is not what it was thought to be—photons of energy. Photons do not exist as discrete entities, and neither does energy."

Jane listened with increasing interest. Although her major in college was journalism, she had been interested enough in modern physics to have taken several electives in that field. She gestured toward Talon. "But, photons and energy do exist. We'd be dead without them."

"Of course, Ms. Stevens, but they are not fundamental entities. May I explain? ... Thank You.

"At Lee-Yang, one trap was made to collect electrons, and another, their antimatter counterpart—positrons. Fast coherent beams of these particles from both traps were made to spew and converge. They 'converted' into an electromagnetic beam of energy composed of photons. So you see, energy is not 'energy' but equal quantities of conjugate matter and antimatter in the 'energy' mode of existence. Of course, neither is a photon a 'photon.' It is an electron-positron conjugate pair at lightspeed.

"Similarly, protomagnetic beams composed of proton-antiproton conjugate pairs can exist, which, at the same frequency, are many times more 'energetic' than electromagnetic beams because protons are many times heavier than electrons. Of course, in compensation, the lifetime of the virtual proton is shorter than that of the virtual electron by the same factor."

Jane felt overwhelmed and a bit exasperated. "Please, Mister Talon, could you just tell us how you went to the future—using less arcane explanations."

"Well, antimatter proved to have antimass."

"Give it to us in lay terms ... okay?"

"Matter gravitationally repulses antimatter."

With a wry smile, Jane stared at Talon. "Forget it—let's continue."

"I'm sorry. I get carried away—one of my bigger faults. ... Anyway, after seven years at Lee-Yang, my research group perfected a proton-antiproton thruster capable of accelerating a vehicle in space for months—to near light speed. We built that vehicle, and it sent us into the future."

Jane shook her head up and down. "Fine, fine ... then, tell us about the trip."

"I remember vividly the day the eight of us left earth orbit for the final test of the matter-antimatter thruster.

"We were to have been gone for less than a year, but we crashed back to a hot, desertic earth, 741 years later—in the year 2786."

Now, Jane was really intrigued. Talon possessed the most vivid imagination of anyone she'd ever met. She smiled. "How did it happen?"

"Well, all seemed perfect—ship, crew, support, and—we thought—the calculations. Our mission was to accelerate toward the Centaurus Constellation at a comfortable one 'g' for three months before reversing acceleration to return to Earth nine months later. Although Centaurus is our solar system's nearest neighbor at a distance of four light-years, we were to have approached it by under one percent that distance—175 billion miles—before reversing acceleration. It was not to be.

"The computer controlled the thrust to give an acceleration of one 'g' and verified our velocity and position by taking star-position and spectrographic readings. Early on, the discrepancies appeared: The Sun's Fraunhofer lines shifted too fast toward the infrared while those of Alpha Centauri did likewise into the ultraviolet. Yet, the anti-proton reserve declined normally. Eighty days out, the light from stars forward and aft winked out, while, those abeam sunk into deep red. Instead of the planned one-quarter lightspeed, we rapidly approached full lightspeed. Our acceleration calculated at four 'g's', but force measurements never deviated from one 'g' ... and our bodies felt nothing amiss either. We traveled half a trillion miles. ... It was uncanny."

Jane was surprised by her feeling of real concern. She was actually absorbed in this fairy tale of Talon's. Whatever his faults and crimes, Talon told a good story. "What did you do?"

"In desperation, we pivoted the spaceship a hundred eighty degrees and headed for home, but we approached Centaurus by another half-trillion miles before the ship's velocity reversed itself eleven weeks later. The second half of our odyssey mirrored the first, and we arrived back in the solar system eleven months after our departure, having traveled a fantastic two trillion miles."

Jane continued to stare at Talon. Then, she realized that her jaw was hanging. "Well, ah ... yes, fantastic ... fantastic indeed."

Talon seemed not to hear but to be totally engrossed in his story. "We could see Earth shimmering in the distance. From the crew came a cry of relief, but our elation was short-lived. Instead of our beautiful, blue, cloud-covered Earth, a near-cloudless planet with vast seas and brown continents hove into view. The shape of North America was familiar except for Florida. ... It was gone.

"Until then, we refused to believe our computers' indications—that we were in the year 2786. However, only cursory observations from a couple of swings around Earth was enough to confirm the awful truth.

"Dejected and expecting no answer, we hailed Earth from a broadcast scanner. Miracle of miracles—an immediate response in clear English amazed us and momentarily buoyed our spirits. The voice confirmed the date and added that our arrival was as expected. Expected? ... Our minds reeled, but we asked for the usual docking instructions—hoping for another 'miracle' ... no such luck.

"Although satellites orbited Earth, none possessed matching docking equipment. With rapidly-waning life support, time was of the essence. We abandoned the spacecraft and crash landed our emergency-entry vehicle in Antarctica at a location specified by the mysterious voice.

"Of course, we hadn't expected to crash, but no runway existed—only miles and miles of sand. At the last moment and to no avail, we opted for a wheels-up landing. The instant we started to cartwheel, I was sure that we were dead ... and we were ... except for me."

Jane chuckled. "So you were the only survivor?"

"Yes."

"No corroborative witnesses ... how convenient."

Talon's eyes flashed. "Well, that's the way it was."

"Yes, I am sure of it, but, please ... do go on."

"I do not know how much later consciousness returned. When it did, I saw before me a nude man suspended in midair ... eyes closed ... skin glistening.

"Memory of the crash returned, so I looked at myself to search for injuries. I could not find myself—I seemed invisible ... as if I were looking through the eyes of another. I moved a leg, then an arm ... nothing. Again, I moved them ... again nothing. The third time, I noticed the nude man mimicking my actions. His eyelids remained shut. I realized mine were shut also, yet ... I could see. I tried to open my eyes, yet ... I could not.

"My father's voice came to me—clear and comprehensible. I understood each word perfectly, yet ... I heard nothing.

"I could see without eyes. I could hear without ears. The other senses: I wondered about them, also. Could I taste, smell, and feel out-of-body, as well? My whereabouts—my very being—intrigued me. Had I entered Nirvana?

"My father spoke to me. I had always listened to my father, so ... I listened.

"He said, 'Welcome, Pierre Talon. We, at Cumulus, have waited many years for your arrival. We rejoice. We celebrate.'

"I asked, 'Am I in Heaven? Are you my dad? You sound like him.'

"Dad's voice answered. 'You are at Cumulus. I am Boniface, the Valid of Cumulus, the Supreme Archivist, and Analysis Council Monitor. My voice is, indeed, that of your father. The use of the voice most respected by the one with whom I communicate is most efficient. ... You need healing before you work. ... You will sleep now.'

"At those words, my eyelids became heavy. I wondered, Cumulus. ... He said 'Cumulus.' ... What is Cumulus? As my senses left me, I became aware of my physical reality ... suspension in a sea of warm air ... nude."

Jane acquired new respect for this man. Never before had she heard such a fascinating story told in such a convincing manner. Yet, she could not—would not—accept it as the truth. Possibly, it was a vivid dream that became reality only in the man's mind. "Mister Talon, your story is absolutely ludicrous ... ridiculous, even. What proof have you?"

"Proof?"

Jane raised her voice. "Yes, Mister Talon—proof, Proof, PROOF. As a scientist, you should know what the term means."

Talon's eyes narrowed.

Jane chuckled to herself. *I'm finally getting under his skin—maybe he'll lose his cool.*

Instead, he said, "I can give proof."

Talon's simple answer jolted her. Convinced that he was bluffing, she decided to lead him deeper into an even more-untenable position. "Then, in heaven's name, why haven't you done so? You could have saved everybody a lot of grief—yourself in particular."

Talon appeared to enter a brief trance before he stated, "Tomorrow night, the Bellevue Cascaders will have won by four to three."

Jane was puzzled. "Are you attempting to predict the outcome of tomorrow's game?"

"It is more than either an attempt or a prediction—it is an established fact."

"... in 2786?"

"Yes, and even after the game tomorrow night."

Talon's sudden grin, seemingly out of character, irked the hell out of her. "How much do you know about the future?" she asked innocently.

"Not as much as I'd like. The human race will have become extinct in 2789, but, if I alert the peoples of the world to their dilemma, they may be able to save our species. However, I know about almost everything that will occur up 'til then, provided the records will have survived."

For the sake of the interview, Jane went along with him. "Of course, you have all this memorized. I mean, you know the outcome of a game in, let's say ... the year 2300?" She literally displayed her tongue-in-cheek attitude.

"Yes, provided a record of it will have existed in 2789 when I will have scanned the Great Archives."

Jane shook her head in disbelief. "Mister Talon, all of your 'will have this' and 'will have that' are quite confusing. Do you really think that way? Will we think and talk that way when we all start flitting back and forth from past to future and vice versa?"

Talon sat and stared at Jane for several moments. He pursed his lips and drummed his fingers upon them.

She wondered about what was going through the crazy man's head.

Abruptly, he said, "Ms. Stevens, I have tolerated your put-down attitude, thus far, because I had respected your professionalism, but you have shown me ... none. This interview is ended. Please, leave." He bolted from his chair, strode to his cot, and plunked himself down—face to the wall.

Jane had difficulty believing what Talon just did. She recovered as best she could. "Ladies and Gentlemen, our first interview session with the accused arsonist, Pierre Talon, has come to a close. Please join us again tomorrow night. I am Jane Stevens for the Informational News Agency. Good night."

The red transmitter lights on the robots winked out.

Jane's fury exploded. "What in hell do you think you are doing? You can't leave like that—in the middle of an interview!" She raised her head and arms to heaven and yelled, "This is what I get for messing with a crazy man."

Talon remained silent—his face to the wall.

Andy burst in. "What's the matter with you two? The senator is furious. He'll be here at any moment."

"That's just fine. Maybe he can talk some sense into this 'Doctor' Pierre Talon. The man is either completely bonkers or trying to bamboozle the whole world. In either case, I won't be a party to it. I have to think of my reputation, you know."

Indignant, Jane flounced out of the cell—her robots, close behind.

15—PREDICTIONS

> Till old experience do attain
> To something like prophetic strain.
>
> —John Milton

Early the next morning, August 14, 2130
Jane Stevens' Informational News Agency
Bellevue, Franklin

Upon arrival at her agency, Jane found chaos. The entire world seemed to be calling and asking for information about Pierre Talon. She was surprised that most callers wanted to know about the results of future sporting events—probably to place sure bets. Many special-interest groups considered Talon a rabble rouser and wanted the interviews stopped. Some were skeptical theoretical physicists wanting to question the man themselves. The sheer volume of calls overloaded the automatic response system. Many callers requested to talk to a human, if not to Jane personally.

Despite her dread of Andy's inevitable arrival, she actually felt relief when, finally, he did appear. His presence gave her an excuse to leave the control-center floor for the haven of her office. In its privacy, she quickly raised her hands—palms out. "Andy … Don't say it! I've had it already today. I'm sorry it happened. I misjudged Talon. I thought I could manipulate him. Don't you see? … I don't want him to make fools of us."

Andy stepped closer and rested his hands on her shoulders. "It wasn't all your fault. Pierre was too sensitive … and too eager to get into the meat of his message to the world. That's been his problem all along.

"Last night, after you left, Senator Yoshimasa and I convinced Pierre we need more proof than just a win tonight for the Cascaders. There's a good chance the final score will be four to three, just as he said."

Eager to see a replay, Jane ordered, "Computer—show the holovideo of the meeting last night between Talon, Drake, and Yoshimasa."

"Negative … you are not cleared," the computer responded.

"For Christ' sake, Andy, let's stop playing games, okay?"

Smug, with a hint of a smile, Andy said, "Computer, show the meeting as requested."

"Negative … a non-cleared person is present."

"Damn that Yoshimasa," Andy said through gritted teeth.

Jane giggled and covered her mouth with her fingertips.

Andy paused before he said, "Okay, let's try this: … Computer—show that portion of subject meeting when Pierre forecasts the results of some future events."

Jane heard her office door click locked and knew that the invisible, photo-electronic, anti-surveillance shield was active. The wallscreen filled with a holographic video of Senator Yoshimasa warning that the information to follow was top secret.

She saw a holoimage of Talon, seated on the edge of his cot—obviously agitated.

"Senator Yoshimasa, I accept what you're saying—you need absolute proof that I was in the future. Evidently, I won't be taken seriously until you receive it. But, you must understand that I must be careful about what I divulge about the future. Should I disclose sensitive information—persons, institutions, or whole industries might be ruined."

The senator threw back his head in a hearty laugh. "I suppose you can tell me how, when, and where I will die."

Talon stared at the senator. Then, he closed his eyes and leaned forward—head in hands, elbows on knees. No one spoke. The silence seemed long and foreboding.

Jane studied Talon's changing expression with interest.

At first, the man showed no emotion. Then, a look of astonishment swept across his face. He frowned, and his eyes popped open to stare at Andy for a long while. Finally, he sighed sadly and shifted his gaze to the senator. "Yes, I can, Senator ..."

On the holoimage, Jane saw the senator's face blanch.

"... but I won't."

The senator was incredulous. "Mister Talon, how could you know this? You can't know that information ... have it in your memory, I mean."

"Yes I can, Senator." Suddenly, Talon stood up. "You want proof that I've been into the future? You'll have it—absolutely—before another week has passed."

Jane listened intently as Talon proceeded to predict the location and description of three, buried archaeological sites containing considerable treasure—an Etruscan tomb, an Incan temple, and, in Japan, a Fujiwaran castle of the Heian period.

Talon said, "You may reveal this information only to the proper authorities at each location. I feel free to divulge the location of these sites because I know that they will be discovered shortly, anyway."

Next, he gave—in detail—the results of three sporting events that were to take place within the following week.

The wallscreen went blank, and the door clicked unlocked.

Jane said, "Well, Talon is really sticking his neck out. Do you believe in those predictions, Andy?"

"How's this for an answer—I've already placed a large bet that he's on the mark with the horse race."

Curious to know why Andy continued to stare at the blank wallscreen, Jane was startled when he snapped his fingers and said, "Well, I'll be danged. I've got it! I've got it!"

"You've got what?"

"You'll see. ... Computer, get me Senator Yoshimasa."

Jane watched the wallscreen light up with the senator's holoimage.

"Yes, Mister Drake?"

"Sir, I know who Pierre's backers were. ... Unknowingly, they are the gambling public. He'd place sure bets on the outcome of games and races. That's how he financed his laboratory and his operations ... with his winnings."

"Did Mister Talon tell you this?"

"No, but, it makes sense."

"Time will tell, Mister Drake," the senator said impassively, "... and have you told Ms. Stevens about the change?"

"Uh, no, Sir ... I haven't yet had the chance."

Startled, Jane said, "What change?"

"Tell her, Mister Drake."

"Yes, Sir."

The senator's image dimmed. The screen darkened.

"What the hell's going on, Andy?"

"Jane ..." Andy hesitated. He looked embarrassed. "You knew that I wanted Kathy to take over the interviews but—I swear—not like this."

Her ire began to rise. "Like what, dammit?"

Andy sighed and spread his hands as if he were apologizing. "The senator assigned Kathy to the remainder of the Talon interviews."

Jane was stunned. "That's ... that's impossible. For Christ' sake—around here, I decide who interviews people. Freedom of the press hasn't yet flown the coop, you know."

"Ya ... sure, but Yoshimasa holds the keys to Pierre—all in the name of national security."

She was really mad, now. "You bastard! You cooked this up with Kathy—behind my back—and the good senator went along because he hates my guts. Well, I hate his, too." She pointed a finger at Andy and shook it furiously. "You won't get away with this. I've got power—more than Yoshimasa could ever imagine." Her neck throbbed. Her pulse pounded in her ears. "That little, two-faced bitch of yours ... said she 'wanted him dead,' said he'd 'murdered my poor, little son' ... bullshit!"

"Please ... Jane, baby! Get a hold of yourself. Sure, the senator wants you off the interviews, but no conspiracy exists. The fact is that, Kathy knows Pierre. She interviewed him a couple of times—seven years ago."

Jane stared at Andy. "What?" she yelled. "Why didn't she ever tell me?"

"She knew him before coming to work for you. Besides, Kathy didn't know that he was the suspected arsonist until last night, when she saw his holoimage during the interview."

"Well, what was her reaction?"

"Jane ... when I got home, she was all excited—said we've got the wrong man—said that Pierre couldn't have done all those horrible things."

"What's that got to do with her taking over the interviews?"

Andy sighed. "The senator was really angry with you last night. He said you were unprofessional and wanted you out. I suggested to him that Kathy might be able to do it—but I meant later—much later. He seemed to like the idea."

Jane forced herself to calm down. She swallowed hard and took a couple of deep breaths. "... Yes, I know I lost it last night, but I couldn't help it."

"I understand. Pierre's story really is incredible. ... Anyway, when I found out about Kathy knowing Pierre, I contacted the senator, and, before I knew it, he'd gotten her to take over the interviews. ... I'm so sorry."

Jane felt Andy's touch on her shoulder. She shivered, then turned, and lifted her face to his. "Andy—Darling—I know that you are not to blame."

Their lips met.

16—BONIFACE

> If you want a picture of the future, imagine
> a boot stamping on a human face—for ever.
>
> —George Orwell

Meanwhile
Franklin State Asylum Number Fifteen, Building 10D
Bellevue, Franklin

Pierre was agitated and angry ... with himself. Throughout his life, he always had tried to control his temper, yet, yesterday, he failed. Maybe Jane Stevens' success in keeping him off balance triggered the incident. He regretted it because the woman's antagonism would make the other interviews that much more difficult. He stopped pacing and flung himself onto his cot.

He stared at the ceiling. Again, his father's voice came back to haunt him. *You are at Cumulus. I am Boniface, the Valid of Cumulus, the Supreme Archivist, and Analysis Council Monitor.* Since yesterday's interview, he could not rid himself of that voice. Again and again , it rang in his ears as if his father were leaning over and whispering to him. Yes, he remembered it well—six hundred fifty-six years into the future—June 4, 2786 to be exact, five miles above Antarctica in the floating city of Cumulus. Pierre closed his eyes.

* * *

Pierre awoke abruptly—his eyes wide in apprehension. He watched the color of the ceiling evolve from one hue of the rainbow to another ... red, orange, yellow, green, blue, violet, and again back to red. The colors of wall and floor traveled the same spectrum.

Cumulus! ... Dad's voice said, "Cumulus." What is Cumulus? Where am I? He remembered that he had been nude, so he glanced at his body. A white robe covered it, now. An oily balm over his feet, glistened. Upon wondering about his face, instantly it appeared before him as if from a ghostly mirror. He recognized himself, but his head, now shaved, shined from the same balm.

In midair, he floated no longer but lay upon a pad which, itself, floated in the center of a cubical room, devoid of windows. He saw nothing else—neither decorations nor furniture of any sort and, oddly enough, no doors.

He stood and examined the room over its entire surface. Nary a crack showed—he was imprisoned.

The changing colors irritated him. *If only the walls wouldn't change color*, he thought.

Pierre was taken aback—the walls remained green, while the ceiling and floor continued their chromatic evolutions. *Maybe I'm onto something.*

Make the ceiling white, the walls ivory, and the floor gray.

Someone or something read his thoughts and obeyed him. He was astounded. …
His imagination ran wild.

This time, he voiced his command. "Play Adagio for Strings by Barber."

He heard the strains of mournful violins fill the air.

"Project John Gielgud's Hamlet."

He saw a skull in that great actor's hands appear before him. "… Alas, poor
Yorick. …"

Oh, my God, I've the knowledge of the world at my fingertips.

"Give news of my fellow crew members."

Anxiously, he awaited a reply. … None came.

"I am Pierre Talon. You rescued me from the crash of a spaceship, which came
from Earth of the past—from the year 2045. The ship carried eight crew members.
How many more survived? … Am I alone?"

Again—no reply, yet Hamlet and Laertes fought on.

"Stop Hamlet."

The room fell silent.

Pierre pounded the wall. He screamed, "Dammit, somebody answer me! Am I the
only one alive?"

A slight noise from behind prompted him to whirl about. The apparition of an
ancient man startled him. He stood erect, yet frail, in a red robe, which swept the floor.
The old one's flowing, white mane blended into his flowing, white beard.

Pierre studied the features of the kindly face of no particular race and perceived in
them an admixture of continents—African, Asian, American, and European. The eyes
under bushy, white brows seemed soft and mellow. For confirmation of flesh and blood
rather than holovision, abruptly, he reached toward the image.

Bone-to-bone contact staggered the man. To Pierre's horror, a huge, dark hole
appeared in the wall. A gigantic, shiny-black robot rushed through and, despite Pierre's
struggles, snatched him off the floor.

Pierre yelled, "I meant no harm. I touched you to see if you were real—that's all.
Please! … Put me down."

Slowly, a withered hand withdrew from the folds of the ancient one's robe and
gestured to the robot. Gently, it put Pierre down.

"You rested well. You need food. Come with me."

Although the old man's enunciations were hesitant, Pierre understood them. He
followed him through the hole and down a long, brightly-lit corridor lined with a profusion of plants. The robot lumbered close behind. They entered an attractive,
well-appointed suite of rooms. Again, plants appeared to be everywhere—their huge
leaves forming a canopy overhead.

"Who are you?"

"No questions … you eat." A scrawny arm waved toward a table upon which was
placed a knife, a goblet, a pitcher of water, and a platter piled with raw fruits and vege-
tables.

Pierre became aware of his hunger and sat to gobble the food. His actions seemed
to mesmerize the old man, who sat opposite and silently watched him eat.

He heard the hesitant voice again. "I am Boniface, the Valid of Cumulus. These rooms are yours ... in the style of your era ... made especially for you. Do they please you?"

Pierre looked around. "Yes—very comfortable indeed, but how did you know I was to arrive—or to survive the crash, for that matter? ... Oh my God! ... The crash! What happened to my crewmates? Are they here? Are they okay?"

"You will forget them. They are not here. They are not okay."

"Did any survive?"

"All were destroyed. You were not destroyed. You are well."

"That's fairly obvious, isn't it? What did you do with their bodies? I want to see them."

Pierre felt grief at the news of his friends' deaths, but the loss of Evelyn was almost too much to bear. With difficulty, he suppressed the vision of her beautiful, delicate body being torn apart.

"All were destroyed. They are gone. Pierre Talon, you will forget them—now, you must learn."

"Sure ... teach me. Tell me how you knew I was to come to this place—to this time. Tell me why I returned to 2786 rather than to 2045. Tell me, do you have the power to reach into the past and wrest a person into your time—at your pleasure? Tell me, Mister Boniface, who are you, and what do you want of me?"

"I am the Valid of Cumulus. The care of the In-valids is my sole reason for existence ... now, it is yours also. The well being of the In-valids necessitates your survival and education. Henceforth, Pierre Talon, you will learn what you are taught."

"In-valids? Who are they? ... Sounds like a bunch of sick people to me."

"The In-valids are the last of the human species, and they all reside here at Cumulus, the last floating city."

"What about you? ... Sure, you're old, but you don't look like an In-valid to me."

"I am not an In-valid, Pierre Talon. ... I am the Valid of Cumulus."

"Yeah, so you keep telling me. ... So what?"

"I am the last of the Valid class of humans. A century ago, many floating cities existed, and each possessed a Valid to care for its population of In-valids. Except for the presence of an apprentice Valid toward the end of an old Valid's life, the In-valids permitted only one Valid per city."

"Why is that? The care of a lot of sick people would seem to require many Valids ... right?"

"A Valid monitors. Machines controlled by computers and the In-valids, themselves, do the actual work. Albeit sophisticated and, in most cases, able to repair themselves, these machines occasionally need care that only a Valid can provide. Reluctantly, the In-valids created the Valid class for that express purpose."

"Why only one per city?"

"A concentration of Valids poses a threat to the In-valids."

"Like taking over and getting rid of them?"

"Yes ... although that is highly unlikely. You see, fertility resides only in the In-valids. During the rite of passage into the Valid class, a valid child is sterilized."

"Could the child refuse sterilization?"

"Yes, but he would be refused entry into the Valid class and converted into an In-valid."

"How?"

"At the minimum, induced paraplegia—ambulant status for In-valids is forbidden."

"Who is your apprentice? Who replaces you when you die?"

"No one. The genetic health of the human race has deteriorated to the point that, now, all embryos are naturally in-valid. The In-valids are incapable of producing my successor.

"Faced with the extinction of the Valid class, the In-valids realized that their days were numbered also. Seventy years ago, they decided not to produce any more children. You see—shortly after I die, they, also, will die, and the human race will become extinct."

"Hold it. Are you trying to tell me that I landed back on a future earth at the time of the extinction of our species?"

"Yes, but you may be in a position to save it."

Pierre chuckled. "Me? ... You've got to be kidding. What do you want me to do? ... Replace you? ... Donate my sperm?"

"Do not make light of our dilemma, Pierre Talon. You will learn everything you can, return to Earth of your time, and save it."

"Return to the past? ... Impossible! I should know; I am an—"

"—an astrophysicist from the year 2045. Yes, and you need to update your knowledge with that regard, too.

"Your first session in the Learning Room will give you—through your natural sense organs—the history of the decline of the species to the year 2045. Prior to the second session, I will show you Cumulus."

"What's in the second session?"

"You will learn the In-valids' viewpoint of history since 2045."

What other viewpoints are there?"

"The Valids', of course ... but, you see, only survivors write history."

With the wave of an arm, Boniface indicated a door. "Pierre Talon, the Learning Room awaits you. Enter, relax, look, listen, and absorb."

Pierre walked over the threshold into pitch black. For an instant, he thought he had been struck blind, then someone touched his shoulder and shook it.

* * *

Pierre's eyes snapped open—something interrupted his reveries.

A robosentry loomed overhead, said "Your lunch is here," and left. The heavy cell door clanked shut behind it.

17—REUNION

O that 't were possible
After long grief and pain
To find the arms of my true love
Round me once again!

—Alfred, Lord Tennyson

The next evening, August 15, 2130

Pierre paced within the confines of his cell. Anxiously, he awaited the arrival of Kathy ... dear Kathy, whom he remembered from years ago—just after his return from the future. He could not believe his good fortune to be seeing her again.

Over the years, he had watched some of her news specials. He recalled that he'd focus her holoimage into the middle of the room and merge himself with it—dance with it. Mouth agape, he'd dive at her gossamer lips, only to engulf thin air. However, the most vivid memory of her was from just before his arrest—the night before. She came to him eager for his love. He gave it passionately, not so much because she was his first in four years, but because she was a tantalizingly intense woman whose insatiable appetite for life's offerings he could not resist.

A loudspeaker broke the silence. "Your guests arrive in five minutes."

Worries about having divulged the outcome of the sporting events bothered him. He knew that chaos could result if Andy and the senator didn't keep quiet about the predictions, especially if they were believed by a large segment of the betting public. In the past, Pierre had spread his own bets inconspicuously over many events so that the odds hadn't been appreciably affected.

Disclosing the locations of the archaeological sites didn't bother him though. He had searched his memory carefully to find sites that would be discovered in the near future anyway—even if he had not indicated their locations.

In the year 2789, before his departure to return to the past, he took to heart the advice given him by Boniface the Valid.

Boniface had said, "Your mission is to return to the past and make as many changes as you possibly can that will benefit the future of our species as a whole. Changes for anyone's personal aggrandizement are forbidden except when necessary for your mission. Good-bye, Pierre Talon. ... Good luck."

Pierre heard the computer speak, "Katharine Carver and Andrew Drake are here."

He wiped away a tear and returned his thoughts to the present.

"Okay, I'm decent."

The heavy door clicked unlocked and slid open.

Kathy and her robots, accompanied by Andy, entered the cell.

Upon sight of her, Pierre stopped breathing for an instant. *She is magnificent ... as I remember her.* He realized how much and how long he had unwittingly suppressed his own sexuality for his obsession ... his mission. Kathy's arrival rekindled in his loins, a fire—long-cold.

56

Andy said, "Pierre, I assume you remember Ms. Carver, so I'll dispense with the introductions."

Despite himself, Pierre lurched awkwardly forward to grasp Kathy's hand. He didn't shake it—just held it for a moment, for as long as he dared. He could not bring himself to speak. He drank in the redness of her lips … lips, which gleamed a wet hungriness. He knew that she remembered "that" night as clearly as did he … her eyes said so … her lips said so. They parted in speech.

"Perhaps Doctor Talon has forgotten. Seven years is a long time."

Pierre awoke from his stupor. "Oh, no … of course I remember … yes, very much so."

Andy's face showed confusion. "Well, I … good luck. This interview will be better than the first, I'm sure." He left, and the door clanked shut.

Now alone with Kathy, Pierre watched her every move as she ordered her camera-transmitter robots to prepare for the interview. Everything about her excited him—the graceful turn of her ankle, the voluptuous curve of her breasts, the elegant flow of her fingers, the intelligent set to her eyes, the sensuous cast of her mouth—with those shining, hungry lips.

Without a word to him, Kathy started the session. "Good evening, ladies and gentlemen. I am Katharine Carver. Tonight, the Informational News Agency presents the second in a series of interviews with Doctor Pierre Talon, a theoretical physicist from the past." She turned toward him, and, when he saw her eyes focus directly upon him, he began to tremble.

"Doctor Talon, congratulations on your win."

He didn't understand. "My win?"

"Don't you remember? … the Cascaders last night—they won four to three, like you said they would."

He laughed. "Oh, yes … but they won, I didn't. I just said what I already knew."

"Anyway, your prediction came true, and that is what's important. Let's start with your childhood. I understand you were born in the early twenty-first century. Can you tell us what the world was like when you were a child? Because of the Wall, little history from that era survives. Of course, we know what our parents and grandparents told us, but, to get a perspective from someone, who was an adult before the Wall occurred, would be a novelty. Doctor Talon, please relate to our audience your unique, eye-witness interpretation of that period in our history."

Pierre wanted to rush to her, envelope her in his arms, and take her … right there, on the spot, before the whole world.

Kathy's expression betrayed her emotions—intelligible only to him … yes, she was reading his fantasy, for it was certainly her own as well.

He smiled.

Kathy recovered first. "Doctor Talon … ?"

"Why, uh … yes, of course, I'd be happy to." He looked into the camera's lens. "I was born in the—then—province of Québec in 2012—that was 118 years ago."

"You are French Canadian, then?"

"No, but my ancestor, Jean Talon, was appointed the first intendant of New France in 1665 by Colbert, Louis XIV's chief minister, and was the one most responsible for the success of its early development. He didn't stay in New France, but my family returned three centuries later. Great grandfather, Guy, left France for Québec in 1967 with his family, which included my grandfather Eric, a little boy of six. My father, Garrett, was the first Talon born in the Americas—in 1989."

"Tell us about your childhood in Québec."

"Well, the winters were still cold, and the people, still hardy. My mother, Chantal née Bourdon, was a devout Catholic and raised me in her image. My father, an officer of the law, disciplined me well. We could have been a happy family.

"When my mother deemed me old enough to care for myself, she became obsessed with the prolife movement, which dominated women's politics of the time. My father fought against the drug scourge. Eventually, he became a soldier but was killed during the Drug War of 2035. Often, I was alone. To blot out the reality of my parents' obsessions, I submerged myself in my studies.

"As a Catholic, my mother opposed induced abortion, although she did believe in passive birth control. My grandmother, a prolife activist, influenced both my mother and me in that regard."

Pierre glanced at Kathy and was startled by her expression of astonishment and … yes, embarrassment. "What is the matter, Ms. Carver?"

"Uh … oh, nothing, Doctor Talon. How about brothers and sisters? Did you have any?"

"I had a little sister—Leanne. After menopause, my mother, older than my father, abandoned the rhythm method of birth control—the only one she allowed herself. Thus, beyond the normal age of child rearing, she bore my unwanted sister. My parents' lack of involvement in Leanne's upbringing ill prepared her for the realities of life.

"My sister never had a chance. When only sixteen, complications from a botched fourth abortion killed her. Leanne's death greatly affected me. I came to abhor induced abortion—for whatever reason. Blindly, I embraced my mother's anti-abortional beliefs as never before. In my era, most people followed either the prochoice or the prolife philosophy. Both sides ignored the more-informed minority in the middle. In those days, we were so naïve that—.

"Doctor Talon, please!"

"What's wrong?"

"You are forbidden to mention these subjects."

He stared at Kathy. "Forbidden?"

In a shy whisper, she said, "Yes … I can't speak of them, but you know …"

Pierre was angry. "No, I don't know. If you mean abortion, birth control, menopause, fetuses, embryos, and the like, then you should know there's something wrong with this society. Apparently, I'm the only person who realizes it."

"Doctor Talon, the transmitter lights are off."

Now, Pierre was really upset. "Damn that Senator Yoshimasa! He agreed not to censor me."

A holoimage of the senator formed in the center of the cell. "Mister Talon," he boomed, "I did not censor you, the National Censorship Board did. Public talks, discussions, and publications that pertain to human reproduction or subjects of a sexual nature have been forbidden since the Wall. We have stamped out the evils of abortion, which so perverted the world of your time."

"That's bullshit, and you know it. Your policy of sticking everyone's head in the sand will doom the human race to extinction."

The senator interrupted. "Mister Talon, that seems to be your favorite expression ... 'doom the human race to extinction.' For the rest of the interview, confine your subjects to those permitted. Is that clear?"

Pierre glared at the senator. "Perfectly."

The senator's holoimage dimmed, and the transmitter lights glowed once again.

Kathy looked at Pierre apologetically.

He returned the gaze as if to say, "I don't blame you—I'm the one at fault." *There went my temper, again.*

"Doctor Talon, please continue."

"I shan't talk of my childhood any longer.

"... I have come to realize that your society is grossly uninformed of the past—particularly of the negative aspects of it."

"What do you mean?"

"Well, records of historical acts that confirm the inherent greediness and cruelty of the human animal have been purged from your libraries and archive centers."

"Perhaps you can't find the records because they never existed—because, basically, people are good and compassionate."

Pierre felt sorry for Kathy—for her ignorance of the past—for the ignorance of everyone in the twenty-second century. "My dear Ms. Carver, I lived before the revisionists butchered the history of our civilization. I believe you call it the Wall—a wall erected between your society and its past. Let me ask you this: Are you content with the world around you? Do you see beauty and bliss far and wide?"

"Well, no, but—"

"Past actions caused every condition in the world today. Likewise, present actions create the world of tomorrow. You do realize that the present is the child of the past, don't you?"

"Of course."

"Then, how can you believe that the past was so perfect, when the present is so terrible?"

"It's not so terrible."

"Not for you and your kind, but for the vast majority of people on Earth, life is intolerable."

"Why? How?"

"When our brains surpassed the capability of those of other animals, damage to our world became inevitable."

"When was that?"

"A million years ago—but the first signs of chaos appeared ten thousand years back, in the cradle of civilization—a veritable paradise. Humans hunted and gathered food there. Majestic forests and sweeping meadows surrounded them. Sparkling brooks and limpid lakes quenched their thirst and soothed their skin. The trials of nature eliminated the sick and the weak. The strong and healthy in body and soul survived and passed these qualities onto their offspring.

"Humans alone created tools to their ends. With the exception of themselves, they vanquished all enemies. Free of constraints from superior beings, they exploited Earth—Water—Air—Fire—and the quintessentials."

"Doctor Talon, you contradict yourself. You paint a wonderful world—not one of greed and cruelty."

"That's only the beginning ... thereafter, it worsens. You see, four million millennia of evolution produced a multitude of fauna and flora in an Edenic world, but only ten sufficed for civilization to crash down all. When hunter-gatherers became farmers, they unwittingly chose the path to extinction. Although agriculture supplied a reliable food source, its advent began the end for humanity.

"Population increased—checked only by war, disease, and murder. Cities sprang up. Division of labor created varied professions, interests, sympathies—and hatreds. Cultivation produced processed foods—obesity and tooth decay followed. Cooking generated mutagens and carcinogens. Crowding spread disease and parasites. Religion, politics, property, and money enabled greediness to flower. Divergent social classes fed prejudices. Social struggles fomented crime.

"Demand for food and fuel increased. The need for firewood destroyed forests and, for farmland destroyed the soil. Deforestation created erosion and a desertic climate. Decreased rainfall forced farmers to irrigate with ground water containing salts. Eventually, the salted soil sustained life no longer." Pierre hesitated for a moment—Kathy's face showed skepticism.

"What you say, cannot be ... natural forces constantly change the surface of the Earth. Human activity could not have inflicted all of the damage that you describe."

"Ms. Carver, humans ravaged the Earth more and longer than you realize. The Near East suffered many millennia of deforestation and irrigation. Its 'Fertile Crescent' became desertic centuries before the birth of Jesus Christ. The rape of Europe started then and took two millennia; that of the Americas began with Columbus and required under one. Primeval forests vanished forever. Fertile land eroded away. Lakes and streams silted up. Fields and pastures leached salts.

"The fatal blow began early in the nineteenth century during the onslaught of the Industrial Revolution. The worst culprits proved to be chemistry and energy-conversion engines. The engines' appetites converted forests, coal deposits, and petroleum fields into polluters of land, sea, and air. Chemical industries invented crop-enhancement and pest-control products. In the naïve belief that these poisons could delay a Malthusian fate—and increase profits—they were spread across the landscape. Instead, they mutilated plant and animal geneticism (sic).

"In the twentieth century, the martial and medical revolutions eliminated our last enemies—war and disease—resulting in a more-serious population and pollution boom. Pollutants permeated the habitat: Filth of human and corporate activity submerged cities. Effluent fouled bush, beast, and beach alike. Like fish oblivious of water, mindlessly, humans tolerated their toxic world. Filth—wretches born in it, who live and die in it, don't notice it."

Kathy appeared to grow alarmed. Pierre hoped so, for it meant that the multitude of viewers might become concerned, also.

"If this were so, didn't people clean up the mess?"

"Yes, of course ... from time to time, in isolated areas, feeble efforts to reverse the carnage succeeded—but only briefly. The greedy and powerful thought only of fleeting pleasures, and Earth's health continued its decline.

"Until the twentieth century, most In-valids died in the womb, shortly after birth, or before puberty. Their defective chromosomes rarely entered the gene pool. Thereafter, medical advances, spurred by pseudo morality, extended the lives of more In-valids.

"At first, the Valids remained oblivious of the In-valids' advances. By mid-twentieth century, however, signs of the increasing power of In-valids appeared: for the blind—Braille's code in elevators and on doors; for the deaf—signing and close-captioning on television; for the crippled—reserved parking, wide toilet stalls, wheelchair lifts, and ramped curbs and building accesses; for the diseased and retarded—more asylums and hospitals. The rights of the In-valids were well established by the end of the twentieth century."

Pierre noticed that the transmitter lights were no longer lit but realized that many persons still watched Kathy and him. "Okay, Kathy, so what I said was forbidden, but I must make people aware of what their ancestors have inflicted upon them. It's too bad your audience won't hear about the twenty-first century—it's the worst of all."

"Then, tell me," Kathy said softly. "I am eager to hear."

"It brought increased deforestation, desertation (sic), and global warming. Worldwide, habitable areas decreased while population increased. Human crowding and misery rose.

"After the Drug War of 2035 and a revival of pseudo religious cult fanaticism, conservatism triumphed over liberalism. Induced abortions, prenatal examinations, and euthanasia were outlawed ... and the In-valid population abruptly increased. The Valids and In-valids of the world continued on their collision course."

Andy entered with a hint of a smile.

His attitude irked Pierre. "Andy, you seem to think that this is all very funny. Somehow, I must teach you and your society how not to repeat the mistakes of our ancestors."

Andy chuckled. "Jeez, Pierre, have you always taken yourself so seriously?"

Pierre sighed. "No, Andy, but if more people had done so in the past, we wouldn't be in the mess we're in today."

18—POLLUTION

Forests keep disappearing, rivers dry up,
wild life's become extinct, the climate's ruined,
and the land grows poorer and uglier every day.

—Anton Chekhov

The next afternoon, August 16, 2130
Jane Stevens' penthouse
Half a mile above Bellevue, Franklin

Jane checked her long fingernails with satisfaction then gazed across her estate. The lawn, like velvet, stretched out to the surrounding flower beds. Rainbow-colored birds cooed and cawed as they flitted from tree to tree. From afar, a doe and her fawn, transfixed, stared at the party preparations.

Jane walked from table to table. The cool blades of grass tickled her toes. She wanted all to be perfect. All was perfect—the crystal and silver sparkled; sharp creases embellished the linen; statuesque appendages graced the ice carvings; …

Arms outstretched, Jane's personnel lined up before her. She examined each fingernail. She was proud of her people—not a robotic or retardic server among them. They were expensive, she knew, but the warmer personality of valids was worth the cost.

A glance at her wrist terminal showed the arrival of the first cabins, halfway down the stratoscraper, 125 floors below.

"To your places everybody, the guests arrive."

Jane smiled as her people scurried stiffly to their posts. The starched uniforms impeded their movements, yet she always insisted upon them. Sandals on at the last minute, she hurried to the turbolift to greet her guests.

* * *

When the torrent of arrivals became a trickle, Jane looked out at the buffet tables and cocktail bars under siege. She visualized a pack of baby wart hogs vying for teats. Everyone seemed to munch, swig, and chatter at once.

First-time guests needed introductions all around, so, to mingle with them, Jane left her post at the turbolift and descended into the crowd. Above all the bobbing heads, she glimpsed Andy's handsome profile, which seemed disdainful of all the scurrying about underneath. From across the lawn, she saw Andy's eyes focus upon her. Adrenaline flowed, and her babbling guests vanished from her mind. She only had eyes for Andy.

Jane smiled. *Andy and I are majestic giraffes eyeing each other on high in arrogant obliviousness of the multitude of mangy wart hogs milling about in the dust below.* She stopped occasionally to acknowledge a greeting as she migrated slowly through the crowd toward him. He had arrived with Kathy, Julie, and Julie's husband—Mario, the son of the founder of Fuerza Cortés. She approached and accorded each either a handshake or a platonic kiss—as suitable. She granted Andy no special treatment—too many prying eyes.

Jane could not help but gaze at Kathy with condescension. She hoped that her guests would not notice, for she prided herself in being always the perfect host to each of them—regardless. Slowly, her critical eye swept over Kathy from head to toe. The woman radiated nothing but beauty and charm. Knowing that all within earshot would strain to hear, Jane said, "Andy, Darling, you must be very proud of the little woman. She seems to have recovered fully from the loss of her son. Despite her age, she looks positively marvelous." She raised her champagne glass in salute and looked Kathy straight in the eye.

Andy cleared his throat. "Yes, I am proud."

Kathy donned a thin smile, yet Jane perceived trembling cheeks as her conniving employee tried to hold the pose.

Jane's attention turned toward the terrace steps. Senator Yoshimasa's arrival created a stir as the little man descended into the crowd. She was surprised that he had the gall to appear. Of course, as always, she had invited him to come, but that was before he forced her off the Talon interviews.

Deferential nods greeted the senator as he made his way toward her. *Offense conquers defense*, she thought. ... Hand extended, Jane met him midway. Her own smile ached, too.

"My dear Senator Yoshimasa, I began to think my party was a failure, but you have arrived to save it, after all. Why are you late, you naughty boy, you?"

Politely, she pretended to listen to his excuses as she bent to intertwine her arm with his and whisk him back to her table. *Walking together across the lawn like this must make a comical sight,* Jane thought, ... *the mangy wart hog and the majestic giraffe.*

Kathy, Julie, Andy, and Mario rose briefly for the expected round of handshakes. A white-gloved waiter, silver salver in palm, waited patiently to offer the senator his snifter of Peshastin Extra Old.

All settled themselves around the table, and the senator raised his glass to Jane. "To you, Ms. Stevens, whose minions know by heart the favorite food and drink of each of us."

"Hear, hear!"

Small talk rose then declined. Despite Jane's revival efforts, conversation lagged—the senator's presence always stifled spontaneity.

Mario came to her rescue. "In your opinion, Senator, how pertinent are Pierre Talon's ideas about the long-term effects of pollution and surpopulation upon the health of the human race?"

Jane felt amused by the senator's familiar expression of contempt. She guessed he must be thinking, *Just because this whelp is his father's son ... he presumes equality to me?*

"Young man, many experts have predicted the effect of crowding and pollution upon our collective health. Mister Talon's views are nothing new."

Mario shot back, "Yes they are, Senator. 'Your' experts did not witness the extinction of the human race. ... Pierre did."

"Perhaps—perhaps not. In either case, you've brought up a moot subject of little interest to me."

"How can you sit there, calmly sipping from your hand-cut, crystal glass, and say you're not concerned that the whole human race is wallowing in its own filth? You—of all people—should do something about it."

The little man leaned forward and set his glass on the table. "Look ... Señor Pavía's kid has no lesson for me—Mizuno Yoshimasa. You youngsters are all alike. You criticize the world but, in ignorance, offer no solutions of your own to its problems. Of course, you seem sincere ... ignorance guarantees sincerity.

"I learned long ago not to argue with the ignorant. The ignorant cannot reason—they possess no foundation of knowledge to back their mental processes ... but that is not the problem. Their stubborn insistence that they are not ignorant is the problem.

"A wise person once said, 'The wise believe they're ignorant; the ignorant believe they're wise.' Indeed ... ignorance is bliss."

Jane looked from one bored face to another and returned Andy's wry smile. She looked at Mario ... no smile there.

"I agree that I'm ignorant, so I must be wise. However, in some areas, I am an expert. You are ignorant of that fact, Senator."

Jane was puzzled by Mario's wink to Andy.

"Yes—I am young," Mario continued. "Yes—I criticize, but—I have solutions, and Pierre Talon has them, also."

"Sure, young man ... you want a law passed that outlaws pollution. Even if such a law were enforceable and enforced, the result would be the opposite of the intended purpose. The accoutrements of our society would be priced out of reach. Poverty, disease, and death would be worse. Anti-pollutive laws were tried. ... They don't work."

"Good enforceable laws can work."

The senator sighed with impatience and leaned forward. "Mister Pavía, let me paint you a little scenario. Permit me to peel away a layer of your youthful naïveté ... no—ignorance, if you will.

"On the one hand, people need food, drink, medicine, cleaners, lubricants, fuels, and many other increasingly sophisticated products. On the other hand, their manufacture, consumption, and final disposition pollute.

"Polluting companies thrive; the ecologically conscious ones disappear. Experience shows that foreign companies can undersell us if we increase our domestic producers' costs with antipollutive laws. The law of economic competition rules."

"Senator Yoshimasa, do you want to hear my solution to the problem—or don't you?"

"I'll stand it if the others can."

Andy intervened. "We have listened to you, Senator, so, surely, we also can tolerate Mario."

Jane was surprised at Andy's "courageous" response and didn't even try to stifle a snicker.

The senator glared at Andy.

Mario continued. "The same antipollutive laws must be imposed upon each particular, worldwide industry within its market area—not its production area."

The senator snorted, raised his eyebrows, and glanced disdainfully at his listeners. "My goodness, you did pay attention in Econ 101, after all. Unfortunately, academicism and pragmatism don't mix. ... In different areas of this 'cruel' world, the disparity between determining factors of consideration make your utopian fix unrealistic."

Mario said, "Senator, your political babble is meaningless gobbledegook."

Jane drew a sharp breath and heard Kathy do likewise. She glanced at the senator.

His tightly-drawn lips were white, but he remained silent, and his arm recoiled instantly at Mario's touch.

"I'm sorry, Senator, I don't mean to offend. Please—hear me out. ... A pollution tax on products made by dirty processes in foreign countries could be collected upon importation—thus countering the unfair advantage of the dirty, foreign product."

The senator snorted. "So, you propose to pay the collected, pollution tax to the clean, domestic manufacturers as compensation for their antipollutive costs."

"Of course, but that's only half of the solution. I propose a double-edged weapon. If domestic producers cheat, tax them and give the proceeds to the clean-producing foreigners. If they all produce cleanly, eliminate the duty altogether."

"And if all produce dirtily?"

"If they're rewarded not to, they won't."

"Nonsense! ... Like I said—a good exercise in Econ 101, but—unworkable in the real world. Young man, you assume, as did Marx and Engels, that the availability of selfless, incorruptible, and competent bureaucratic watchdogs is a fact of life. The communist world collapsed a century and a half ago because it believed in such naïve fallacies. ... Yes, greed is too powerful an emotion for legislative action to control. Mister Pavía, these good people have listened to your textbook solution to pollution. Let them hear mine.

"The basic culprit is the advance of two technologies—medical and martial— responsible for Earth's excessive population and, therefore, its rampant pollution."

Mario's eyes sparkled in triumph. "You got that from Doctor Talon."

"Young man, it is mere common sense. After 1900, medical advances saved people who, otherwise, would have died younger. After 1945, the overkill of nuclear weapons rendered total war unattractive to the greedy as a means to their ends. The lack of massively-destructive wars since then has saved hundreds of millions of lives.

"Disease and war ... these two checks on the explosion of our species' population have been absent for two centuries. During that time, simultaneous to a five-fold increase in human population, its earthly habitat shrunk in half."

The senator pointed to the sky. "Look up there. What do you see?"

Julie said, "The sky ... of course."

"You see? ... You are so used to looking at the sky through filters, you aren't even aware of the dome."

Jane looked up. "Yes, when I was a little girl, I watched when grandmother had this dome installed. The original one couldn't absorb the more-powerful, ultraviolet rays. This dome, 150 feet in diameter, covers the entire penthouse area—half an acre."

"Most people can't afford that kind of protection," the senator said. "They are condemned either to live in gloom or risk ultraviolet burns.

"In the last decade, the population growth has slowed, so we should be pleased ... right? ... Wrong! The birth rate continues higher than ever, but the death rate has outpaced it. Tens of millions of people die every year of starvation, neglect, and environmental poisoning.

"Humans resemble bacteria in a petri dish—explosive growth until food is gone, habitat despoiled, then ... extinction."

Excited, Mario blurted, "So, you have surrendered your constituency to a Malthusian fate."

The senator put a hand on Mario's shoulder. "My boy, I surrender nothing. As your hero Mister Talon has said, our fate was sealed when the human species triumphed over the others. Like hurricanes and earthquakes, excessive population and pervasive pollution became inevitable.

"In a way, we are alike, Pierre Talon and I ... we both know that our race is dying ... but with one difference."

"What is that, Senator?"

"His faith in our ultimate salvation."

19—ABANDONMENT

Fly the rank city, shun its turbid air:
Breathe not the chaos of eternal smoke
and volatile corruption.

—John Armstrong

Six hundred fifty-six years in the future, June 5, 2786
The floating city of Cumulus
Five miles above Antarctica

Pierre, with Boniface at his side, stood behind the parapet, which surrounded Cumulus. Through a window, he gazed in awe at the desolate Antarctic continent three miles below. Beyond the murky atmosphere, he discerned outcroppings of Earth's remaining glaciers under immense sand dunes. Here and there, he saw clusters of towering, mushroom-shaped skyscrapers pierce layers of pukey-green haze. The buildings were ballooned—like flowers atop slender stems. Top-heavy, the taller ones had broken in half and fallen over.

Oh, my God, Pierre thought, *am I having a nightmare? Is this really how life on Earth will end?*

He noticed that Boniface also gazed over the desolate landscape but failed to read the old man's emotions through the heavy, white beard. Then, he realized that Boniface had viewed this morbid scene, perhaps, thousands of times before and, no doubt, was inured by now.

"Boniface, who lives in those cities?"

Slowly the placid countenance turned to face Pierre. "Nobody. Over a century ago, the last one was abandoned—in the year 2672, to be exact."

"And no one lives elsewhere on Earth?"

The ancient one appeared to be impatient. "Pierre, I've already told you—the In-valids of Cumulus and I are the sole survivors of the human species."

"Yes, I know. You told me before—yet I have difficulty believing it."

The old eyes softened again. "First, you learn; then, you believe."

Pierre pointed out the window. "Those collapsed buildings look like wilted flowers whose stems could no longer support them. Why did they fall over? Why were the cities abandoned?"

The old man wet his lips and started to speak. "Down there, life became intolerable. Heat, pollution, and sand storms worsened over the centuries. The carbon-dioxide content of the atmosphere now stands at five percent—a lethal level. Forced to move farther from the equator and to higher altitudes, my ancestors—your descendants—erected ever-taller stratoscrapers. To escape noxious gases at the surface, they inhabited only the bulbous top parts. Eventually, the structures peaked at four thousand feet—technically they could be made no taller—but, for the sake of human survival, taller ones had to be constructed."

"Couldn't people have migrated into the mountains?"

"They did, until those higher reaches teemed with the dying poor and diseased. The wealthy possessed the means to go elsewhere. They developed state-of-the-art technologies and applied them to their survival. The field of antineutronics was the most promising and enabled the construction of taller buildings and, eventually, of floating cities such as Cumulus."

"Antineutronics? ... I'm an expert in antiprotonic propulsion—are the two related?"

"Yes, Pierre, but much has been discovered about antimatter since 2045. In the twenty-third century, Doctor Giulio Manzoni from Françitalia, a southwestern province of Eurasia, formulated the Principle of Universal Duality in which he suggested that antimass is an attribute of antimatter."

Pierre flushed with curiosity. "What do you mean ... 'universal duality' ... 'antimass'?"

"Exactly what the terms imply: The Universe is bilaterally symmetrical such that its total mass and volume are zero."

"Boniface, that is absurd; the Universe couldn't exist if it contained neither mass nor volume."

A look of sympathy came into the tired old eyes. "I'm sorry, Pierre, for a moment I thought you were familiar with Doctor Manzoni's work. I forgot—you are a physicist from a prior era, so let me bring you up to date:

"The Universe is composed of matter and antimatter such that the sum of their respective attributes and anti-attributes equals zero—"

"Zero? ... I still don't understa—"

"You would, Pierre, if you'd just let me finish. ... As I was saying: Matter possesses attributes or—if you will—dimensions of mass, temperature, charge, length, and time. The anti-attributes of antimatter are antimass, antitemperature, anticharge, antilength, and antitime."

Pierre smiled. "That's a lot of antis."

Boniface ignored the remark and continued the thesis. "For a moment, suppose there is—someplace—a bunch of matter that possesses precise magnitudes for its attributes—it has a certain mass at a certain temperature, possesses a certain charge, occupies a certain amount of space, and ages with time. That's a fair description of most anything ... right?"

Pierre was intrigued. "Sure—I guess so. ... Please continue."

"Good. Now, suppose a similar bunch of antimatter exists whose anti-attributes possess the same magnitudes as do the attributes of the bunch of matter. Would you say, then, that the two bunches are identical?"

Pierre wanted to appear knowledgeable. "No, of course not—one is made of matter, the other—of antimatter."

"But their respective attributes and anti-attributes possess the same magnitudes, so what distinguishes matter from antimatter?"

"The signs would be different ... you know—positive, negative—clockwise, counterclockwise. ..."

Under thick umbrageous eyebrows, the ancient one's alert eyes twinkled mischievously. "You've finally got it."

"Got what, Boniface?"

"The differences between matter and antimatter. Don't you see? ... The signs of the attributes and anti-attributes oppose each other in every dimension. So, if you combine the two bunches, what happens?"

"They annihilate each other, of course."

"In a manner of speaking—yes, but 'annihilation' is just the popular name of the process. In reality, no annihilation would—or could—take place. Instead, the bunches 'convert' from the matter mode of existence into either an energy mode or a virtual mode."

"What's the difference?"

"In the energy mode, a particle and an antiparticle do not exactly coincide in space. A distance—the wavelength of the 'energy' beam—separates them. However, if the wavelength is zero, the particles exist in the virtual mode—coincide spatially—and virtually disappear, leaving nothing behind."

"Not even energy?"

"No ... not even energy. You see, the sum of their attributes and anti-attributes is zero—mass cancels antimass, temperature—antitemperature, time—antitime, space—antispace ... Nothing remains, not even 'empty' space—not even a void.

"A matter person in a matter environment experiences the same physical laws as does an antimatter person in an antimatter environment. Only if all attributes are opposite in sign to anti-attributes is this possible.

"However, if a matter person looks into an antimatter world, he sees an amazing sight—like a movie film projected in reverse. An antiblackhole appears as a whitehole, an anti-Big Bang—as a Big Crunch. Antipeople seem to get younger, finally, to disappear at birth. Conversely, an antimatter person looking into a matter world also sees time reversed."

"Boniface, this is fantastic. This must mean the age of the matter part of the Universe is equal and opposite to the age of the antimatter part. Added together, the age of the entire Universe is zero. ... Oh, my God! The Universe is ageless."

Boniface appeared excited, too. "Not only that, Pierre ... total entropy is zero as well. Although entropy and anti-entropy both increase over time, anti-entropy increases over antitime, so, as far as our matter world is concerned, it decreases and cancels out entropy."

"Boniface, Doctor Manzoni was right: The Universe is a perfectly balanced, symmetrical dual universe and ... a wondrous place indeed."

The old eyes gleamed. "Pierre, it is more balanced and symmetrical than you realize. Not only are attributes conjugates of anti-attributes, so are the various forces, of their respective antiforces. Although the forces of gravitation and antigravitation are attractive within their own environments, matter gravitationally repels antimatter. The electromagnetic and anti-electromagnetic forces follow similar but opposite rules. Electrons electromagnetically repel other electrons; positrons—other positrons, but electrons attract positrons.

"In sum, within each of the two environments, conjugate particles gravitationally attract and electromagnetically repel, while, when spanning the two, the opposite is true—conjugate particles gravitationally repel and electromagnetically attract."

Pierre could contain himself no longer. Tears came to his eyes. "If only Evelyn and Dimitri could have heard this. They would have been ecstatic."

"Your crew members?"

"Yes, but those two were more than just 'crew members.' Dimitri Adam was my second in command and a true friend. He was an ecosystem specialist of Russian-British ancestry. Evelyn Chang was an expert in life-support technology. Her parents had emigrated from Hong Kong to Vancouver, Canada where she was born, and I—." Despite himself, Pierre choked up.

"You liked Evelyn, didn't you?"

"Boniface, I loved her … dearly, I loved her."

"Did she love you?"

"I don't know, but, in time, she might have."

"Did Dimitri and she love each other?"

Boniface's question jolted Pierre. "I don't know; why do you ask? They're both dead, aren't they? They're all dead?"

"Yes, they are all dead, and their bodies have been destroyed—you cannot view them."

Pierre sighed. "It's just as well. I want to remember Evelyn as she was—beautiful and vibrant." Silently, he gazed across the sand dunes of Antarctica.

"Come, let us eat. You must be hungry." Boniface shuffled away, and Pierre followed him down the long forest-like corridors of Cumulus.

"Why all the vegetation?"

The old man seemed amused. "Without it, we'd all be dead—it removes carbon dioxide from—and supplies oxygen to—the air."

"Can't your advanced technology produce machines to do that?"

"Yes, but we've found that plants do a better job. Interaction between plants and animals automatically balance the components of the atmosphere. We always have the optimum amounts of oxygen, nitrogen, and carbon dioxide in our air."

"That's wonderful, Boniface. How does it work?"

"For goodness sake, Pierre, didn't you learn anything back in 2045? … Plants and animals 'know' of each others needs and produce them in just the right quantities."

"What do you mean?"

"Well, take Cumulus, for instance. We've a closed ecosystem here. If the human population increases, plants detect more carbon dioxide and less oxygen. They then absorb the excessive carbon dioxide and release more oxygen and, in the process, grow in proportion to the animal population. Of course, if animals kill the plants, they—the animals, I mean—in essence, commit suicide."

"Then, that's what happened to Earth?"

"Yes, Pierre. Earth is also a closed ecosystem, and we humans have destroyed so much of its carbon-containing resources that life is no longer possible. Only the huge limestone deposits, which corals took hundreds of millions of years to produce, save this planet from the fate of Venus—an atmosphere that melts lead."

Once again, they arrived at his quarters. On the table, plates of fruit and a pitcher of water awaited them. They sat and ate.

20—DINNER

> We were to do more business after
> dinner; but after dinner is after
> dinner—an old saying and a true,
> "much drinking, little thinking."
>
> —Jonathan Swift

Six hundred fifty-six years in the past, August 21, 2130
Andrew's apartment
Seattle, Franklin

Katharine was home watching the Saturday-afternoon races with Andy. In the main event, the first-three horses finished exactly as Pierre predicted—to the split second. ... It was uncanny. Andy amused her. He had won a bundle and could barely contain himself. He made a bigger bet on Pierre's prediction of the results of Monday's football game.

Katharine's outlook had improved. Not only was she conducting her most spectacular series of interviews ever but was doing so with this man whom she had once loved and grieved for as long dead. She felt exhilarated by Pierre's miraculous reappearance, yet she was bothered by how last week's session had ended. She knew that Pierre wanted the interviews to succeed, but, seemingly, he didn't want to obey the rules—didn't even want to know about them.

Katharine stared at Andy. He seemed changed—now, less attractive, even boorish. Before Douglas's death, she had hungered for Andy's carnal frenzies. At day's end, after caring for her son, gratification of their mutual lust had dissipated her frustrations and allowed her peaceful sleep. She realized that, since then, she had gradually cooled to his savage fervor.

Pierre's sudden "resurrection" rekindled her cherished memory of their night together so long ago. By comparison to Pierre's lovemaking, Andy's seemed crass and insensitive. She now craved Pierre's tenderness, his sensitivity, and his calm, lingering sensuousness punctuated by climaxes of orgasmic ecstasy. *Yes ... that night is memorable.*

Katharine feared that Andy might notice her feelings toward Pierre, so she leaned over and planted a platonic kiss on his cheek. "You're quiet today ... still thinking about the interviews?"

"Yup." He grabbed her thigh and brusquely ran his hand up her leg.

She cringed.

Abruptly, he withdrew. "What the hell's the matter with you lately?"

"Nothing ... I'm not in the mood right now."

" 'Seems you're never in the mood anymore."

"Don't be silly, Darling ... I'm just all tensed up over Pierre's interviews, that's all."

"Ya? Well, you should be ... neither Jane's nor yours was a raving success."

71

Andy's eyes glazed over. "Ya know … it's hard to believe Pierre traveled to the future and back, but his predictions do seem to hold up—look at the horse race just now … it was fantastic. Still, he doesn't organize his presentation properly—talks about anything that comes to mind. No wonder he is considered to be insane. Something has got to change though … the senator's riding the hell outta me."

"Andy, you've got the wrong man," Katharine blurted.

"So you keep telling me … but, no, Pierre's the right man alright."

"I mean … he didn't kill anyone. He didn't kill my son. Somebody else did. Maybe he did travel through time, but Pierre could not have killed anyone—I just know it."

"Kathy, how can you 'just know it'? How can you be so sure Pierre isn't responsible for your son's death … divine revelation?"

She was perplexed. *Up 'til now, Andy had supported Pierre. Suddenly, he seems to have turned against him. Why? Is Andy jealous? Has he guessed about Pierre and me?* "No, Andy, not divine revelation, but I've always been a good judge of character … you know that. Maybe I'm just psychic. Besides, when I interviewed Pierre seven years ago, he seemed so sincere—so unselfishly dedicated."

"Kathy, what the hell's the commotion in the kitchen—I can't even hear the God damn' holovision?"

"Sorry. I hired two, advanced cookrobots to help with dinner. I want a gourmet feast for Julie and Mario tonight. Most of the food is from the Moon, so I want expert preparation."

"Jeez, Kathy, from the Moon? That's a lotta money."

"Sure, but we haven't entertained them since their marriage. I want a proper start with them. You know I haven't been easy to get along with, lately."

"Amen to that. … Dammit, Kathy, can't you get those robots to be quiet before Julie and Mario arrive?"

* * *

Katharine felt good. The dinner had been gourmet. She thought that Julie, tense upon arrival, now appeared mellow and relaxed. She ushered her guests into the living room for brandies and liqueurs.

"Mother," Julie asked, "when is your next interview with this Talon fellow?"

"Tuesday night … Jane doesn't want it to compete with Monday-night football."

"Well, his views about his youth and the past are interesting, but I'd like to hear what he has to say about the future."

Andy said, "Be patient, Julie, he'll get around to it. Right now, Pierre is priming the listeners for the really bad news."

"I hope so. The whole world needs to be scared about the future. We all seem to go about our day-to-day business without concern for society's health. I think we—"

"Julie," Mario butted in, "everyone is aware and worried, but each waits for someone else to solve the problem. Collectively, we are concerned, but, individually, we are selfish. In the past, many species destroyed themselves because of some flaw in their survival instincts. I had thought humans could rise above this law of nature, but, now, I have my doubts. We—humans—don't respect our environment … and that will prove to be our survival-instinct flaw … if, indeed, proof can occur when no one exists to witness it. But, just as Senator Yoshimasa said, I fear this fellow's efforts are futile. Nevertheless, I do wish him luck."

Apparently, Julie and Mario had warmed to their subject, so Katharine kept quiet and listened. She hoped they'd avoid the one subject upsetting to her. She noticed that Andy was watching her. Suddenly, she realized that her eyelids drooped. She glanced at her brandy snifter—empty. *How many have I had? ... one or two?* Julie's not-so-furtive glances her way prompted alertness, yet, her eyes kept closing.

"Mario darling, I agree with you but hope we're both wrong," Julie said. After another cautious glance at Katharine, she stated offhandedly, "I do think that abortions, embryonic examinations, and euthanasia of in-valid newborns should be legalized."

Her daughter's remark shook Katharine from her lethargy. She intercepted Andy and Mario's looks of dread to each other. She sensed Julie's eyes on her again so, with difficulty, remained stoic.

Evidently reassured, Julie continued. "If we are to minimize the world's in-valid population, it only makes sense. Most of the people I know have at least one in-valid in each of their families.

"Nature tries to keep the species healthy but is hampered by society's clumsy attempts to save 'God's children.' Look at us. ... We're wallowing in the deformed, the sick, and the insane. As soon as possible after conception, they should be kept from ever being born."

Despite her self control, Katharine groaned and thought, *Murder—what a "sweet" way of putting it.*

Mario shot a glance at her, then turned back to his wife. "I agree with your diagnosis, Julie, but not your cure. A hundred years ago, society already had gone your route. Why do you think those restrictive laws were passed back then? ... The excesses had become intolerable—even sickening.

"Take prenatal exams—those indicating the 'wrong' sex or hair or skin color, or some other asinine reason caused abortions in the thousands. Others in the hundreds of thousands occurred as birth-control substitutes—why spoil a good sex act with birth-control measures when one always can fall back on an abortion? Many submitted themselves to abortions because they were too young—or were too old—or lacked sufficient money or weren't married yet or hadn't been married long enough. This world indeed would be desolate if every newborn were wanted."

"Perhaps ... but a better world it would be," Julie countered. "Fifteen billion souls exist on this earth—thrice the number of a century and a half ago. Most starve in crowded squalor and mercifully die young.

"Deforestation and increased planetary heating—both caused by overpopulation—have created more uninhabitable deserts. Overuse of the land has further shrunk our habitat like an overgrazed pasture. Nature now limits our numbers because we have failed to do so. Last year alone, 150 million wretches committed suicide or died from starvation or disease. We have two choices—continue this madness or selectively prevent in-valid humans from beginning their brief, miserable lives."

Katharine had enough. After her daughter's latest drivel, she could contain herself no longer. Her stupor evaporated, and she shouted, "Julie, shut up—you're talking nonsense, again."

21—CULLING

To kill a human being is, after all,
the least injury you can do him.

—Henry James

An instant later

Julie felt her jaw drop. "What did you say, Mother?"

"I said—"

"Never mind. I heard what you said but can't believe that you said it." One by one, Julie looked at the others. Andrew stared at his feet. Mario frowned, but his faint smile seemed to egg her on.

"Julie, it is I who cannot believe what you said. Where do you get such crazy ideas?"

Julie knew that she should feel compassion for her mother's ignorance, but she could not. Over the years, her mother had steadfastly refused to face reality. No doubt, Douglas's existence had been the reason, but, now, her little brother was dead—there were no more excuses. "Dammit, Mother, can't you wake up to what's happening to us? You're a good reporter and interviewer, but you can't continue to be, if you stick with your outmoded anti-abortional beliefs. I try to remember that grandmother and great grandmoth—"

"You leave them out of it."

Andrew spoke. "Look, Kathy, you believed what your mother told you, but she and her mother lived in other times. Today is different."

Her mother shot a glance at Andrew. "So, today we can kill babies. Is that it? ... Besides, who asked you? This is between my daughter and me."

Julie was amused by the look on Andrew's face—one of hurt and surprise. She glanced at her husband, but Mario's expression remained the same—his slight smile still egging her on. Yet, she knew that he didn't necessarily support her views. No doubt, he was proud of her ability to stand up to her mother, who had so dominated her before their marriage. *Perhaps*, she thought, *Mario is content to see himself as the catalyst in this transformation of our mother-daughter relationship.*

"Oh, Mother, there you go again—using distorted rhetoric. Eliminating a defective embryo is not killing a baby."

Her mother shook a disapproving finger at her. "God is against killing babies. God's law forbids abortion."

Julie could not suppress a laugh. "That a 'God's law' against abortion exists always was a common misconception among the prolifers of the past. God has no such law—it was dreamed up by ignorant people embracing false religions of their own invention. God's law supports the survival of the species—not that of individuals. God guards the health of a species by performing more abortions than we humans ever have done. The medical profession, abetted by prolifers and their lawyers, breaks God's law. Civilization and false religions make its aberrations possible."

74

Her mother's eyes widened. "You blaspheme. From where did you get these sacrilegious beliefs? Have I raised a godless monster? Are we becoming a godless world?"

Despite her mother's theatrics, Julie remained unmoved. "You hate melodrama, so calm down and listen to reason for a change.

"You see, Mother, while Mario's been working at Fuerza Cortés, I've been spending my days learning about the controversy that has surrounded abortion for the past two centuries. It wasn't easy. The Wall did its job well, but some documents remain. Despite my prejudices, I've tried to educate myself with dispassion and objectivity."

Julie saw that her mother's eyes were closed but detected a tear leaking from under an eyelid.

"Even before conception, nature—or, if you prefer, God—starts the culling process. Before the sex act transpires, formidable obstacles to mating exist: The environment must be survived to adulthood—predators and disease kill the weak and sickly. This is not cruel, but necessary to a species' survival—individuals die that the species might live.

"Only the strong and desirable mate. In the higher species, males fight for the right to mate and do so with healthy females or with one 'alpha' female, who, in turn, fought with her sisters for the right. The losers of these fights do not breed among themselves. To do so would condemn the species to rapid extinction.

"I have not yet mentioned the abortional stage—an important link in this culling process."

Her mother opened her eyes and stabbed looks of disapproval her way. "You equate humans to animals? ... Humans are special. God created us to rule over animals. Those barbaric rules of survival don't apply to humans—every human life is sacred."

Julie felt angry. "No, Mother, you are wrong. Humans are but one link in a series of species that evolve from one to another through Natural Selection. Ironically, our 'advanced' civilization is halting the process—bringing the human species to extinction. I am sure we will be extinct by 2789 ... just as Pierre Talon affirms will happen."

Without conviction, her mother said, "I see." She added curtly, "Explain God's abortions—if you can."

Julie smiled. Sarcastic though the request be, her mother actually asked her for an explanation. "Well, the culling process continues during and after the sex act. Much sperm is defective. The defective rate for humans is higher than that of any other primate species. In addition, during the last two centuries, as a result of the continuous degradation of our environment, the defective human-sperm rate increased from twenty-five to fifty percent. The defective ovum rate sustained a lesser increase.

"Over the eons, a mechanism evolved, which keeps most of the defective sperm from ever reaching the ova—a mechanism based upon the physicality and chemistry of the sexual organs.

"To facilitate summary fertilization, the ovaries could have been located near the cervix—where sperm are deposited. But, no—nature placed them as far away as possible, thus sperm must hunt for ova over long distances. You'd imagine that nature would pave the way. But, no—the fluids of the uterus prove to be toxic to sperm—only the more hardy and less defective survive the trek.

"So, what has medical science done? ... performed in-vitro fertilization in a petri dish, where an ovum must summarily accept a sperm that—you might say—hasn't earned its 'stripes' yet. In-vitro fertilization causes an increased, defective-zygote count."

Her mother seemed confused. "Zygote?"

"Yes ... zygote. Don't feel bad, Mother; long ago, most prolifers didn't know the meaning of the term either. Their misguiding, misguided leaders preferred to use—erroneously—the word 'embryo' or, better yet—'fetus' ... stirred up more antipathy, you know."

"How is that? ... A fertilized ovum does become a fetus."

"Sure—just like an unfertilized ovum or sperm is the basis for an adult human, but, before becoming a fetus, new life must pass through a brief zygotic stage and a three-month, embryonic stage during which time the life form resembles any species of developing vertebrate. Only in the last six months of pregnancy does the embryo become a fetus and acquire human characteristics.

"Now you can understand why the prolife fanatics liked to throw around the word 'fetus' when, in most cases, the term didn't apply."

"So what is a zygote?"

Julie found it hard to believe that her own mother, a modern educated woman, could have remained so ignorant of the subject. Certainly, her experience with her deformed son had made her close her heart and mind to the obvious ... or was she just playing dumb on purpose. "A zygote is a fertilized ovum, which has yet to procure a source of food. The majority of inviable zygotes are incapable of finding and retaining nourishment. Today, in most cases, a woman, whose ovum is fertilized, never knows it. The faulty zygote simply fails to attach itself to the uterine wall and flushes out with the menstrual flow."

"Then, this flushing out is your God's abortion?"

"No," Julie answered, "but it is—as you would say—God eliminating a defective, potential life form. An abortion cannot happen with a zygote because it isn't even part of the woman yet—not attached to her uterus. A woman cannot have an abortion before she has become pregnant or, in other words, before the zygote attaches itself to the uterus and transforms into an embryo."

Her mother spoke with affected sadness. "Ah, she is ready for God to perform the abortion ... at last."

Julie ignored the sarcasm. "If that is necessary to maintain a healthy species—yes. Two centuries ago, ten percent of human pregnancies ended in abortion. One century ago, the rate climbed to thirty, and, now, it is fifty percent."

Her mother seemed dismayed. "You see, Julie, the prolifers were right. Even with our strict anti-abortional laws, a growing number of abortions are performed. Can you imagine what the world would be like if the abortionists had gotten their way? Certainly, by now, pregnancies would end in abortion far over the fifty-percent rate."

Julie laughed disparagingly and tried a little sarcasm of her own. "Ah, Mother ... you are the naïve one, aren't you? I'm referring to natural—not—induced abortions. If the name has a greater impact on you, let's call them God's abortions. Most women don't even realize they've had God's abortion. They lose the embryo early, so the only symptom is a slightly heavier menstrual flow than normal. Of course, if the abortion occurs later on, cramps, nausea, and a definite embryonic issue may signal that an abortion has occurred."

Her mother's expression changed to one of feigned wonderment. "Do natural abortions of fetuses occur often?"

Again, Julie was gratified that her mother had asked her for information yet doubted the sincerity of her request. "No. Nature eliminates most defective new life in the zygotic and embryonic phases of development. The relatively small amount of inviable-life rejections in the late fetal phase are called stillbirths, not abortions."

Her mother seemed hurried to change the subject. "In sum, at the end of the embryonic phase, nature has finished most of its 'culling' process—as you call it."

"The culling process never stops. Defective fetuses that survive birth no longer enjoy protection by the mother's womb. In nature, the environment eliminates the in-valid newborn quickly—a mother cat refuses the teat to a malformed kitten or—the kitten is unable to feed itself, in the first place.

"Our 'civilized' societies, under the guise of compassion, force medical science to keep defective life alive. These in-valids are the death knell of our species. The devastating human surpopulation of Earth, in large part, resulted from—"

"Fine, fine … I understand what you're trying to tell me, Julie. I'm tired. I'm going to bed."

Her mother struggled to her feet, bid everyone good night, and headed down the hallway to her bedroom.

Julie detected a definite stagger to her gait.

Vivre est une maladie dont le sommeil
nous soulage toutes les seize heures.
C'est un palliatif. La mort est le remède.
—Sébastien-Roch Nicolas Chamfort

Moments later

Katharine sat on the bed and buried her head in her hands. She had faked excessive drunkenness—an improvised device—in an attempt to explain her lack of response to her daughter's opinions about a particularly painful subject. Another confrontation would have damaged even further her already fragile relationship with Julie. She had planned the dinner to pacify rather than embitter.

What else could she do? She didn't want to appear submissive, yet she knew the drunkenness ploy would only delay the inevitable clash. *Oh, if only Julie and I could be friends! She's all I have left in this world.*

Katharine whispered, "Computer, pipe the living-room conversation to my receptors."

She recognized Mario's voice through her aural implants, "… you are right, Andy, my Catholic upbringing does affect my philosophy, but so does common sense.

"Maybe you remember the Extermination Era in India. Julie and I are too young to remember, but I, at least, have studied the subject.

"Despite forced abortion and birth-control programs, the subcontinent's population came to surpass two billion. In desperation, the Indian government authorized euthanasia. Of course, the motives were noble—if ill-conceived. Unfortunately, many used euthanasia for political ends."

"How is that?" Julie asked.

"Well, upon the word of greedy or spiteful bureaucrats, whole families and, even villages, were 'legally' wiped out. Death squads roamed the countryside and killed anyone deemed 'in-valid.' The lack-eyed and lack-limbed disappeared. A limp, gray hair, or wrinkled skin condemned millions.

"I don't believe that a society can properly legislate and police euthanasia. The culprit is the corruptibility of the human animal. The power of human thought enables our rationale to expand in many directions—even to satisfy individual, selfish ambitions. We can tolerate only deaths from the randomness and impartiality of disease and natural disaster—from God's will."

Katharine listened for Andy's voice. His silence seemed unnatural—Andy always loved a good discussion. Maybe the subject was too risqué for him. Possibly, for her sake, he might be unwilling to express his own convictions. Perhaps he was silent because Julie was expressing them in damned-good stead.

She felt a sense of awe for the precocious maturity of her daughter's views. Her little girl had grown to womanhood behind her back. She listened to Julie with heightened interest.

"Well, I certainly don't approve of death squads smashing their way into people's homes searching for senile grandparents huddled in dark corners. On the other hand, families must be allowed to make decisions concerning their own in-valid offspring. Society should not have the power to martyr parents by forcing them to keep their defective issues alive.

"Then again, many religious zealots believe that to care for their deformed children earns them respect, martyrdom, and eternal salvation. In reality, they are duped by society through a religion's peer-pressured brainwashing. The limited resources squandered on the in-valid condemn to miserable deaths the millions of starving, valid babies on this jam-packed planet. Ironically, the in-valid die miserably, anyway."

Each of Julie's words pained Katharine, and, in the privacy of her bedroom, she wept openly. Mario's voice was, again, a welcome respite.

"Julie, an unborn must be allowed to develop naturally and be born. If a newborn is deformed to the point where normal care cannot sustain its life, that normal care should be continued until the baby dies a normal death. I agree that heroic, state-of-the-art, medical measures should not be brought to bear. That is nature's way ... God's way."

"Mario, dear, that is pure crap, and you know it. Your 'nature's way' is the cruelest of all, and it can be extremely cruel. A carnivore, more often than not, starts eating its victim while it is still alive—a perfect example of 'nature's way.'

"No, the more compassionate route is the earliest possible recognition and suppression of in-valid life forms. Most can be detected and aborted long before the end of the embryonic stage of development. Of course, waiting to abort until into the fetal stage is criminal, but the earlier decision is not—it is compassionate for the suppressed life form, its parents, and its siblings—present and, most particularly ... future."

For a moment, Julie stopped talking, and Katharine wondered where her little girl had learned this new-found knowledge of hers."

"Mario, darling, if you could raise either a valid child or an in-valid one—but not both—which one would you choose?"

Hidden in her bedroom, Katharine waited anxiously for Mario's response, but her receptors remained silent. She knew that the question must be a trick and that Mario knew it, too.

Finally, she heard Mario's answer: "The valid child, of course."

"My dear husband ... that is a wise choice because, otherwise, you would have condemned any potential future, possibly valid, children to death. ... You see, if our first child is in-valid and you decide to keep it, I would support your decision for the sake of our marriage, but I would never, ever, have another child—possibly the very one that could have been valid.

"My mother, by keeping her in-valid son Douglas, possibly—just possibly—condemned to death ... any future valid siblings that I might have had."

Beyond caring that her cries would echo into every corner of the apartment, Katharine rocked to and fro on her bed and emitted prolonged wails of anguish.

23—LEVITATION

It beareth the name of Vanity-Fair,
because the town where 'tis kept,
is lighter than vanity.

—John Bunyon

Six hundred fifty-six years in the future, June 5, 2786
The floating city of Cumulus
Five miles above Antarctica

Pierre chewed his fruit slowly. Something about Boniface's explanations bothered him. He looked up. "If I understand correctly, Manzoni's Principle of Universal Duality states: Equal quantities of matter and antimatter constitute the Universe, and, because they repulse each other, never the twain shall meet."

Boniface's eyes sparkled. "Almost correct—I wouldn't say 'never.' "

"What if all matter and antimatter in the Universe, through some magic, could be made to coincide spatially?"

"The Universe would wink out—disappear without a trace."

"Then, the Universe doesn't really exist."

"It exists only because its matter and antimatter components are kept apart."

"What keeps them apart?"

"Antigravity, of course."

"So, where's all the antimatter? Up to 2045, little was detected."

Boniface stroked the extremities of his long white mustache, which flowed down into his beard. "You see, Pierre, as the Universe formed, matter and antimatter repulsed each other and pooled into separate groups. Over time, these groups attracted more and more of their kind until they became galaxies and antigalaxies. These formed into clusters and anticlusters and, finally, into superclusters and antisuperclusters."

"Can antigalaxies be detected from Earth? How are they distinguished from galaxies?"

"Pierre, they are farther away from us than is any galaxy. The few that can be detected are barely discernible—and, at that, by the same kind of radiation as is emitted by galaxies. Remember, electromagnetic radiation is half matter and half antimatter—alternating occurrences of electrons and positrons at the speed of light."

"Wait a minute ... at the speed of light, particles possess infinite mass."

"Ah, yes ... individually they do, but as conjugate pairs in the energy mode, their mass and antimass cancel, so the energy beam's effective mass is zero."

Pierre chuckled. "Boniface, do you have an answer for everything?"

The old man frowned and said, "If I did, by now, all of the In-valids would be Valid.

"Boniface, tell me how antineutronics made those buildings down there so tall."

"I was wondering when you were going to ask. Well, as you know, a bound neutron within an atomic nucleus is stable. However, removed from a nucleus, a free neutron becomes unstable and soon decays into other—stable—particles. In 2252, twenty years after Manzoni's work, a stabilization process for free neutrons gave them indefinite lifetimes. For the first time, many neutrons could be held together by their mutual strong-force attraction to form a super-massive ball. Because the ball contained no protons, no electromagnetic force existed to attract electrons and form atoms."

"How are neutron balls held in place? Certainly, they must be very heavy."

"Yes—unlike atomic nuclei in their electronic clouds, Planck quantum distancing doesn't exist; therefore, microscopic amounts of them weigh tons. Also, because neutrons contain no electrical charge, magnetic traps cannot retain them. A ball of free neutrons would sink toward the center of the earth until annihilated.

"In 2260, the process for collecting free neutrons was successfully employed on antineutrons. Of course, our matter environment quickly annihilated them, but, not before they were observed to rise rather than fall—as do neutrons."

"So, Manzoni's theory that antimatter possesses antimass became law."

"Exactly, Pierre ... and a new technology blossomed—antineutronics ... but efficient containment vessels for neutrons and antineutrons did not arrive on the scene for another twenty years. In 2281, when they did, their simplicity stunned the world—the neutrons and antineutrons, in a way, contained each other."

"What about mutual annihilation?"

"No problem. ... Here's how it's done: Suspend a minute, solid sphere of antineutrons in the center of a larger—although still microscopic—hollow ball of neutrons."

"Suspend—how?"

"That's the simplicity part. ... Through matter-antimatter repulsion, the two, concentric, spherically-symmetrical balls remain in equilibrium—spatially separate."

"Ingenious, but, again I ask you—What's this got to do with increasing the height of a building?"

"I'm getting to that, Pierre. ... Earth's gravity repulses balls containing more antineutrons than neutrons and, in essence, produces lift. You can mix trillions of these balls into an amorphous liquid and harden them into blocks of ordinary-looking material. Attached to buildings, the blocks hold them up ... rather, they pull them up.

"Naturally, this technology didn't happen overnight—it evolved slowly. The production and safe retention of large amounts of antimatter didn't happen until 2316. Levitated vehicles appeared in 2369, and buildings got help against gravity in 2395. By 2474, enough modules existed to make a building 'weightless.' Thereafter, veritable floating cities existed, as buildings cut their 'umbilical cords' from Mother Earth."

"Boniface, that is fascinating, ab-so-lute-ly fascinating. ... Then, those broken buildings down there were not designed to stand by themselves."

"No, with the levitation modules removed, they collapsed like houses of cards. ... Pierre, we must be going—another learning session awaits you."

"I'm tired. I'll do it tomorrow."

"No, Pierre Talon, you'll learn more today. Have no fear, you will learn without effort—this time, we'll bypass your normal senses. Your brain will absorb knowledge from high-frequency information beams.

"Come."

The woman that deliberates is lost.

—Joseph Addison

Six hundred fifty-six years into the past, August 24, 2130
Jane Stevens' Informational News Agency
Bellevue, Franklin

Jane's curt summons surprised Katharine. Rarely, was she asked to present herself in the boss's office—usually, Jane conducted business through the holoscreen.

"Do come in, Kathy. Please … sit down."

Katharine sat and wondered about what "stupidity" she was guilty of to merit a scolding.

Jane had her back turned to Katharine and was looking out the window. As if her announcement were of slight importance, she said, offhandedly, "I'll be interviewing Talon tonight."

Katharine felt her temples throb. She leapt to her feet. "What! You can't do that. My interview is already planned. I get along with Pierre—you don't. What will the senator say about this?"

"He's in San Francisco."

"He'll still find out."

"Of course, but too late to do anything about it because you, my dear Kathy, will not show up for the interview."

"Oh, yes I will."

Jane pivoted and faced Katharine. She snarled, "In that case, I'll fire you on the spot."

Katharine was dumbstruck. She groped for a response, but Jane was quicker. "Look, I want Talon exposed for the fraud he is. He killed your son, for God's sake, so I thought you'd be the best choice to discredit him, but, after your dewy-eyed performance last week, it's obvious you can't—or won't."

"Oh, Jane, Pierre's not guilty. I know he—.

"Shut up!" Jane rushed toward Katharine, grabbed her shoulders, and shook them. "Look at me, Kathy. I want to know what went on between you and Talon seven years ago."

Katharine pulled away. "Nothing! … besides, it's none of your business."

Jane's eyes gleamed in triumph. "Aha, you are hiding something. Before … you wanted him dead. Now … you call him by his first name and can't sing his praises high enough—what gives, Kathy?"

Katharine jutted out her chin. "Nothing!"

"Okay, okay … if you insist, but, tonight, I'm putting an end to his nonsense about the future."

Katharine took her courage in her hands. "Jane, what's the real reason? … Are you jealous?"

"Of you?"

"Yes."

Jane snickered. "Why should I be?"

"Andy, of course." Jane's hollow laugh galled her.

"Naturally I'm attracted to him. What woman wouldn't be? But, my stable is full of virile men—I needn't stoop to steal another woman's."

Katharine arched her eyebrows. "Then, you're taking this interview away from me because you want all the glory for yourself."

"My dear, I've got all the glory I need. ... No, I must chastise both Talon and Yoshimasa. I'm going to show the good senator he can't dictate to me about how I should conduct my business. ... Go home, Kathy. ... Watch the interview tonight and witness the fall of Talon's credibility."

Katharine bit her lip and, without a word, stomped out of Jane's office.

* * *

Home alone, Katharine awaited Jane's interview session with Pierre. Andy had gone to help Jane prepare for it. He said that he wanted to coach her about tact, patience, courtesy, and, in general, better, on-camera manners. She suspected that he really wanted an excuse to see the bitch.

From the sofa, she scanned the wallscreen in monitor mode. The sound track in her aural receptors switched to match each screenframe as her gaze shifted from one to another. Nothing interested her. She looked away, and her receptors fell silent.

Katharine felt nauseated. Her little world was crumbling around her. Saturday night, it had begun with Julie and, today, was continuing with Jane. Everything that Katharine supposed was there, appeared to be vanishing: Her daughter seemed irreversibly lost to her. Her job with Jane's agency was rapidly becoming unbearable. Her relationship with Andy was deteriorating ... . She felt a sense of panic and wondered why her life always seemed to migrate from one crisis to another. Was the fault hers entirely—or should others share the blame?

She did know, though, that a revolution had launched itself in her soul. Her interests, tastes, morals, her fundamental philosophy about life, and ... even her reason for existing were being put to the test. She felt empty, was gutted of her strength, and lacked the will to live. All things precious to her flashed before her mind. One by one, she had lost the more important—husband, son, friends, and now—her daughter.

Saturday night, Julie made her aware that, had she not kept her deformed son, she might have had other children. This possibility never before occurred to Katharine. For the past three days, the revelation tormented her. Her brain repeated the same questions over and over: What is the more terrible—keep a son, who is in a vegetal state, and, consequently, vow never to have another child or—reject that son and have another— perhaps normal—child? As a result of keeping Douglas, did she "murder" her third child by never conceiving it? These questions tore at her very entrails.

Katharine hoped that she realized the truth at last. Finally, she realized that, during all these years, she had existed myopically in a deceptive cocoon. Why hadn't she considered what might have occurred had she abandoned Douglas? True, he might have been worse off, even died earlier than he did—but would he have realized it? Would he have suffered?

On the other hand, Katharine knew that her marriage would have been a success, that her husband would not have had the accident that killed him. She knew she would have had another child ... maybe more. She knew that her daughter and she would have remained good friends.

If she could relive those years, would she change anything? Katharine had mulled the question over many times. She always came up with the same, painful answer: *I suppose I wouldn't*, she had thought. *To plan one's life based upon the possibilities of the future is difficult. Experience and family morals are the biggest influences in one's life, and I know my decision to keep Douglas was based on these.*

Was her childhood education balanced enough to have allowed her to make the right decision? Was her mother's and grandmother's advise—no, command—to keep the baby, a good one? In the past, the answers were clear-cut but, now, seemed elusive.

Thoughts of Pierre cheered her, but being unable to be with him quickly quenched the feeling. And, what about Andy? Despite his uncouthness, he was a good man. Yet, in her heart, she realized that if she were forced to choose between the two men, Andy would have to go.

Katharine glanced at the wallscreen and recognized Jane in one of the screen-frames. The time for the interview had arrived. "Activate frame fourteen," she ordered. The image in the screenframe expanded to fill the center of the living room, and Pierre Talon's isolation cell appeared to be transported into the apartment.

She knew no warmth emanated from the cell, yet, upon seeing its holo-image, she felt a pleasant glow. She didn't know why. The room had hard, cold walls with hard, cold furnishings, so from where did the feeling of warmth come? She didn't know.

She was impressed by—even proud of—Pierre's confidence in himself and his mission. She admired his no-nonsense treatment of Jane in the first interview. She felt good whenever she saw him.

The possibility that Pierre might be the arsonist killer of her son was very real, but she chose to ignore it. Subconsciously, she knew that she would deal with the problem, when and if necessary.

She shifted her attention to Jane, who looked ravishingly beautiful ... and rich enough to attract any man. There she is, seven years my senior, still looking so youthful. Is it her workouts? Is it her African blood? Experts say that persons of mixed race are healthier, handsomer, and smarter than the inbred.

25—TIME

Time present and time past are
Both perhaps present in time future,
And time future contained in time past.

—Thomas Stearns Eliot

A moment later

Katharine realized that Jane had already started the interview. She listened.

"… to reduce the number of calls to my agency, I will, at this time, answer the more popular questions.

"Two weeks ago, in an effort to prove that he had visited the future, Pierre Talon gave to the authorities detailed predictions. Thus far, they have proved to be correct. Of course, we can reveal to the public neither the nature of the predictions nor their results.

"Many believe that these successful outcomes do not prove Mister Talon's claim. They say that his fake searches of his brain for 'facts' are unconvincing. Nobody is capable of remembering, much less recalling, the incredible number of precise facts he presumes to have at his mental finger tips. How does he grab predictions from nowhere? Even if his public records or historical accounts from the future do exist, he does not have them here—in the asylum—at his disposition.

"The very implausibility of his claims suggests that, somehow, he has conned us. Possibly, someone outside the asylum rigged the 'facts' and secretly communicated them to Mister Talon. Other popular questions concern the technology that Pierre Talon used for his 'voyage' backward from the future into the past."

Katharine wondered whom Jane was quoting, when she said, "Many believe …" and "They say …" and "Other popular questions …" *Shabby journalism!*

"The physics community is anxious for his explanations. To help us arrive at the truth, we have invited one of the more-prestigious, theoretical physicists of our time to question him. She will prove Mister Talon to be a fake.

"Before I introduce our guest, who is standing by in Göttingen, I have some questions for Mister Talon. His answers will be my contribution to the proof that he is a fake."

Jane turned toward Pierre, who seemed calm and collected.

Katharine held her breath.

"Mister Talon," Jane said, "I want you to relate to my viewers—now, tonight—the closing statistics of the Monnetville Stock Exchange for the next five open days including indices, major stock prices, volumes purchased and sold … the works."

Pierre's cold expression made Katharine shiver. She knew Jane had guts, but, this time, she was going too far. Does she have approval to ask these questions? … and how will Pierre handle her demand? Will he reject it out of hand?

Katharine watched Pierre attentively. He remained motionless for a long time—eyes closed. She noticed Jane snort and shake her head in disgust. Finally, she saw Pierre open his eyes.

85

He spoke slowly. "Yes, I have all that information, but I cannot reveal it—chaos in the world economies would result."

Katharine was startled by the maniacal glint in Jane's eyes. Her boss pounced. "Ah-ha, I knew it. You can't fake the answers, can you, Mister Talon."

"I agree that I can't, Ms. Stevens, and I'm not. They are established facts. However, should I publicly reveal such information, I would be guilty of manipulating the stock market. More importantly, the information I possess is based upon my not revealing the future or, more precisely, the information not being acted upon. A public revelation would prove nothing because it, in itself, would cause the outcome to change."

Katharine was amused to see Jane's apparent confusion over this cause-and-effect paradox of temporal loops.

"Very well, you may have your way. After the interview, I'll arrange for a secure place for you to record and store your statistics until the week has passed."

Katharine was surprised when Pierre agreed. ... Could his claim possibly be true? ... that he did indeed visit the future?

She noticed the holoimage of a petite, gray-haired, asian woman project itself next to Jane and Pierre's.

Jane turned to face the famous physicist, and her teeth flashed anew. "Ladies and Gentlemen, I am honored to present the very distinguished Doctor Bai Nyugen in Göttingen. As most of you know, Doctor Nyugen is the 2124 Nobel Prize Laureate in astrophysics, president of the Max Planck Society in Göttingen, chairholder of the Nathan Rosen Institute in Jerusalem, and senior member of the prestigious Feynman Consortium in Pasadena. ... Welcome, Doctor Nyugen."

"Thank you, Ms. Stevens."

Jane's exudation of confidence rankled Katharine. She dearly hoped that Pierre would—again—put her in her place.

"Doctor, you and I conversed this morning. If you please, could you repeat the specifics of the conversation to Mister Talon?"

"Of course." Doctor Nyugen turned toward Pierre. "I am honored to meet you, Doctor Talon."

Katharine was taken aback by the title accorded Pierre. Since the beginning of the interviews, this was the first time she had noticed anyone other than herself refer to him as "Doctor." She felt a sense of satisfaction when she saw a frown replace Jane's smug expression.

Doctor Nyugen continued. "I have read some of your papers, Doctor. They are very advanced for that period."

The two physicists ignored Jane and proceeded to exchange compliments and banalities as if time were of small concern.

Jane looked exasperated. Finally, she interrupted the little tête-à-tête. "Please, Doctor Nyugen, we must be moving along."

Katharine giggled.

The illustrious guest excused herself and launched into a long, technical lecture as to why travel into the past is impossible.

Katharine was surprised by Pierre's patience as he waited courteously for Doctor Nyugen to finish.

Then, he said, "I agree with you one-hundred percent, Doctor Nyugen, but you see—"

Jane cut him off. "That settles that. Next week, I will reveal the remainder of the proof that Mister Talon did not visit the future."

As Jane talked, Pierre raised his hand in mimicry of a little, scrawny-necked school boy and, in a timid voice, said, "Ms. Stevens, ma'am … please, ma'am, may I have my rebuttal time, now?"

Katharine laughed at Pierre's put-down. She was, indeed, feeling better.

Jane said, "There is little to add, Mister Talon, but—please, do go on."

Pierre addressed himself to Doctor Nyugen. "You confine your reasoning to the matter world and not to the antimatter world. Is that right?"

"Yes, of course. One cannot travel in an antimatter world. … Antimatter is only a quantum-level phenomenon."

"Do you agree, Doctor Nyugen, that, if antimatter were a macroscopic phenomenon, time in an antimatter world would flow opposite in direction to time in a matter world?"

"Well, Richard Feynman theorized such a proposition almost two centuries ago—but—solely on the quantum level … and that has been proven only recently."

Pierre asked, "How about superclusters of antigalaxies?"

"… galaxies composed of antimatter?"

"Precisely, Doctor Nyugen."

"None have been observed, and their existence is improbable."

"Why is that?"

"Well, if they did exist, we most certainly would have witnessed, by now, a tremendously explosive collision between a galaxy and an antigalaxy and a near complete annihilation of the two—but we have not."

Pierre continued his prompts. "What about gravitational repulsion?"

Doctor Nyugen was emphatic. "There is no such thing."

"You continue to confine your reasoning to the matter world. You see, Doctor Nyugen, matter is gravitationally repulsed by antimatter, so galaxies and antigalaxies are forced not to collide."

For a moment, Doctor Nyugen's expression was confused, then it changed to one of somebody who had just discovered religion. To Katharine, however, the more gratifying expression was Jane's—a sign of her unhappy premonition of Pierre's ultimate victory.

"Are you telling me that the Universe is perfectly symmetrical, Doctor Talon?"

Pierre grinned. "Absolutely."

"Then, all antimatter attributes are diametrically opposite to those of matter—in every basic dimension … mass, temperature, charge, length, and time." Doctor Nyugen's tone of voice was appropriate to the recitation of the Lord's Prayer.

"That is correct, Doctor Nyugen. … Giulio Manzoni, himself, will not say it better."

"Who is Giulio Manzoni?"

"Not 'is' … but, 'will be.' … Oh, he will write a little paper in 2233 entitled, 'The Duality of the Universe.' "

"Important?"

"… set the world on its ear." Pierre beamed.

Doctor Nyugen looked at Jane. "Ms. Stevens, I must say that this conversation with Doctor Talon is a great revelation to me. I agree with him: Time travel into the past is possible."

Jane looked puzzled—and crestfallen. "Doctor Nyugen, I seem to have missed something here. … What changed your mind?"

"It's fairly obvious—if antimatter has antimass, antigalaxies will repel galaxies, which makes the existence of antigalaxies possible. If they exist, one can travel to them and, while there, go backward in time."

"But—how?"

Doctor Nyugen's response showed her impatience. "My dear lady, by just staying there awhile, that's all … it is automatic."

Although Katharine could not grasp the particulars of Pierre's victory, she reveled in it and in a feeling of warm contentedness, as if the achievement had been her own.

26—DREAMWORLD

The hope I dreamed of was a dream,
   Was but a dream; and now I wake,
Exceeding comfortless, and worn, and old,
   For a dream's sake.

—Christina Rossetti

Six hundred fifty-six years into the future, June 5, 2786
The floating city of Cumulus
Five miles above Antarctica

Boniface turned to Pierre. "Before you enter the Learning Room, I must explain the sessions: You will visit the past in the years 2431, 2473, and 2550—the three most-significant dates in the independence of the In-valids. Participation in these historical vignettes will instill in you a good perspective of the past that you do not now know."

Pierre was incredulous. "From the Learning Room, I can travel into the past?"

"No, you will remain here, but all of your sensory nerves will be artificially stimulated by human sensations that were recorded during those times. You will experience real feelings of real persons from past eras as if you were actually they."

"Will I be able to distinguish between these time trips and reality?"

"Yes. In these learning sessions, you will receive only the recorded sensations of others. You will be unable to control their actions, which are historical facts and cannot be changed. In essence, your mind will be a passenger in the brain of a strange body—not its pilot."

"I won't be able to control my host body? Oh, that's just great. What if this guy gets himself in real trouble … could I bail out?"

"Certainly, Pierre. Just thinking about it would return your own senses to you. However, if you did, you'd rob yourself of valuable experiences.

"In-valids, of course, use a different technology in their Dreamworlds. Entering them, they live completely vicarious—yet realistic—lives. In fact, their continual trips into these virtual realities keep insanity at bay."

"You mean, they can leave their flawed bodies behind and live in a fully-interactive, simulated environment?"

"Absolutely. In-valids can assume to have beautiful, healthy bodies and minds of their choice. As a matter of fact, most In-valids remain in dream states for long periods and become convinced that they are valid persons living valid lives. To them, returning to the real world seems like a bad dream—a nightmare—and off they go again … back to their simulated Utopias—their Dreamworlds."

"Boniface, does every In-valid lead a vicarious life?"

"No, some of the less-deformed ones resist the temptation, but, as they age and are subjected to amputations and transplantations, most finally succumb to its appeal. However, one particularly strong-willed In-valid continues to face her existence despite her advanced age. Of course, her heavy responsibilities prompt her to remain alert."

"Who is she?"

"Her name is Strata, and she is the Protector of Cumulus and Head of the Decision Council."

"Will I meet her?"

"Yes—eventually ... but not physically. She exists extra corporeally—her brain having been disembodied for over a century, now."

"How old is this Strata, and what do you mean 'disembodied'?"

"She was born 254 years ago in 2532. Her brain, extracted from her cranium, is bathed in a warm encephalofluid and fed hormone-rich, oxygenated blood."

"She must possess artificial sense organs."

"—as do all disembodied In-valids, Pierre. Strata, as the Protector of Cumulus, must see and hear all. Unlike a normal human with two each eyes, ears, and nostrils, she is connected to hundreds of artificial ones—possibly thousands."

Pierre shuddered. "Do you think she's listening to us, now?"

Boniface appeared unconcerned. "Perhaps."

Apprehensively, Pierre glanced about. "And you, Boniface ... how old are you?"

"I am 190."

Pierre studied the frail-looking man with increasing fondness. "Tell me about yourself, Boniface."

"Very well. ... Strata's ancestors came from a land contaminated by radioactivity. Subsequent generations produced more and more stillbirths and babies with worse and worse deformities.

"Strata, herself, was more fortunate than her feebleminded cousins and siblings—her brain was intact ... even brilliant. However, she was born without eyes, with an exposed spinal column and almost nonexistent vertebrae. Her three, stubby arms ended in useless flippers."

Pierre was revolted. "Boniface, how could that happen? How could generation after generation inherit such terrible deformities?"

"Do you remember the tragedy of Chernobyl in the Ukraine toward the end of the twentieth century?"

"Of course. ... It occurred a quarter century before my birth."

"Then, you know that it was the first significant, radioactive contamination of Earth. Thereafter, nuclear technology vulgarized until it became available to almost anyone. Through apathy, ineptitude, and negligence; one-by-one, other, more-serious 'Chernobyls' occurred. Additionally, terrorist groups possessing atomic weapons held whole cities for ransom. They annihilated some of the world's largest, along with tens of millions of people ... just to satisfy the vanity of various, obscure—and quite mad—war lords.

"Yes, Pierre, humankind of yesteryear poisoned the land: Certainly, many 'Chernobyls' and terrorists' atomic explosions occurred ... but centuries of small, innumerable, individual, seemingly-benign abuses of the land, sea, and air also accumulated, and they helped to effect our ultimate catastrophe.

"Unfortunately, the changes, from one generation to the next, were so small that they barely worried the uneducated masses, who were preoccupied by greed and the traumata of day-to-day survival. Except for fanatical revolutions, the apathetic majority always defeats the concerned minority."

"Boniface, you paint future Earth a dismal place—I hesitate to enter the Learning Room."

"You mean 'past' Earth, don't you? ... Of course—after civilized humans arrived—it did become a dismal place. Myopic juggling of their burgeoning knowledge of physical and chemical processes devastated the Earth and its genetic legacy. The remaining, untainted, food-producing regions of the world dwindled to insignificance. Forced either to poison or to starve themselves, the peoples of the world survived as best they could. However, genetic damage could not be avoided, and the in-valid count continued its upward spiral."

"That is horrible, Boniface. I never knew the effects of pollution could be so cumulative, pervasive, and devastative. To be sure, back in the year 2045, pollution increased, but the majority considered it more of a nuisance than genocidal. Everyone thought that he, only one person, could do little to rectify the situation, so he did nothing—expecting the other guy to do it."

"Pierre, that was only half the problem. ... Also, everyone thought that he, only one person, contributed little to overall pollution, so he polluted—expecting the other guy not to."

"You were going to tell me about yourself, Boniface; instead, you've told me about Strata."

"To tell about Strata is to tell about myself. You see ... Strata is my mother."

"Your mother? ... How could that be? She is an In-valid—and you, a Valid."

"Pierre, ever since the demise of the last, real Valid over two centuries ago, Valids issue from viscera of In-valids, not of other Valids. When I was conceived, human genomic sequencing had not yet deteriorated enough to preclude the occasional occurrence of a valid zygote. Although Strata was incapable of bearing me, her ova did receive the very finest sperm. The best of her valid embryos gestated in an extrauterine placenta and produced me ... but, enough about me—the Learning Room awaits.

"You will enter the mind of John the Martyr, founder of the In-valids' struggle for independence and grandfather of Joan the Liberator. John the Martyr was the first to revolt against the tyranny of the Valids and demand justice and equality for his people."

"When did he live? What happened to him?"

"Pierre, after this learning session, your questions will be more than answered."

27—PANDEMONIUM

Even God cannot change the past.

—Agathon

Six hundred fifty-six years into the past, August 26, 2130
Franklin State Asylum Number Fifteen, Building 10D
Bellevue, Franklin

Pierre finished breakfast and was anxious for the news. The Monnetville Stock Market had just closed. Certainly, his predictions and the day's statistics would differ. How could it be otherwise?

The day before, in spite of the security precautions, his secret stock-market predictions were publicized. Pierre was shocked. The financial world was agog. Worldwide pandemonium reigned.

To Pierre, half of the world condemned and vilified him, while the other half, praised and sanctified him. As the pro and con forces fought back and forth, the values of the stocks that he had mentioned fluctuated wildly.

He was worried that the world would discredit him when the results of the market's closing statistics were found not to match his predictions. He felt that the fault was not his. Someone had betrayed him. *Was it that bitch, Jane? ... or the senator?* Pierre was sure that Andy was not the culprit.

The speakers came to life. Pierre heard the voice of the robosentry. "You have two visitors—Senator Mizuno Yoshimasa and Mister Andrew Drake."

Grim-faced, the senator entered with Andy close behind. Pierre suspected that Andy was stifling a smile. The man winked—confirming Pierre's hunch. Without a word, Pierre's visitors simply looked at him. Then, Andy's smile surfaced. Apparently, he wanted to remain behind the senator to hide the beginning of a belly laugh.

Pierre's curiosity got the better of him. "Okay, what happened? ... Bad, uh?"

Andy rushed past the senator and grabbed Pierre in a bear hug. "Pierre, baby ... you did it! I don't know how—but you did it. It was beautiful ... ab-so-lute-ly beautiful. That last hour, I thought I would die. Those stocks went up and down like an undamped yoyo. When the gong sounded, the stats were perfectly in the groove, just like you said they'd be—the volumes, the various industry standings, the closing values ... everything. I had difficulty believing it happened, but you were right on, baby, right on!"

The senator was trying to get Andy's attention. Finally, he yelled, "Mister Drake, would you please be quiet!" He grabbed Andy by the shoulder and, despite the senator's small size, flung him aside.

"Mister Talon, do you know what this means?" the senator ranted.

"Of course ... I have shown proof that I visited the future."

"Perhaps, but you caused the world's major economies to teeter on the brink of disaster. Tomorrow will be a day of planet-wide pandemonium. The markets might be forced to close early."

"Senator," Pierre said firmly, "none of this is of my making. I could not have revealed those predictions, and you know it. ... You even know when I take a piss and by how much, as you are so fond of saying."

Andy laughed uproariously.

The senator frowned and said, "When it concerns you, Mister Talon, I'm not sure about anything anymore—except that the financial markets must be stabilized. Can you reverse this monstrosity ... maybe a public announcement renouncing your predictions—"

"No, my dear senator," Pierre said, "the damage is done; the world must ride your 'monstrosity' for the rest of the week. ... I didn't push for this 'travel-to-the-future proof'; your people did—particularly Jane Stevens."

The senator snorted. "Ha! Jane Stevens—one of mine? Don't be ridiculous. If she could use those long fingernails of hers to pluck out my eyes, she would. We've been at each other's throats for years ... but, now, I've got her."

Andy asked, "How's that?"

"I've barred her from further contact with Mister Talon. Ms. Carver will take over the interviews permanently."

"Under what pretext?"

The senator scowled. "I don't need one ... but, if you want one, take your pick—improper conduct, national-security measure, or stock-market manipulation."

"Have you proof of the manipulation?"

"No, but who else could—or would—have done it?

"You or I could have."

Pierre broke in. "Well, I certainly couldn't have.

The senator said, "Of course not, but you didn't have to play her game in the first place."

"—and loose all credibility? I don't think so. Look, I didn't want to prove anything but was forced to. My message is a long-overdue warning to the peoples of this planet—not an exercise in qualifying myself. However, if I'm not taken seriously without 'proving myself this' or 'proving myself that,' then I shall provide whatever proof is necessary for my ends. That proof, which—I was promised—was to have been provided only to a select few, somehow was given—through no fault of mine—to the whole world.

"I hope that these shenanigans have come to an end. I must continue my mission. Senator, you promised me your support and access to the people. Now, give it, or I refuse to live up to my end of the bargain."

"What bargain is that?" Andy asked.

The senator whispered to Pierre, "Shut up, you fool."

Ignoring him, Pierre lied, "Oh, nothing much, Andy. I just give the good senator, here, free fortune-telling séances, that's all."

The senator glared at Pierre, grabbed Andy by the arm, and steered him toward the door. "Mister Drake," he bellowed, "we are leaving."

Pierre laughed harder than he had in a long time.

* * *

Although communications to Pierre's cell were blocked, Andy's early morning visits for the remainder of the week kept Pierre informed of the course of the stock market fiasco. Despite the chaos, the closing statistics always were as Pierre predicted. On the second day, the Monnetville Stock Market closed two hours early in an unsuccessful attempt to short circuit the predictions. Other attempts to thwart them failed also. Apparently, the efforts to circumvent or take advantage of Pierre's predictions served only to make them a reality.

Pierre could not understand why his predictions were succeeding. The very act of revealing them prompted the public into making different, financial decisions, so the statistics should be different from those in the predictions, which were based upon those available to him before he returned to the past. Although Pierre considered himself to be an expert technician, he knew the difficulty of understanding the cause-and-effect paradox of a person from the future looping back to the past to affect the future, ad infinitum. He was in a quandary.

Pierre was content to remain in the asylum so long as the interviews continued to his satisfaction. However, should events turn against him, he wanted the luxury of possessing feasible escape plans. He tried to signal the picogremlins he knew were still in his body, but they would not respond. His robosentries and his room's surveillance system couldn't be corrupted either—he was unable to obtain the necessary tools or privacy. He needed an ally. Andy appeared to be the only available candidate.

Pierre assumed that Andy and he had become good friends, but he wasn't sure of the man's feelings. The two seemed to agree with each other on most issues; however, in respect for the inhibitive surveillance that they both knew was monitoring them, their conversations necessarily remained awkward and superficial.

Pierre believed that his hint of a collusion with the senator might arouse Andy's curiosity enough to stir him to action. He waited for some sign of a secret message from him, but none came.

On two occasions, Pierre recklessly asked Andy if the surveillance system ever "broke-down"—the first time, "of age"—the second time, "of sabotage by one trustee or another." Apparently, neither time did Andy fall for Pierre's suggestions—perhaps he hadn't the guts to stand up to the senator.

The ant's a centaur in his dragon world.
Pull down thy vanity, it is not man
Made courage, or made order, or made grace.

—Ezra Pound

A week later, Sept 2, 2130

Pierre awakened with a start. He heard soft scratchings outside. Moments later, the lights switched on, and the heavy cell door clicked unlocked. Pierre sprang from his cot and cautiously slid the door open a crack. He saw Andy and a swarthy, young man of handsome build standing in front of the robosentry stationed at the door. Andy was whispering to the young man. Pierre strained to hear.

"Mario, are you sure this'll work?"

"Hell, no, but the picotech robots indicated it would."

At the words "picotech robots," Pierre's heart skipped a beat.

"If it doesn't, we'd better be ready to grab Pierre and haul ass."

"Quick, Andy, go in and try to hail your control center. I'll guard the door."

Andy brushed past Pierre and whispered, "Ssh ... no noise!" Andy stopped in the middle of the cell, faced the wallscreen, and drew himself up to his full height.

The seconds ticked by. Nobody moved. Silence reigned.

Pierre noticed beads of sweat on Andy's brow.

The young man thrust his head into the cell. He berated Andy in a forced whisper, "Andy, do it now, dammit ... now!

Andy nervously licked his lips and whispered, "Computer, identify yourself."

The wallscreen lit up.

After what seemed to be an eternity, the speakers came to life. "This is Operation Save-Pierre Control Center."

Andy shook a fist in the air and yelled, "Yahoo, it works!" He ran to Pierre, gave him a hug, and introduced the young man.

"Pierre, Mario's a genius. He reconstituted the remains of your infiltrate-and-seize picotechnology. See?" Andy gestured at the wallscreen. "... It works!"

Pierre was amazed. "That was some mean feat. I thought that I had destroyed it completely."

With affected modesty, Mario said, "Well, the picotech robots did all the work."

"Don't shortchange yourself; I know what you did ... and they're called picogremlins, not picotech robots."

Mario laughed. "Well, whatever they're called, they sure do the job."

Pierre frowned. "You'd better run a status check."

"Right," Mario agreed. "Computer, run the Save-Pierre test algorithm."

As the screenframes came up, Pierre examined them and grinned. "Nice work, Mario. ... So, we control this building and two diverging escape routes. How about the rest of the asylum complex?"

95

"We infiltrated the asylum's entire control system with your ... ah 'picogremlins.' They lie dormant awaiting seizure orders. In this building, the seizure is passive unless an emergency exists."

Andy asked, "What is passive seizure? ... sounds like an oxymoron to me."

Mario laughed. "Andy, I'll answer only if you tell me what an oxymoron is."

"You've got a deal."

"Well, passive seizure means that we control, but the asylum's surveillance system 'thinks' that it controls and that everything is normal ... although it isn't. The system's queries receive real or simulated responses depending upon which ones keep the alarms from going off."

"What response is the surveillance system getting, now?" Andy asked.

Pierre pointed to his bed using pantomimed movements. "Don't you see me sound asleep? ... No, I guess not—it's too dark in here."

Under the bright lights, Pierre and his new-found allies laughed noisily and danced in a circle in the middle of the room.

Mario said, "Andy, we needn't worry about detection of the picogremlins, either. They are amorphous-based rather than crystalline in structure like our less sophisticated nanotech robo—er, nanogremlins."

"—meaning?"

"—meaning that any detection probes would garner only innocent-looking, structureless reflections. Furthermore, even though picogremlins consume practically no energy, they are ambient-powered and leave no power-drain traces in the host system."

"How can they be so small and yet so effective?" Andy asked.

This time, Pierre answered. "Andy, picogremlins are roughly a million times smaller than the primitive microgremlins of fifty years ago and a thousand times smaller than today's nanogremlins. However, any type gremlin or computer virus is useless if it can be detected and, thus, be neutralized. In essence, picogremlins sacrifice multitasking for stealth.

"Nanogremlins, although microscopic in size, are like a herd of noisy elephants— all identical, all capable of coping with anything they encounter—except enemy picogremlins. On the other hand, picogremlins are as a colony of quiet, unseen ants— each ant different, each ant designed for a single task."

Like a patronizing grandfather, Pierre smiled at Mario and Andy. "As a boy, I saw the last of the wild elephants, while you two can only visit domesticated ones ... and 'wild' ants? ... Well, they're just as plentiful as ever.

"The asylum's control system, of course, is monitored and protected by patrolling bands of soldier nanogremlins—very effective against other invading nanogremlins. However, they can't even detect our picogremlins, which, as incredibly tiny, mobile, single-task computers, travel with impunity through the host control system—probing here and there until they find their targets. Then, like leeches, they latch onto the enemy's nanotechnology architecture and superimpose their picotechnology counterparts. Finally, they design viruses and install them throughout the network."

Pierre rested his hands on the shoulders of his two, new friends. "Gentlemen, thanks to you, I now control this asylum. The rest of my stay here takes on new meaning. ... If only Senator Mizuno Yoshimasa knew that his next visit will be to my lair rather than to my cage."

29—POSSESSED

Zwei Seelen wohnen, ach! in meiner Brust.

—Johann Wolfgang von Goethe

Six hundred fifty-six years into the future, June 5, 2786
The floating city of Cumulus
Five miles above Antarctica

Pierre entered the Learning Room, lay on the couch, and closed his eyes. Gradually, a feeling of cold and emptiness swept over him—an emptiness of the wit, not of the gut. Never before had he experienced such a void—such loneliness. He knew not who, why, and where he was. His reason to exist fled. His will to live died. A depression of manic proportions engulfed him. At that moment, had he the power to do himself in, he would.

Then, he felt a bolt of excruciating pain flash through his brain. He heard a moan of agony escape his lips. He gripped the armrests until he thought his knuckles would shatter. As consciousness faded, he sensed new warmth course through his mind.

* * *

Pierre awoke in great pain and saw before him a row of seven, pallid persons draped in black robes—hair, grizzled—skin, wrinkled. Perched high above, they glared down at him from behind a massive bench. He heard the middle one speak:

"Bailiff, you may proceed."

"Hear ye, hear ye, hear ye. On this date, May twenty-ninth in the year of our Lord 2431, John Thorpe, the defendant, is tried for charges of high felonious crimes of murder and treason against the Republic of Urbane and its people."

Pierre noticed that, without ordering his head to move, it slowly did so to look at the bailiff and then back to see the judges again. Each movement shot pangs of agony through his spine.

"John Thorpe," the presiding judge asked, "what is your plea?"

"Your honor, my client John Thorpe pleads not guilty to the charges."

Pierre's head pivoted painfully to the right, and he looked into the face of the attractive, young woman who just spoke. *Why is John in constant agony like this? I can hardly bear it.*

She looked directly at him and whispered, "John, have courage. You have many supporters. We'll fight this to the end ... and win."

For an instant, Pierre was taken aback by the name "John." He wanted to scream, "I'm Pierre, not John," but he could not. Then, a strange voice resonated through his skull. It shocked him:

"No, Nataly, I will be condemned and executed. The Valids possess the necessary proof, for I never tried to conceal my actions. Worldwide publicity of my trial and execution is all that I ask. Hopefully, my death will galvanize my followers into a force with which the Valids will be compelled to reckon."

97

Pierre could not feel his legs. He tried to look down to see them—his head and eyes would not respond. Neither could he touch them—his arms also refused to obey. He realized that he had no control of his body—that, indeed, his body was not his to control.

The pretty lady named Nataly talked to him again. "Please, John, don't be so fatalistic."

The judge quieted her with a glare. "The prosecution will present its opening statement."

To his right, Pierre heard a man voice a passionate speech. It portrayed John as a murdering monster who malevolently organized retards and other In-valids to revolt and commit acts of terror against society.

While Pierre listened with heightening interest, his head moved, and he saw his lower body. *Oh, God, I have no ... John has no legs.* To his horror, he saw no pelvis, either. For the first time, he recognized the pungent odor that he was smelling—stale urine. He noticed the shabbiness of John's wheelchair—decrepit with worn tires and ripped padding.

Slowly, Pierre became aware of John's physical being. He surmised that ulcerated bedsores were responsible for the omnipresent throbbing of his backside. He noticed that John's movements were premeditated and sparse and hoped they would continue that way—Pierre abhorred pain. John was indeed a man with a tormented soul—of this Pierre was agonizingly aware.

The prosecutor's voice drew Pierre's attention back to the proceedings:

"... I will prove beyond any possible doubt that John Thorpe, not of sound body, but of perfectly sound mind, did, of his own free will, premeditatedly and maliciously plan and order the execution of the following, felonious acts: grand theft, arson, smuggling, piracy, assault and battery, and torture and mayhem and murder. Further, John Thorpe, alone, did preach rebellion, did incite riots, and did foment sedition, all of which caused widespread uprisings of retards, criminals and other sorts of undesirable subhumans resulting in much loss of life, limb, and property."

Pierre sensed that he was about to whisper. The words welled up in his throat, and he understood them the instant before they left his lips. "Nataly, please ask the Court a question. Ask what my punishment will be if I am found guilty of the most heinous crime with which I am charged."

Nataly appeared startled. "Please, John, let me present my opening stateme—"

"No! Do it!" Pierre felt his teeth grind and his fists open and close—his brain numbed by sharp stabs of excruciation.

Nataly stood. "If the Court please, may I ask a question?"

"Yes, you may, madam."

"If my client is found guilty of the worst offense with which he is charged, what would be his punishment?"

The presiding judge leaned to the right and then to the left to confer in whispers with his peers. He looked down and said, "If the defendant John Thorpe is found guilty of the offense you just mentioned, his head will be separated from his body."

The explosion of one, simple word from John's mouth startled Pierre. "How?"

The judge stared directly at him and shot back, "By the guillotine, Mister Thorpe, by the guillotine."

"I wish to change my plea, your honor."

Nataly appeared hysterical. "No, John, no! I won't let you do this. Think of your little son—he needs you."

"Calm yourself, Nataly—my son is in good hands. I can do more for him dead than alive ... and for myself, too."

The judge smiled. "And what plea might that be, Mister Thorpe?"

Pierre wanted to cry out, "No, no, John, don't do it. Think of me—I suffer everything you suffer," but he was incapable of uttering his thoughts.

"I am guilty, your honor."

Immediately, an uproar filled the courtroom. Nataly sobbed into her hands. The judge gavelled the bench again and again, and the room returned to order.

"Guilty of what count?"

"All of them, your honor."

Again, the clamor forced the judge to gavel the room into silence. He turned to the prosecutor. "What is the State's response to this turn of events?"

The prosecutor rose, faced the defendant, and smiled in triumph. "Your honor, in light of Mister Thorpe's forthrightness, the prosecution recommends that the Court consider the defendant's plea as a de-facto attempt to bargain for a lesser sentence. The State agrees to his request and recommends leniency in the form of a sentence of life imprisonment."

Pierre heard air rush into his lungs. His chest expanded against the straps, which held him upright in the wheelchair. He feared he would faint, but an explosive utterance from his lips shook him to attention.

"Dear God, no! I am guilty. I must be punished as specified by law."

Pierre's eyes filled with tears. His vision blurred ... his chest heaved ... his view tilted upward. He heard John's silent prayer enter his soul: *Oh, dear God in Heaven ... by the silent brush of the blade, let this torso—so tortured—tumble away from me ... by the cold caress of stern steel, let my blood—so base—run to remorseless rest ... and my head—so hurt—dwell in the warm womb of Mother Earth.*

Pierre couldn't see—John had closed his eyes—yet he detected incantation-like whispers while the judges decided John's fate. As he awaited their verdict, he felt John's heart pound furiously.

Finally, the middle judge spoke. "The defendant John Thorpe will direct his attention to the bench, and his counsel will rise."

Pierre saw again.

"The State wants us to believe it shows leniency and, therefore, 'compassion' by recommending a 'lesser' sentence. The Court believes that, in this case, death is the lesser and more compassionate sentence and that the State is perfectly aware of this."

The prosecutor interrupted. "Your honor, I did not mean to—"

"Quiet—you risk a charge of contempt of court. You made your motive quite clear. Nevertheless, your recommendation is rejected as being moot. In this instance, the law is precise—the sentence cannot be mitigated. If the defendant is found guilty, the penalty is death.

"The defendant's admission of guilt does not necessarily constitute de-facto guilt. The task of this Court is to decide whether or not the prima-facie evidence does, indeed, support the defendant's plea. In this case, the Court does concur. Therefore, the defendant John Thorpe is found guilty of all charges for which he was indicted. Have you anything to say before sentence is passed?"

"No!"

The courtroom was deathly silent.

"Very well. ... By the power vested in the Court by the people of the Republic of Urbane, you, John Thorpe, are condemned to death by separation of body from soul."

The crowd roared.

The judge stood and pounded the bench. "Order in the Court. I will have order in this Court."

Slowly, the tumult subsided.

"That's better. ... John Thorpe, do you intend to throw yourself on the mercy of this Court or to appeal its judgment?"

"No!"

"John. Please!

"Nataly, be quiet."

The judge continued. "Very well. ... Due to the revolutionary state of mind of our citizens and the unique circumstances surrounding the defendant's crimes, the sentence must be carried out in due haste. The execution takes place at dawn ... tomorrow."

Again, the judge gavelled ... this time, to no avail.

Despite the din of the milling crowd, Pierre heard the prosecutor shout at the judges:

"You fools! You fools! You create a martyr. The Christians have John the Baptist. Now, the In-valids have John the Martyr. We are lost, you fools—we are lost!"

The courtroom was in chaos. Losing control, the judge yelled, "Bailiff, bring in security."

Pierre gritted his teeth as John's arms suddenly shot straight up and remained there like two flag poles.

A booming voice roared, "Shut up, everybody—John wants to talk. Let John talk!"

Another voice screamed, "We don't have to wait 'til dawn, let's kill the murderer now."

Behind him, Pierre heard the use of clubs as the security force cleared the room of the more recalcitrant spectators. Slowly, the uproar subsided.

Pierre's back ached, but the arms remained up.

"John Thorpe," the judge said, "you may speak."

The arms collapsed.

"Your honor, I claim the Right of the Condemned."

A brief hubbub ensued. "Kill him, now." ... "Let him say his piece." ... "Let's lynch him." ... "He carries the sentence of death—he has the right to address the Court."

The gavel came down. "By constitutional right, you, John Thorpe, who are condemned to death, may address this court. ... At this time, mount the dais and rebut your accusers."

L'amour vient de l'aveuglement,
L'amitié, de la connaissance.

—Roger de Rabutin, comte de Bussy

Six hundred fifty-six years into the past, September 5, 2130
Andy's apartment
Seattle, Franklin

Andy said, "Computer, I need a bicabin in ten minutes."

"Confirmed."

He turned to Katharine. "This'll be the first year you aren't coming with me. Are you sure you can't get away?"

"Absolutely." Katharine sensed that Andy really didn't want her to go with him. Probably, he was just mouthing what he presumed she wanted to hear. For some time, their relationship with each other had been declining. Both possessed voracious sexual appetites, so they still made love, but the act had become mechanical—more to satisfy the senses rather than the soul. Yet, she still loved him even though, most of the time, his coarse manners irritated her ... but, sometimes, depending upon the moment—and her mood—they'd become an aphrodisiac too exciting to resist.

"Your cabin has arrived."

Andy and she entered the cabin. It sped off toward the spaceport.

For the next three days, Andy would amuse himself in the famous casino city of Silverado on the southern shore of Great Slave Lake in the Awokanak Province of Nunavut. Until now, she had always gone with him to attend the annual National Fire-fighters Convention—wherever it was held. Normally, his departure without her would have upset her. This time, it didn't.

However, when she learned that he would stay at the vast Athabasca Grand Hotel, she almost changed her mind. The complex housed over thirty restaurants—many world-renowned—whose cuisines were prepared with satellite-grown food guaranteed free of noxious chemicals and radioactive elements. Of course, the drinking water came from spent, hydroxygen fuel because, like in most areas of the world, the ground water was toxic. All of the hotel's recreational areas were either indoors or protected by the latest dome technology.

For thirty years, thousands of the world's more-wealthy families had lived year round at the Athabasca Grand in the reassuring knowledge that they were protected from the more-dangerous aspects of Earth's increasingly-hazardous environment. Nevertheless, their rates of cancer and in-valid births increased almost as fast as those of other, less fortunate, families—no matter what the hotel claimed.

Katharine thought, *Oh, well ... I'd better stay here to see what Pierre has in mind.* She still could not understand the bizarre incident, which prompted her decision to stay behind. It had occurred in her bedroom the day before, when she was getting ready to go to work.

* * *

Andy had already left the apartment. She had showered and was drying herself, when Pierre's voice startled the hell out of her. She spun around, speechless at the sight of his grinning face on the wallscreen. The computer had not only failed to notify her of an incoming message but, worst of all, had started two-way communication without her knowledge—while she was stark naked, in the—supposed—privacy of her own dressing room. "Computer, shut down visual immediately."

Nothing happened.

Katharine groped for her dressing gown.

Pierre said, "Please, Kathy, don't be alarmed and don't ask me how. I'll explain later. ... Kathy?"

"... Yes, Pierre."

"Please ... don't go with Andy."

"Why?"

"You know very well ... 'why.' I am asking you, Kathy—don't go with Andy to his convention. ... Trust me."

Katharine startled herself by saying, "I'll stay, Pierre, if that's what you want." Her voice sounded remote—as if her faculty for speech were disembodied. For an instant, she did not realize why she had agreed so quickly to his request ... then, suddenly, she knew.

* * *

Jolted, Katharine returned to the present to find Andy shaking her shoulder.

"Hey, don't take it so hard, baby. I'll be back in only three days, and it's not your fault you've got to stay for the rest of the interviews. ... I can't figure Jane though—she seems paranoid about Pierre."

Katharine couldn't help but smile. Even though the senator held no place in her heart, she was happy to see him inflict upon Jane her comeuppance. "Maybe so, but she should have known not to buck Yoshimasa. Counting on 'freedom of the press' to guarantee continued access to Doctor Talon was naïve. Yet, she tried everything but couldn't get around his national-security ploy."

"Hey ... it was no ploy. Pierre knows secrets, which, if divulged to the wrong people, could very well compromise our national security."

"What secrets?"

"I can't say, Kathy ... secrets are secrets. Besides, I barely know anything about them. Mario, with his technical savvy, understands them more than I."

The cabin sped within view of the spaceport. One after the other, Katharine watched shuttles depad like rockets in a fireworks display. Their vapor plumes eventually would form into clouds, which would provide much-needed rain to the area.

"Ya know, Kathy, I feel sorry for Jane. The allegation that she revealed the stock-market predictions to the public is ludicrous."

"Why? ... Christ, Andy, you, yourself, said that she was paranoid."

"I know, but she wouldn't cut her own professional throat. Besides, no proof that she did it exists."

Andy's support of Jane rankled Katharine. "For the senator, well-founded suspicions are enough. He is aware that Jane's grandmother founded the news agency and that Jane is still its majority shareholder, yet he decided to press for her permanent removal from the Talon interviews. Certainly, he had just cause."

"Maybe so, Kathy. Obviously, the senator and she are, now, irreversibly pitted against each other. Knowing his power and deviousness, I hope that she comes to no harm."

Katharine didn't answer but kept quiet until Andy was ready to board the shuttle.

He stepped close and put his hands on her shoulders.

She put her arms around his neck and kissed him full on the lips. She felt his hands slip under her buttocks and wondered if people were watching them.

Andy pulled her off the floor and thrust his hips forward.

She pulled her head back, and, with a smack, their lips separated. "Get going, you big lug."

Andy grinned and turned to board the shuttle.

After it disappeared to the north, Katharine left for home. To her surprise, at the first wye switch, her cabin shunted to another line—one not leading to the apartment. "Computer, I am going to Seattle. ... Confirm."

The computer voiced, "Negative, you are going to Franklin State Asylum Number Fifteen."

What is the matter with this system, anyway? "Computer, who countermanded my order to go to—"

"I did."

She recognized Pierre's voice and saw his holoimage on the cabin's microscreen. She even saw him on her wrist terminal. "Oh, my God! You can control my cabin from your cell. Can you control any cabin? What else can you control? Pierre, how can you do this?" she yelled.

"I'll explain when you are here."

"But, how am I to get in? Except for the interviews, the senator's got you in isolation, so—" Katharine burst out laughing—she finally understood. "Pierre, don't you say it. ... I will. ... You control the asylum's robosentries, too. Right? ... Christ, Pierre, you can control anything you want, can't you?"

Pierre said simply, "Yes, Kathy, I can."

The cabin shunted to the asylum's spur line, penetrated the environmental shield, and slowed to a stop. Katharine alighted and, with apprehension, approached the asylum's main entrance. The heavy, steel gates were closed, and a robosentry, thrice Katharine's size, barred her path.

She stopped in front of it and stared into its dark lenses.

It remained motionless, yet its joints creaked eerily.

She was terrified.

Then, it spoke. "Ms. Katharine Carver, you are cleared to proceed." With a rumble, the robosentry slowly stepped aside, and the doors clanked open.

Under the protective dome within the asylum complex, Katharine navigated herself between buildings and through mazes of intersecting pathways. With pounding heart, she passed several checkpoints without reaction from the robosentries. As she neared the building that contained Pierre, panic gripped her. She could walk no faster. She began to run. Once inside, Katharine sprinted the length of the corridor toward Pierre's cell.

When she saw his cell door, she raced toward it as if hyenas nipped at her heels. With waning strength, she flung herself at the closed door. At the last instant, it slid open, and Katharine soared over the threshold into Pierre's arms. She clung to him and, with chest heaving, devoured huge gobs of air.

Finally able to speak, she said, "Oh, Pierre, I was so scared. They were watching me—those unseen eyes. It was silly of me, I know, but I couldn't get here fast enough."

Katharine wondered at his silence. She tilted her head back and looked up at him. His expression was no surprise. She had seen it on Andy's face and before that—on her husband's.

Katharine was barely aware that the door had slid shut and, with a click, had locked itself.

31—GOMORRAH

The tree of liberty must be refreshed from
time to time with the blood of patriots
and tyrants. It is its natural manure.

—Thomas Jefferson

A few hours later

Pierre couldn't feel his arm. Kathy's weight had cut off its circulation, yet he hesitated
to reclaim it and awaken her.

He hadn't slept. Alertness was paramount. He imagined the worst-possible warning: Senator Yoshimasa's cabin just arrived at the main gate. You have 300 seconds to
get your visitor out the rear exit—299—298—297....

After all, Kathy was there, in the middle of the day—asleep—and nude, at that. He
listened intently, but the speakers remained silent—thank God.

Pierre gazed fondly at Kathy. He supposed that she would not sleep so peacefully
were she to know that his powers were less than believed. *This is sheer madness,* he
thought. *If the warning should come at this instant, Kathy'd not get out in time.*

Pierre kissed her forehead. "Wake up, Kathy. At a moment's notice, you must be
ready to leave, and I must be presentable. The senator could surprise us—anytime—
with an unannounced visit."

They dressed quickly, tidied things up, and sat down at the table.

Kathy reached across it, grasped his hand, and pulled herself to him.

They kissed.

"Pierre?"

"Yes."

"Am I still the only woman you've had since you left the past?"

"What do you mean—'still'?"

"Don't you remember? I asked you the same question seven years ago."

"And what did I say then?"

"That I was."

"You still are." *How did we get on this subject, anyway?*

"Did you have a lady friend before you left for the future?"

"Not really. I loved a young woman once—but only from afar."

"What do you mean?"

"In preparation for the trip into space, our crew worked closely together for long
hours. One of the more brilliant physicists was petite Evelyn Chang. She was beautiful—a porcelain doll."

"You loved her?"

"Yes ... ardently."

"Did she return your love?"

"No, but we didn't have time for such luxuries. Getting the spaceship ready took all our waking hours. Besides, other suitors pressured her, and the last thing she needed was another one bothering her."

"Maybe you were her choice, and she was just waiting for you to show interest in her."

"Hardly. Dimitri Adam, who was infinitely more charming and handsome than I, liked her, too. Actually, Evelyn seemed to like us both, but only platonically. We were too engrossed in our work to pursue amorous interests."

"How about during the trip? It was very long, wasn't it?"

"Yes … eleven months."

"… long enough for Evelyn and you to get together, no doubt."

Despite himself, Pierre's ire surfaced. "Did I have an affair with Evelyn? Is that what you want to know? … No, I didn't, but not for lack of trying. Whenever I was around, she managed to be with the others and on a different work shift at that."

"Did Dimitri finally succeed with her?"

Angrily, Pierre blurted, "I don't know and don't care. Christ, Kathy, Evelyn is dead—they're both dead—the subject is dead—forget it."

"Why Pierre, you're still in love with Evelyn, aren't you?"

"Kathy … I said 'Forget it.' "

She withdrew her hand. "Do you want me to leave?"

"No, of course not. I'm sorry, Kathy. I want you to … I've much to tell you."

Kathy said, "We must prepare for the next interview—it's tomorrow night. Could you start by telling me what you hope to accomplish during these interviews?"

"Yes … , all along, I've tried to, but something always happens to stop me. First, I want you to know about where I've been … to whom I've talked … what I've learned … and how I've learned it." Pierre could sit no longer. He rose to pace the length of the room and back. "You see, Kathy, you must feel what I feel … believe what I believe … think what I think. Time is short. I have much to do. … You must help me."

Suddenly aware of his incoherence, Pierre stopped pacing and glanced at Kathy. Her quizzical expression betrayed her alarm. He stepped closer and searched her eyes. He found anxiety but, no fear.

Kathy held his gaze and said, "These interviews must be a smashing success. Pierre, you can help me make them so by telling me everything. What was the early twenty-first century like? … Please, calm yourself. Tell me about life back then."

He sat down and sighed. "In some ways, life then was worse than today."

"How is that?"

"Well, our society was in crisis. Decades of libertarianism revealed the basic dissoluteness of the human animal. Fighting each other to standoffs, polarized special-interest groups squandered Earth's resources. Radicalism crested, rationalism troughed, and compromise was scorned.

"Effective contraception, legalized abortion, parental declination, and the eclipse of scholastic discipline transformed a hard-working, God-fearing society into a mob of voracious pleasure seekers. Informed and responsible constituencies shrank until no longer could our democratic processes be monitored properly.

"Eventually, the revolution came, but not from hedonism. Rampant crime and an ineffectual justice system sparked the revolt. Commanding thug armies, drug lords controlled many countries. Expanding drug ghettoes engulfed entire cities. Gangs roamed door-to-door enforcing drug consumption. Deaths from overdoses entered the norm. Murderers, rapists, torturers, and drug pushers proliferated. If arrested at all, they received mere slaps on the wrist and freedom to continue their reigns of terror."

Kathy was wide-eyed. "I never knew that. In school, they never taught us that."

"Well, what were you taught? … that the world has forever been a utopia?"

"No, but—"

"Christ, Kathy, don't you realize that your government hides every negative aspect of your society from you—from everybody. Only a small, select group of powerful people make the important decisions—to further their own, greedy ends. The masses have no say anymore. What do you think the National Censorship Board does anyway? … only enforce the Wall and keep people from mentioning the words embryo, fetus, or abortion in public?"

"Okay, Pierre, so our day-and-age isn't perfect, but what did your world do to fix things? Since the future inherits from the past, evidently, not much."

Pierre sighed. "You're right, Kathy, yet—at first—the people did try to fight back. Law enforcement agencies fed suspected criminals to a judicial system that was biased in their favor. Few rights were accorded to the criminals' victims. Economics dictated the ineffectiveness of the courts. Criminal money attracted the more-talented lawyers. Underpaid, overworked, and less-competent prosecuting attorneys could not compete.

"The successful defense lawyers became the judges, so courts favorable to the accused perpetuated themselves. In obsessive fear of punishing the innocent, the judiciary allowed sharp lawyers endless appeals for their convicted clients. The result was no justice at all.

"At the onset of the twenty-first century, an outraged public prompted the creation of stricter laws, more effective police, harsher judges and juries, and more prisons."

Pierre noticed the wallscreen light up—a robot was coming down the hall with his dinner. He turned toward Kathy. "The door will open in a minute, and a robot will bring my dinner and leave."

"Then, I must hide." She looked around anxiously.

Pierre laughed. "Don't worry, I've programmed the robot to detect only what I want it to … you won't be noticed."

Kathy glanced at the door, then laughed nervously. "Really? … You can penetrate their security like that? It's amazing."

"Not at all … it's the future."

The robot came and went.

Although the food was not of the best, Pierre was accustomed to it and ate with gusto. To tide Kathy over until she returned home, he offered her a morsel or two.

She refused them.

Pierre wiped his mouth. "Anyway, it did no good."

"The stricter laws and all that?"

"Right … the crime lords responded with massive assassinations. They ordered the killings of thousands of judges, lawyers, legislators, and members of juries. Law and order vanished. The police, in disarray, hunkered down. The representatives of the people had failed in their duty to protect them.

"Although at its nadir, civilization was not completely lost. The revolutions of 1789, 1917, 1991, and 2035 are stark testimony to the truth that power ultimately emanates from the people.

"The Drug War of 2035 began in the United States. Americans were better equipped to retake their country from the grip of organized crime. Their Bill of Rights guaranteed them the right to bear arms; thus, many ordinary citizens possessed weapons. Unfortunately, as in Nazi Germany a hundred years earlier, government records held the identities of those who possessed them.

"As protests spread, mobs formed. They demanded action.

"Concerned crime lords obtained the identities of the arms holders. Then, like Hitler's Brownshirts, squads of executioners swept through the neighborhoods. They confiscated weapons and murdered their owners."

"Who was Hitler?"

Pierre sighed and shook his head. "He was a murderous dictator of RENA's germanic province, which, at the time, was a sovereign nation. He plunged Europe into chaos and stole its people's freedom. You see, the most basic guarantee of the continuance of a people's freedom is the right—no, the duty—of every, law-abiding citizen to possess arms ... in secret. Before society learns this lesson, how many more tyrants must rise and patriots must die?

"Militia groups managed to form, and the Drug War of 2035 was on. Eighteen months later, the people prevailed, but the world was in a shambles. During the war, many died—including my father."

Kathy reached out and touched his fingers. "Your childhood must have been very sad. Did such turmoil really exist back then ... before the Wall?"

Pierre had difficulty believing her naïveté. He became angry, again. "Do you really believe I'd waste my time telling fairy tales like Jane Stevens is so sure that I do? I guess that, since the Wall, all the history you get is watered-down names, dates, and places."

Kathy looked sheepish. "Perhaps that is why history never interested me, but go on ... what happened after the Drug War?"

"A blood bath ... the victors, on a rampage, executed the drug lords, their thugs, and many ancillary criminals. They hunted down and slaughtered turncoats and fifth columnists. Mutual enemies struck at each other over long-festering hatreds. Eight years later, when I left the past, the world was still in a shambles.

"In postwar United States, a Continental Congress amended the Constitution to sweep away libertarianism, which had so corrupted society. It abolished many freedoms that were guaranteed by the Bill of Rights because the people had proved themselves incapable of using them wisely. The regular Congress, free to pass laws to constrain the irresponsible actions of the people, did so with abandon."

Kathy brightened. "Yes, I remember learning about that in school—the suppression of The Bill of Rights."

"Well, the Continental Congress did not suppress all of the amendments; it reinforced some, especially the Second Amendment."

"Which one is that?"

"The right to bear arms. Long ago, I memorized it. It read:

'A well regulated Militia, being necessary to the security of
a free State, the right of the People to keep and bear Arms
shall not be infringed.'

"However, the Drug War of 2035 proved that the amendment was too weak to
accomplish its intended purpose. The more-effective, updated version, in part, reads:

'... the right of the people to keep Arms in secret and to
bear Arms shall not ...'

and

'... a person who ever has been found individually guilty
of a felonious act of violence against another person or persons may have the right to obtain, keep, and bear arms
infringed ...' "

Kathy said, "Wouldn't armed camps spring up and fight each other as in medieval
times?"

"That was the big controversy, of course ... but it didn't happen that way. You see,
Kathy, when law-abiding citizens, early in life, possess and learn the proper use of fire-
arms, they effectively control crime and the abuse of power."

"Why?"

"Because law-enforcement agencies cannot do it all. People must protect themselves but do so in a responsible manner without trampling the rights of others."

"But, Pierre, how that can be guaranteed?"

"It can't, but, by mandating our institutions to return their functions to those origi-
nally intended, society can protect itself more effectively."

"Is that what happened after the Drug War?"

"Yes. An overhauled court system meted out justice rapidly and appropriately. The
Supreme Court, confined to interpreting the intent and constitutionality of laws, maintained the separation and balance of power within and between governmental entities.
It no longer served as the ultimate appellate court for civil suits and criminal prosecu-
tions.

"Each of the newly-established, civil-court systems specialized in one aspect of
the law—familial, medical, technological, contractual, commercial, liability ... each
with its own, final appellate court. Litigants paid for all civil-court costs, and losing
plaintiffs of capricious or frivolous suits, paid all of the defendant's expenses.

"The criminal courts treated violent and non-violent crimes separately in two inde-
pendent court and prison systems. The acceptance of plea bargaining, state's evidence,
insanity pleas, and reduced sentences declined. Those accused of violent crimes
through prima-facie evidence remained in jail—without bail, and, those convicted, in
prison—without parole. Habitual criminals received life, while those who inflicted
pain or death on others received, in turn—death. Inmates worked to earn their keep,
and recalcitrants survived on minimum subsistence.

"While the social climate remained ripe, the reformers continued in their zeal:
They constrained genetic engineering, slashed birth-control research, outlawed abortions, euthanasia, and prenatal examinations. Speedy and severe punishment befell
flouters of these new laws."

Kathy asked, "How old were you during this social upheaval? Were you bothered by it?"

"When the war broke out, I was a twenty-three-year-old doctoral candidate in physics and exempt from military service. Therefore, I was little adversely affected by it. Except for the death of my father, I was glad that it had occurred because, finally, the world was rid of the drug scourge and all of its criminal trappings.

"My mother was proud that her efforts helped to outlaw induced abortions. I was happy for her and satisfied by the outcome of her struggle. Of course, my sister could not have been returned to life, but other young women were spared—or so I believed."

"I'm so sorry about your sister. You must have loved her very much."

Pierre's eyes misted. He swallowed hard and mumbled, "Yes—very much. … The poor girl could not leave her mistakes behind."

"What do you mean?"

"Well, men can leave their 'mistakes' behind, thus, they always have been more prone to promiscuousness than women. Because of the social consequences of their 'mistakes,' historically, women were the founders and enforcers of sexual mores.

"Then, in the mid-twentieth century, medical advances vulgarized the practice of birth control and, for the first time in history, allowed the abasement of women's sexual mores to a level near those of men. Rising libertarianism heralded promiscuity, venereal disease, induced abortion, and the decline of the marital and familial institutions.

"The resultant 'liberation' of women caused leveling of the sexes and loss of the delicious mysticism once felt by one sex toward the other. A hazy, unisex image replaced the strictly-male or -female one. Homosexuality, endemic to overripe, blasé civilizations, exploded."

"My God, Pierre, I had no idea that the past was so wicked."

"Well, Kathy, it got worse. … Before the Drug War, teenagers considered easily-available abortions to have been forever accepted. They believed that, after puberty, promiscuous sexual activity was natural. They scorned birth-control measures in the knowledge that, if 'something happened,' abortions could be had without parental consent or knowledge.

"However, as the demand for abortions increased, so did prolife pressure upon the medical profession to halt them. Competent doctors and nurses, tired of the constant hassles, fled the field. Charlatans, quacks, and, eventually, filthy butchers filled the void. They preyed upon naïve, teenage girls and poor, illiterate women—those not worldly enough to understand the necessity of practicing birth control rather than subjecting themselves to continual, health-draining abortions. Ironically, they, also, were the least capable of protecting themselves from these quacks. My sister was one of them."

"The world in that era was terrible, Pierre, but you have certainly opened my eyes. I doubt that many people today realize that our restrictive sex laws are a result of the Drug War. How old was your sister when she died?"

"Sixteen—after her fourth abortion." Again, he fought back tears.

"Yes—I remember your mentioning that before. … Abortions are wicked, Pierre—for whatever reason—they're terribly wrong."

"Not always."

Kathy appeared startled. "Yes ... always. You sound like my daughter. I thought you were against abortion."

"After my sister's death, I was ... categorically, but I am not the same person that I was back then. Now, I am like no other person alive. My experiences in many time periods have given me hindsight, foresight, and sight in between.

"Now, I realize that neither a pure prochoice nor a pure prolife solution to the abortional controversy was an optimal one. In today's polluted world of a teeming, increasingly in-valid population, the old argument that all abortions must be prohibited because all human life is sacred has become moot.

"On the other hand, young, healthy women in the prime of their procreative lives must be protected from their own follies. The illegality of teenage abortion is the only effective method of decreasing unwanted, teenage pregnancies. Only this method encourages teenagers to be less sexually active and more birth-control conscious. Unfortunately, as always, a price must be paid: Some girls will die or be maimed in illegal abortions.

"The prime objective in any policy concerning abortion must be the maintenance of a stable or decreasing world population of valid persons. Toward that end, this society needs a common-sense abortional policy that will—."

Kathy interrupted. "I hope you don't propose to suggest such a policy tomorrow night."

"Well, yes, I—"

Kathy spread her hands in a gesture of futility. "The censors will bar it, Pierre ... you should know this, by now."

"But, it's the only way. Humanity will die without it."

"It's your travels through time, isn't it? They've convinced you."

He stared at Kathy for a moment. "Yes!"

"Okay, then ... tell me about your abortion policy for society—but don't tell tomorrow's audience."

Pierre hesitated. He wondered if Kathy was the right person to hear what he had to say. He was aware that, for many years, she had nursed an in-valid son and justified her actions by announcing to anyone who'd listen, her zealous opposition to abortion and euthanasia. He said, "You might not like what I'm going to tell you."

"No doubt, but I must be open to new morals that evolve to meet the needs of a changing society."

Pierre was proud of Kathy. At last, her reasoning process seemed to be maturing. "Good. ... First, if you were the only person on Earth, you could have absolute rights. However, when fifteen billion souls crowd into the world's shrinking habitable areas—many of whom are starving or in-valid, an individual's rights must be balanced with those of others and, more pertinently, with the species as a whole."

Pierre noticed that Kathy fidgeted. Obviously, she was uncomfortable listening to what he had to say. "Understand that, under this policy, no pregnant woman is forced against her will to have medical examinations or an abortion, and no viable fetus may suffer an induced abortion unless a board of medical examiners, as prescribed by law, deems the procedure necessary for serious therapeutic reasons."

"Such as the imminent death of the mother?"

"Yes, that would be one. ... Upon learning that she is pregnant, a woman should be encouraged to have an immediate medical examination. Her doctor would rapidly determine the health of the mother and her embryo and recommend either a continued pregnancy or an induced abortion. If the doctor recommends, and the woman accepts, an induced abortion, it may be performed upon an embryo—but not upon a fetus. If she refuses the doctor's recommendation to abort and bears an in-valid child, the cost of that child's care shall not be paid by taxpayers."

"But, Pierre—"

"Please—let me continue. ... A woman past childbearing age or one who has birthed, at the least, one valid baby may elect to have an abortion before onset of the fetal stage."

"No! That's murder. You can't—"

"Murder, you say? How about the millions of valid children that die for lack of care or of food because of society's obsession with the in-valid ones? The world's overtaxed resources cannot save both. Decades ago, your society made the difficult choice. Unfortunately, it was the wrong one.

"The right one was to deny induced abortions of valid embryos to young, healthy women who had not yet given birth to a healthy baby, and ... in all other instances, encourage them to abort. The salient points of such a policy are: a practical compromise between the prolife and prochoice extremists, elimination of in-valid life in its earliest stage, suppression of teenage or late-term induced abortions, and reduction of large families and of pregnancies in older women.

"The early detection and suppression of an in-valid embryo saves parents from the trauma of deciding the future of a deformed newborn, from imposing unhappy, martyred lives upon earlier children, and from the sacrifice of denying themselves future valid children.

"What is the matter, Kathy? You appear to be ill."

J'accuse.

—Émile Zola

Three hundred one years into the future, May 29, 2431
The Court for Treasonable Acts
Republic of Urbane

John Thorpe bit his lip and grasped his wheelchair's drive rings. *I don't want them to see me tremble. I must have courage. Dear God, don't abandon me now. I have only a few hours more ... only a few hours 'til bliss envelops me.*

Seeing Nataly rise to help, he said, "I go alone, Nataly. ... Please sit down."

"But, John, your condition—"

"Don't touch the chair—my condition is fine."

John strained and pushed. Soon, he got his chair rolling toward the front of the courtroom—toward the dais. He looked at it—less than a foot above the floor, but, for him, it was like a mountain. He felt his cheeks ripple with effort and pain as he clenched his jaw and accelerated the chair toward the ramp. With a clatter, the little front wheels bumped onto it—followed by the big, rear ones. He strained to keep from rolling back—but to no avail.

"Bailiff," the judge said, "help Mister Thorpe to the stand."

"Bailiff, stay where you are," John ordered. He glanced at Nataly.

Her eyes swam in tears. Her shoulders heaved in emotion.

His own eyes closed. His own shoulders mustered all the strength he possessed for another run at the ramp. This time, momentum thrust him—almost—to the top. The rear wheels lacked inches, so, to rest, he momentarily applied the brake. Then, benefiting from years of practice, he simultaneously released it and muscled his wheelchair to the summit.

From his vantage point, John looked out and scanned the crowd. He saw old friends—most in wheelchairs or on gurneys with heads propped up—but a few were Valids or supported by crutches. He recognized enemies, too. Whether friend or foe, all silently riveted their gaze upon him for some time. Finally, as if from a hidden signal, most everyone cheered.

"John Thorpe, you may address the Court."

"Thank you, your honor."

For a pregnant moment, John surveyed his audience, which silently awaited his words. He spoke:

"Many of you see in me a vile monster, which shortly will receive its just reward. Perhaps you are right, but, before you render final judgment, let me tell you how and why I became what I am.

"I, unlike most people, am an avid student of history. You might ask ... why?

"Well, as a child, I had access to historical records as did few others. My mother worked for the censorship administration. To her disgust, she witnessed the systematic

113

destruction of our civilization's remaining historical records. At risk of life, she brought home materials ordered destroyed.

"I watched antique, two-dimensional movies from centuries past and marveled at all of the Valids in them. I remember vividly one particular movie where a scene contained a huge crowd of people—all on their feet! In my youthful naïveté, I wondered, from where had come all of these Valids? My mother then told me that, centuries ago, almost all humans were valid and the few in-valid ones became so through injury or disease ... after birth. I wondered why. Thereafter, I consumed all history I could find and discovered facts that, for decades, our government has tried to hide. For instance, the fact that the atmosphere is half a percent carbon dioxide is common knowledge. Yet, few of you know that, half a millennium ago, it contained one-twentieth of that. No wonder, outdoors, we gasp for breath."

John heard a Valid from the crowd yell, "Thorpe, stop your damn' whining so we can all go home."

Another screamed, "If I had the chance, I'd shut him up."

The judge's gavel came down. "Order! Order in the court. This man is condemned to death. His last opportunity to express himself is now. By law, this court must listen. If you don't like it ... leave."

John gazed about the courtroom.

No one moved.

"Mister Thorpe, please continue."

"Thank you, your honor. ... Also, few of you know that only three percent of the population was in-valid in the year 2000, and rose each succeeding century to fifteen, then thirty, fifty, and, finally, eighty percent today.

"Two centuries ago, Earth's human population peaked at eighteen billion—the 'petri dish' that was Earth had run over. Chemicals could push no further the yield of the land. Indeed, these poisons had finally rendered useless, fields and pastures. The thoroughly contaminated environment caused tens of millions to die each year. Expanded zoological shelters failed to save the remaining wildlife.

"A century later, tropical Earth became completely desertated (sic). Temperate zones continued to succumb also, and humanity clustered higher in the mountains and nearer to the poles.

"Today, the Earth supports barely three billion souls. The crutched, the gurneyed, and the wheelchaired dominate a typical street scene. Millions of other miserables lie hidden in obscure places, awaiting painful—but merciful—deaths.

"Over the years, the wealthy and powerful succeeded in protecting themselves from the worst aspects of our planet's slow demise. At first, the differences between rich and poor were money, power, and luxury. Yet, poor persons of intelligence could grasp opportunities and become rich. ... Hope lived.

"Then, educators and employers began using genomic quartal sequencing to cull the genetically 'unsound' from the 'sound.' Thus, from birth, individuals were irreversibly branded as learners or retards, employables or unemployables, Valids or In-valids. ... Hope died.

"Only the genetically similar were allowed to mate with each other, thus various classes of mutants appeared—actual human subspecies."

John raised his voice to a high pitch. "I accuse Valids of availing themselves of safe, satellite-grown food—to the exclusion of In-valids. I accuse Valids of sheltering themselves from the Sun, the atmosphere, and the incessant dust storms by living and working in huge complexes high in the sky—to the exclusion of In-valids. I accuse Valids of maliciously establishing and intensifying a ruthless policy of apartheid based upon their idea of which persons are genetically valid."

For some time, John noticed the prosecutor fidget. Finally, the man rose. "Your honor, I object—a court of law is not the proper forum for a history lesson, especially one of such bias. May the condemned confine his remarks to an attempt to justify his felonious actions?"

"I agree. ... Mister Thorpe, please limit your talk to your rebuttal."

"Very well, your honor. One by one, I will address myself to each charge brought against me.

"Grand theft: I organized raiding parties to steal the basic necessities of life hoarded in warehouses across the land. I had food, clothing, and fuel—reserved for Valids—distributed to the poor and needy.

"Arson: To draw the attention of the Valids, I ordered their hoards of luxury goods—quite useless to the masses—put to the torch.

"Smuggling and piracy: Contaminated, earth-grown food is responsible for the breakdown of genomic sequence patterns—and, thus, the creation of mutant In-valids. The limited amount of untainted food grown on satellites and the Moon is allocated to Valids only. I wanted In-valids to have some, too. Therefore, I had the transport shuttles hijacked and their contents smuggled to Earth to feed my people.

"Assault, battery, mayhem, and murder: Valids resisted my followers, and, quite naturally, clashes occurred between them. Although most losses were robotic, maiming and killing of humans on both sides were inevitable. This violence was not premeditated, but resulted from the heat of the struggle.

"Torture: I intended no torture. Unfortunately, in addition to robots, I needed retards to do my bidding. Some of them, to extract information from mum captives, went beyond my orders. Again, these acts were not performed for their own sake.

"Rebellion, rioting, and sedition: Whenever a government responds only to a privileged few for the detriment of the majority, sedition not only becomes necessary to make unjust society just but, a moral duty as well. Should a downtrodden people fail to obtain a peaceful redress of justified grievances, they must use whatever means are available to them. Rebellion, rioting, and sedition may be their sole choices.

"I am before you today because I found battle with tyranny preferable to the abhorrence of complacently accepting injustice. To welcome the embrace of death from these circumstances is, indeed, a sweet luxury."

The judge smiled. "To me, your indulgences seem to have borne bitter fruit ... however, to each his own. ... Before we close, answer me one question, Mister Thorpe."

"Which one, your honor?"

"Why? ... In God's name, why?"

John's eyes welled with tears, and he almost stifled a sob. "... Despite my wife's and my genomic patterns, we produced a valid baby—a son—perfect in all aspects. He was full of life and eager to learn.

"However, try as I might, I failed to get him accepted into a school for Valids. Using forged credentials, a Valid friend finally succeeded where I had failed. My son became one of the school's best pupils, but jealous schoolmates discovered his In-valid origins. One day, a gang of upper-class boys abducted and beat him. To assure he never be mistaken for a Valid again, they poked out his eyes and crippled him. He was only seven years old. ... My wife killed herself."

John wept.

"Who were those boys? They can be brought to justice."

"You needn't bother, your honor. ... With great resolve, my friends have already ushered them into the ranks of the In-valid."

33—CONCEPTION

O wombe! O bely! O stynkyng cod
Fulfilled of dong and of corrupcioun!

—Geoffrey Chaucer

Three hundred one years into the past, September 6, 2130
En route to Julie and Mario's apartment
Bellevue, Franklin

In a rush, Katharine left the news agency and boarded a monocabin for Julie's apartment. She was worried about her distraught daughter, who had called and asked for an urgent talk—in private.

Julie had refused to divulge her problem on screen. Apparently, she believed it serious enough to warrant her mother's undivided attention—in person.

Although anxious, Katharine felt gratified that her daughter had asked her for help. Ages had passed since the last time Julie had confided in her. *What is bothering my little girl?*

Julie wasn't Katharine's only worry. With nary a word, Jane disappeared to God-knows-where. The explanation was that she'd gone on a "business" trip. Katharine didn't buy it. When she told Pierre, he offered to find Jane. Katharine was astounded at how easily he located her—only one terse question to his screen sufficed. Jane was registered under an alias at the Athabasca Grand Hotel, which was the same hotel that housed Andy. Katharine wasn't upset by the news—she had expected it. Actually, it obliterated her sense of guilt over her own affair with Pierre.

She wondered about Andy. Will he be feeling guilty about now? Knowing him, she didn't believe so. Upon returning, would he attempt to enter her bed? If so, would he confess his infidelity beforehand? She wanted to break with him but had no money to get her own place. *What should I do? Why do I always find myself in such dilemmas?*

The cabin shunted to the spur line and stopped at Julie's stratoscraper.

* * *

"Oh, Mother, I'm so unhappy."

"Is it Mario? Has he hurt you? Is he seeing another woman?"

"No ... nothing like that, but he has made me pregnant."

Katharine knew that she should not be surprised, but she was. That her daughter already could have a child of her own hadn't yet dawned on her. However, now, Julie's announcement made Katharine realize that the opportunity for her to play the role of a better mother was now at hand.

Then, a sense of panic gripped her. *Has confrontation time arrived, too. This is no time to complicate my daughter's emotions. She came to me for help. I must help her ... soothe her ... make her my little girl again. Dear God, please ... give me the strength to be a good mother ... please—no confrontation.* All of these jumbled thoughts coursed through her mind in an instant, and she promptly replied, "That is wonderful news, Dear. Mario and you must be very happy."

"Mario is ecstatic, but I certainly am not."

Katharine saw lines of anxiety in Julie's face. She tried to allay her fears. "Julie dear, to have a child is normal. You are young and healthy with a young, healthy husband—you have no reason to worry."

"Oh, Mother, you should be the first to know that visible signs of youth and health aren't enough anymore. My chance of having an in-valid child is greater than when you had Douglas."

"Julie, please! … Don't compare your situation with mine. When your father and I were young, few realized by how much our environment had deteriorated. In our ignorance and complacency, we frolicked unprotected in the Sun, breathed unprocessed air, and consumed food and drink tainted by carcinogens. Almost too late, our generation learned about the damage society was inflicting upon us and took appropriate counter-measures. Your generation now lives in a cleaner world."

Katharine gazed fondly at her daughter, who stared dejectedly at the carpet. She stroked her hair.

Julie turned—sobbing—and buried her face in her mother's bosom.

"Your baby will be fine, Julie. You have nothing to fear. From the day of your birth, your father and I kept you isolated from the worst aspects of our world. We rarely ate earth-grown food. We used natural soaps, few medicines, and virtually no chemicals. Most of your childhood was spent indoors breathing quality air. I see no problem. … Think positively, for Heaven's sake."

Julie sat up and wiped her eyes. "Don't try to sweeten the pill, Mother. I'm old enough to take my medicine and face reality. I know that you've always wanted the best for me, but the best was never available—not for grandmother, not for you, and, certainly … not for me. You are sweet to try to ease my anxiety, but your voice gives you away—when you lie, it quavers. My baby is in harm's way—you know it—I know it … yet Mario appears to ignore it."

"What do you mean? I thought you said that he was ecstatic."

"Ecstatic about becoming a father, yes … but unable or unwilling to recognize the dangers involved."

Julie began pacing.

Katharine empathized. … Oh, how she empathized yet felt helpless. She refused to allow herself involvement in any differences between Julie and Mario—a mother-in-law intrusion that could only turn to tragedy.

Julie continued to pace. "Oh, Mother, I can't stand being pregnant without knowing. How can I sit month after month, getting bigger and bigger, without knowing?"

"Knowing what?"

"Dammit, don't act so God-damned naïve. I didn't come to my mother for hand holding. I need real help—someone to find a doctor who'll examine me. Mario is no help—says 'it's against God's will. Illegal examinations beget illegal abortions' he says."

I must be careful, Katharine thought. *I agree with Mario, but, if Julie should know, I would again alienate myself from her. What shall I do? … try to force my moral beliefs on her? … or compromise my own by deferring to hers? Either my daughter controls me, or ... she leaves me. Either way, I lose.* "What if the examination indicates a deformed embryo?"

Julie whipped around to stare at her. The question seemed to jolt her daughter. "My God, Mother, do you realize that's the first time I've ever heard you pronounce the word 'embryo.' What is this world coming to?"

Katharine felt suddenly exhausted but forced herself to face Julie in her usual, resolute manner. "It's a perfectly good word—means an early stage of a new life's development."

"You needn't explain—I know already, but, to answer your question ... I'd get an abortion."

Katharine inhaled sharply to voice her protest but held her tongue. She knew that Julie was waiting for her reaction, so she reflected well before giving a calm answer. "Of course you may decide for yourself, but you must realize you'd be committing a crime. Our culture has always been against abortion. It was tolerated—even legal— during the last quarter of the twentieth and first quarter of the twenty-first centuries, but the prochoice movement was eventually stamped out. Most people have always been revolted by abortion."

Julie emitted a hollow laugh. "From where did you learn that? If you say 'from Pierre Talon,' I don't believe it. In reality, he probably said that, before abortion was legalized, most people were revolted by 'back-alley' butcherings that maimed and killed women because safe, legal abortions were unavailable."

"Come now, Julie, those women were breaking the law ... God's law—'thou shalt not kill.' If they were maimed and killed, they received God's punishment."

"You're being unreasonable and silly. At this rate, we'll never see eye-to-eye. ... Mother, are you just going to stand there being stubborn, or are you going to help me find a doctor?"

"Julie, I think it's unwise to break the law like—"

"Dammit, I need my mother's help. Are you going to give it, or should I go elsewhere?"

"Yes, Julie, I'll give it. ... I'll find you that doctor."

34—DECEPTION

O what a tangled web we weave,
When first we practice to deceive!

—Sir Walter Scott

Three days later, September 9, 2130
The office of Doctor Sullivan
Seattle, Franklin

Katharine was disappointed in her search for a doctor for Julie. Her contacts recommended a number of unsavory quacks, who—she felt sure—never saw the interior of a medical school. The most impressive one proved, the worst—his superb credentials and glowing recommendations had been elegantly forged.

She dreaded contacting Doctor Sullivan, her son's former doctor, but he seemed to be her only option. Just the sight of him was sure to revive bitter memories of Douglas's worst moments.

I must not look back. Dear Julie, my last and only child, is my duty now.

Katharine entered the office of Doctor Sullivan and, despite his warm greeting, felt apprehensive. Something was wrong. Having conferred with Doctor Sullivan countless times in the past, she knew he was the same doctor that had treated her son, but—somehow—he was changed. No longer did she see in him the distinguished savior of unfortunate infants and parental soul soother she had known. The man before her appeared as a base opportunist and exploiter of the miserable. She almost fled but recalled why she was there.

Katharine informed the doctor of Julie's pregnancy and fears, then asked for his help.

Immediately, he was defensive. "Ms. Carver, you ask me for a prenatal exam for your daughter? ... Oh, no, I could never get into shadow medicine. I am a respected doctor for the in-valid. I have my reputation to protect. Besides, obstetrics isn't my specialty."

"What difference does that make? You won't be delivering the baby anyway. No one would find out. ... Doctor Sullivan, we have known each other for many years. I would never betray you, and neither would Julie."

"The prenatal exam, itself, does not worry me—the possible consequences of it does. If I should find a deformed embryo, your daughter would demand I induce an abortion, and that, I will never do. However, once I examine her, I am open to blackmail."

"Doctor, do you believe she would do such a thing?"

"Blackmail me to get an abortion? ... Why of course she would. No matter good intentions, she'd be desperate, and desperate people take desperate measures."

"What if you should find a normal embryo?"

The doctor smiled. "Then, Ms. Carver, there would be no problem."

"Exactly," she agreed.

A long silence ensued.

"Ms. Carver, if that is all ... I am busy, you know."

"No, that is not all. ... Doctor Sullivan, examine my daughter and tell her everything is fine ... no matter what."

"I can't do that."

"Why not?"

"Because, if the birth produces a deformed baby, she would know I misled her."

Katharine reached into her handbag, retrieved a bag of gold coins that she had saved for emergencies, and threw it on the desk.

Matter-of-factly, the doctor counted the coins, licked his lips, and looked up at her. "I require more than this."

"How much more?"

The doctor's eyes narrowed to slits. "Well, Ms. Carver, how much more do you have?"

Why, that greedy, little devil. "That's all I have—my entire savings."

Doctor Sullivan studied her for a moment, then placed the bag of coins in a drawer. "Very well. I believe you. I will do as you ask."

Katharine should have felt grateful, but she did not. Instead, an acrid taste invaded her throat. "I need your assurance that my daughter will never know this conversation took place."

"My dear Ms. Carver, I believe that the secrecy of this conversation is in both of our interests."

Katharine rose and turned to leave.

The doctor ran after her.

"Will you want to know the result of the exam?"

"Absolutely not."

"Even if ... ?"

Katharine gazed at the doctor with as haughty a look as she could muster. "Yes ... 'even if—' After all, you cannot violate the confidentiality of your doctor-patient relationship. ... Good-bye, Doctor Sullivan."

35—MARTYRDOM

I tell you, and I pray God it be
not laid to your charge, that
I am the Martyr of the People.

—Charles I of Great Britain

Three hundred one years into the future, May 30, 2431
The Urbane National Penitentiary, Complex M
Republic of Urbane

Pierre looked out from John's eyes and saw himself enclosed in a prison cell. That it was early morning surprised him. Only a split second before, he had been at John's trial—in the late afternoon of the previous day. Evidently, John's sensations hadn't been recorded between times. He watched two robonurses leave. No doubt, they had groomed John and just finished installing him in his wheelchair. Pierre felt better—probably the robots also did something to ease John's persistent aches and pains.

Nataly and an older man entered. The heavy cell door clanked shut behind them.

He heard himself say, "Karl, I am so glad to see you. How is Hannah? ... and my little Alex?"

"Hannah's fine and so is your son. ... John, how can you think of my wife and me at a time like this? You and your son are all that's important, now."

Pierre was surprised to see the man approach, hug his head, and plant a kiss on his brow. *Certainly John has known this Karl and his wife for some time. They must be raising his son.* John's words interrupted his thoughts. "No, Karl, from now on, only Alex and my friends are important. ... My time is past."

Pierre's gaze shifted to Nataly, and he listened to his lips say, "Nataly, you look beautiful this morning."

The young woman rushed forward, knelt, and looked up to him as if to God Himself. She kissed his hand.

Pierre knew that his feeling of guilt about being on the receiving end of Nataly's admiration was silly, but he couldn't help it—her adoration was intended only for John. Then, he recalled that many others before him must have entered John's mind, too. Had they felt guilty about eavesdropping on Nataly's emotions, as well?

"I'm so ashamed, John. I failed you in court yesterday. Please forgive me."

Again Pierre's head resonated with John's voice. "Nothing needs forgiving, Nataly. The trial proceeded exactly as I planned." Pierre felt John's hand stroke Nataly's hair. "Karl, I hope you have kept Alex from hearing about my trial. My son is too young to worry about the fate of his father."

"I couldn't keep Alex from accessing the telechannels. He hung on every word of your speech. Of course, if he were capable of seeing your image, he would have been ecstatic. Hannah and I have told him all about your struggle for recognition of in-valid rights. Alex knows everything. He's ten years old now ... he understands."

122

"Karl, my only regret is that I cannot see my son before I leave this existence. I want him to know that I have not abandoned him. I want him to know that I love him."

"Alex is mature for his age ... probably from his suffering. He knows you love him and understands why you did what you did and why you want to die. John, your son is proud of you."

Pierre's eyes glazed.

Nataly spoke. "What about your followers? How can they continue the fight without you?"

"I'm not indispensable. ... No one is. Someone will emerge to lead them. Leaders, like heros, are not born—they are ordinary persons amid extraordinary circumstances. They do what they must. So long as Valids oppress In-valids, the struggle will find leaders."

"But, John, they've captured and executed most of your lieutenants, already. No one remains to replace you."

"The rise of a new leader takes time, Nataly, but it will happen."

Karl said, "Why did the Valids bring you to trial? Why didn't they summarily execute you, too? And, why revive such a bloody and barbarous way of execution? The guillotine hasn't been used in centuries."

"The Valids are desperate—our rebellion almost succeeded. My trial and execution are well publicized showpieces designed, not only to demoralize the In-valids but, to show the world the legality of my condemnation and punishment. The use of the guillotine, of course, is simply an extension of the Valids' garish methods."

Pierre saw two men enter.

The younger one said, "Mister Thorpe, time is short—the Sun rises in one hour. The prefect has come to speak to you."

The other man said, "John Thorpe, yesterday, you rebuffed your right of appeal. I now offer you a last chance for a reprieve. At this time, will you appeal your case?"

"No! ... Absolutely not."

Nataly interrupted, "John, please—"

"Nataly, my decision is final."

The prefect said, "Very well, Mister Thorpe, but, remember, once you are led from this cell, your right of appeal ceases."

The first man said, "Your guests must leave in ten minutes."

The two men left.

Karl said, "Do you hear the crowd in the square, John? Hundreds or, perhaps, thousands surround the scaffold. You believe that they will cheer you as you pass, don't you?"

"Of course—they're my followers."

"Your remaining followers have already gone underground. To cheer you publicly means death. No, John, those people out there in wheelchairs and on gurneys are Valids—disguised as In-valids. They will vilify you."

"I might have known. Their propagandistic schemes know no bounds, but don't worry—the world will see through their theatrics."

The door slid open, and Pierre saw the man who had accompanied the prefect.

"Your guests must leave."

Nataly began to sob.

Karl hugged Pierre and whispered words of encouragement, "John … John, have no fear. It will be over quickly … painlessly."

"Yes, no more pain. … Karl, I thank you and Hannah for raising my son. Now, he is your son. Take good care of him … and of Hannah … and of yourself. Someday, we will meet again … in a better world."

Pierre felt Nataly's tears rub into his cheeks. Her embrace caused much pain. She seemed incoherent—all she said was, "Oh, John, no! Don't let it happen. Don't let it happen."

Karl took her by the arm and ushered her from the cell.

Pierre was alone. He wondered what John was thinking and why he couldn't enter his thoughts. After all, weren't thoughts just another input to memory—like the five senses?

He felt anxious—time was running out for John. He wondered whether or not Boniface expected him to remain in John's mind to the end of his execution. He certainly wasn't looking forward to the experience.

Maybe I'll leave John's mind when he mounts the scaffold. No, I'll wait until his neck is beneath the poised blade. … Perhaps Boniface is testing me to see if I have the courage to feel the blade's bitter bite. Oh, God … what should I do?

The door rumbled open. A robosentry entered and said, "John Thorpe, the Sun rises in thirty minutes. You will come with me." It pushed Pierre's wheelchair down the prison corridors and through the gate into the courtyard. Pierre would have gasped from the terrible heat that hit him, but John's only reaction was the instantaneous formation of beads of sweat upon his brow.

In the middle of the courtyard, Pierre was struck by the image of the scaffold surmounted by its instrument of death. Under the glow of floodlights, the guillotine stood out in sharp contrast to the black sky. Pierre knew that he would have trembled at the sight, but John did not.

How can John be so calm about his own death?

Pierre winced in pain as the robosentry pushed the wheelchair over the rough cobblestones of the courtyard. Upon entering the glare of the lights, he heard the crowd roar.

"There he is, the little traitor." … "To death with him." … "John Thorpe, may you fry in hell forever." … .

The robot pushed John's wheelchair toward the scaffold. Despite the double row of robosentries, which flanked the passage, the crowd threw at John all sorts of filth. Most missed, but some did not.

While Pierre could smell the stench of rotten eggs in John's nostrils, he felt the sting of an overripe tomato, which splattered his cheek. The impact of a well-thrown rock numbed his arm, and his mouth burned from the acridness of heaved vomit.

Pierre thought that he'd pass out. *I've got to hang on. I must show Boniface that a person from the twenty-first century can take it as well as anybody.*

A frenzied man, apparently forgetting about his in-valid disguise, sprang from his gurney, vaulted the sentries, and sprinted toward John.

Pierre hoped that John could put up a defense—however feeble it might be. From the corner of his eye, he perceived the robot's arm whip out and smash the face of his attacker. The man crumpled in a heap—short of his target.

The mob howled, and other "In-valids," miraculously "cured," jumped up and surged forward. The robosentries interlocked arms and held back the rioters until the wheelchair arrived at the foot of the scaffold steps.

Pierre felt the restraining straps loosen and a huge arm pluck John from his wheelchair. An instant later, John was in his robot's arms atop the scaffold watching the snarling pack lunge at him with lupine-like leaps from below.

The floodlights switched off, and Pierre viewed the macabre scene from the growing twilight of dawn. *It is time. ... Am I strong enough to remain with John to the end?*

Despite the accompanying cacophony, Pierre heard an official speak. "John Thorpe, have you any last words before I must do my duty?"

"Yes. ... SILENCE!"

Pierre was taken aback by the sudden roar in his head. John had inhaled sharply and thundered in a deep voice, which echoed loudly to the far reaches of the courtyard. Certainly, the mob was surprised also, because the tumult subsided enough for John's speech to be heard.

"People of Urbane, I make no apology for my actions. Had I not come forward to lead my people, another would have done so. My execution is but a pause in our predestined march to freedom. My passage will allow a stronger—perhaps more vicious—leader to emerge from the oppressed masses. He will guide you to victory.

"With pleasure, I accept the soothing death that awaits me—for my wretched frame, in rebellious pain, harbors life no longer. After I am gone, envision me—if, in your hearts, you can ... as the martyr of the people."

In mock appreciation from the crowd, polite claps and cheers greeted Pierre. Soon they degenerated into rhythmic slaps and jeers and repeated shouts of, "Kill him! Kill him! Kill him! ... ."

Rapidly, Pierre found John lying on his chest, staring into a bloodstained tub. The back of "his" neck tingled—or so Pierre supposed. A bile-like bitterness flooded "his" mouth. He heard "his" heart pound its last, life-giving surges of blood to "his" brain. The feeling of imminent doom falling from behind was overpowering and drove him into a panic. He repeated to himself, *I will not leave; I will not leave—I will endure!*

A voice said, "Look at the horizon and tell me when you see the Sun."

Were he in control of John's body, Pierre knew that he would be too terror stricken to move, but John's head turned calmly toward the east. In a daze, Pierre noticed the dawn's glow gradually brighten until, finally, the Sun's orb peeked at him. John's tongue responded.

"The Sun is risen."

For an instant, Pierre heard a swish, then—a thud. He felt no extra pain, but the feeling of falling in slow motion abruptly ended when John's head banged—painfully—into the bottom of the tub. He stared up and briefly saw the stump of John's neck before blood splashed hotly into "his" eyes. The cheers of the crowd receded into silence. The nagging aches and pains abandoned him. His agony evolved into sweet bliss. Mercifully, Pierre became blind, deaf, and numb.

The emptiness and coldness returned, but the earlier depression and morbidity did not. He wasn't even lonely. Indeed, he was elated—all suffering had ceased.

> But fornication, and all uncleanliness,
> or covetousness let it not be once
> named among you, as becometh saints.
>
> —Ephesians 5:3

Three hundred one years into the past, September 13, 2130
Jane Stevens' Informational News Agency
Bellevue, Franklin

Upon Jane's arrival at the agency, Katharine greeted the woman with innocence and charm. "Good morning, Jane. I hope your trip was successful. When did you get back?"

Jane smiled. Actually, she smirked. "Last night. Yes, I had a pleasant trip ... thank you, Kathy."

"That's good." *The bitch! Of course she had a good time. If she was after pure animal sex, Andy could certainly deliver.*

Later in the morning, Katharine greeted Andy at the spaceport. She welcomed him home with a kiss that was less than ardent. His response was not a paradigm of passion, either. *He knows that I know.*

En route home, both sat in pregnant silence. Katharine stared straight ahead yet sensed Andy's furtive glances. Finally, she caught him in the act—their eyes met.

Andy spread his hands—palms up. "Look, I didn't invite Jane to Silverado. When she learned you weren't going, she couldn't resist coming as a surprise." He cut short a chuckle.

Katharine rolled her eyes. "God, Andy, how you do flatter yourself."

"You needn't be so self-righteous, Kathy. We haven't been exactly fawning lovers, lately. I'm not blind, you know. I've been watching your growing infatuation with Pierre. When you declined to go with me to the convention, I knew that something was afoot."

"So that's your excuse. Well, you're wrong. Before you left, I was never unfaithful."

"... and after?"

"Dammit, Andy, before I ever met you, Pierre and I loved each other."

"... and you love him still."

"Well, yes, I—"

Andy slapped his knee. "Then, that's it."

"What do you mean?"

"We can't possibly live together anymore: You have a new lover."

Katharine was livid. "You lousy son of a bitch. You've been fucking Jane for the past week, and, now, with your slappable, martyred expression, you say I have a new lover. You ... you hypocrite, and Pierre is ten times the lover you are. Every time you

126

took me, I imagined myself in his arms. All your fornications sicken me ... you sicken me, you pompous ass."

Andy's face reddened. His whole body quivered. He waved a finger in her face and barked, "Why you ungrateful bitch! Out! I want you out of my home ... tonight, do you hear me ... tonight!"

Katharine's heart leapt. Where could she go? She had no money. She blurted, "Tonight? Hell, I won't stay another instant—I'm out, as of now!"

* * *

Katharine hated to have to do it, but what other choice had she? "Are you sure that I'm not imposing?"

"Don't be ridiculous, Mother. We won't need the nursery for several months yet. By then, you'll have your own place."

Mario said, "And don't worry about your things, either. I had them put in Fuerza Cortés's warehouse out at the spaceport—free of charge."

Katharine was ashamed. "You two are too good to me."

"We're just happy that you left Andrew, Mother. How many times, since Douglas died, have I asked you to?"

"Look, all that is done and over with—let's talk of happier things."

Julie smiled. "Good, let's eat. You'll enjoy dinner, Mother. Mario bought me a new cookrobot. It prepares all kinds of fantastic dishes that the old one couldn't."

Katharine sat opposite Mario with Julie to her right. The table looked wonderful. "Mmm ... this is delicious."

Julie beamed. "That is one of the advantages of having a husband high up in the Fuerza Cortés company."

Mario spoke. "The coffee is genuine. How do you like it?"

Katharine took another sip. "Wonderful. I don't believe I've ever tasted real coffee before. Where did you get it? I bet it cost a lot."

"It's priceless, but I get it free. Fuerza Cortés owns an experimental coffee plantation on the Moon. This is from its first harvest. As a matter of fact, the whole dinner came from the Moon." Mario smiled, reached for Julie's hand, and squeezed it. "After Julie told me that she was going to have a baby, I insisted she refrain from eating earth-grown food. We don't want to take any unnecessary chances."

"It must be very expensive."

"Normally, yes—but being my father's son has its privileges."

Katharine was curious. "Relations with your father have improved, I presume."

Mario arched his eyebrows. "Considerably. Obviously, he's hedging his relationship with his future grandchild. However, he does... ."

Katharine stopped listening. She sensed her daughter's gaze upon her. She turned to face her and perceived a hint of a smile. *What are her thoughts? If they're about me, I hope I'm treated kindly.* Katharine pondered over the contract she had made with Doctor Sullivan. Her hands trembled, so she lowered them to her lap. She shivered.

"Kathy, are you cold? You look pale. Could I get you one of Julie's sweaters?"

"No ... thank you anyway, Mario."

"Mother, I must confess—tonight, you seem like a different person."

Katharine tensed. *Does my guilt show?* "What do you mean, dear?"

"Well, in the past you appeared old and stubborn—with old-fashioned ideas. Now, you seem wise and capable."

Mario said, "Perhaps watching the Talon interviews changed your perception of your mother."

"No, it isn't that. Maybe it's because she finally mustered the courage to leave Andrew. Maybe it's my pregnancy. I feel a greater kinship toward her, now. I'm going the same route as she—being a mother, I mean." Julie touched her mother's arm.

By reflex, Katharine almost jerked it back. *Her loving touch ... I don't deserve it.* As Julie continued to talk, Katharine could barely keep from cupping her hands over her ears.

"... nine months gestation is not only required to develop the fetus but to prepare the future mother psychologically for the responsibilities of motherhood. Doctor Sullivan says that my embryo is doing well. Oh, I'm so happy."

Mario said, "I wish you'd stop seeing him. Something's wrong about that man."

"Don't be silly, Darling, Mother vouched for him, didn't you, Mother?

Katharine stared at Mario. *God, does he know something?* She shivered. "Ah ... yes, of course."

37—DESPOLIATION

'Ye have robb'd,' said he, 'ye have slaughter'd
and made an end,
Take your ill-got plunder, and bury the dead.'

—Sir Henry Newbolt

The next morning, September 14, 2130
Katharine's office, Informational News Agency
Bellevue, Franklin

Katharine busied herself putting the finishing touches on her new documentary about forests.

She had researched the evolution of Earth's plant life from the end of the last ice age to the present. She was pleased with her work and hoped that her report would shock the world as much as the Talon interviews were doing.

Pierre's encouragement had given her the idea for the documentary in the first place. As a matter of fact, most of its content was affected by his great knowledge of history that had occurred prior to the Wall.

So far, Katharine managed to avoid Jane, but she knew that she would be forced to face her before the day was out. The documentary was ready for scheduling, and Jane wanted to see it beforehand.

Startled, Katharine watched Jane stride in—unannounced.

"Isn't it ready … yet?"

A spurt of adrenaline shot through Katharine. *Speak of the devil.* Although Jane's sarcastically-strident voice caused the arteries in her neck to pulsate, she smiled and said, "Yes, Jane, it's ready. I worked overtime on it because I knew you were anxious to review it, but it wasn't scheduled for completion until next week, of course."

Jane frowned. "Who told you that?"

"Why … why you did … just a few days ago."

Jane kept her eyes averted. "You're mistaken."

Katharine forced false enthusiasm. "Jane, this one will draw big, too. The Talon interviews have alerted the viewers to the plight of humankind, and they thirst for more."

"Frankly, I think they're sick of it, but let us get this over with. Give me a run-down—and be quick about it."

"Sure, Jane." Katharine sensed that Jane was maintaining her foul mood with difficulty. She was sure that Andy was prejudicing Jane against her but hoped that the woman was professional enough not to be affected for long by his petty concerns.

* * *

Katharine was surprised. Although she had shown Jane the proof, the woman still refused to believe the seriousness of the problem.

129

"The atmosphere contains only one-tenth of one percent carbon dioxide—that's not much."

"But, Jane, that's four times the amount that was present in the mid-twentieth century and enough to cause real damage. Don't you see? The initial impetus for the increase was deforestation and burning of fossil fuels. Look at the resultant chain reaction: The blanket of carbon dioxide trapped the solar heat beneath it and heated the atmosphere, which, in turn, heated the oceans. The warmer oceans released trapped methane and, thus, supplied even more carbon dioxide to the atmosphere. Earth's coral reefs, which absorb carbon dioxide from the sea, are dying. It's a cycle that's spiraling upward—out of control."

With exaggerated swirls of her long, spindly arms, Jane said sarcastically, "What do you mean 'spiraling upward' … 'out of control'?"

"Well, humans have forced nature out of balance so much that human-made infusion of carbon dioxide into the atmosphere caused nature to add even more. Now, the process is unstable."

"How can you be so sure?"

"The statistics confirm it: The carbon-dioxide increase is not linear or even exponential—it's the rate of increase that's exponential, and, Jane … there's a hellava difference between the two."

"Like what?" Despite her foul mood, Jane seemed unable to hide her curiosity.

"Like the death of the human species, that's what. During the interviews, you heard Pierre say that, by 2786, the atmosphere will contain five percent carbon dioxide—enough to wipe from the face of the Earth, all higher life forms."

Jane hooted. "I don't give a damn what Talon says. What did your own research tell you?"

"Not much. Most records pertaining to what I want to know were destroyed long ago, but Pierre, on the other hand, is a veritable fountain of historical knowledge."

"Christ, Kathy, the man's been declared insane by the world's top psychiatrists. Don't you realize that he's telling you fairy tales?"

"No, he isn't. When I mention some obscure fact that I've gleaned from an archive, immediately he fleshes it out in a most plausible and convincing manner. Jane, his sincerity is absolute."

"Tell me … from where does he draw his information in such detail?"

Katharine hesitated—because she didn't know. "Just listen and judge for yourself."

"Very well—you've got ten minutes."

Katharine jumped at the chance. "Jane, Pierre showed me that only plants shield us from asphyxiation. Up to the twenty-first century, plants consumed the carbon dioxide that animals produced. Contrariwise, animals consumed the oxygen plants produced. Nature was in balance … but, no more.

"Although most large animals have disappeared from the Earth, increased human population has more than taken their place in the consumption of oxygen and … energy. Historically, humans obtained energy by burning fossil fuels—first, wood; then, coal; and, finally, petroleum. The process of burning and breathing released huge quantities of carbon dioxide, but few oxygen-producing processes remained.

"During the last century, the oxygen content of the atmosphere declined by one-fifth—from twenty-one to seventeen percent. Oxygen depletion and carbon-dioxide buildup created the emphysemic pandemic late in the past century. Of course, since then, the advent of hydroxygen has alleviated the problem—but only temporarily."

"Okay, Kathy, I admit we have more carbon dioxide, less oxygen, and increased atmospheric warming, but we're still emerging from an ice age. That is what has caused forests to degenerate into deserts. Humans played no role in the degradation of northern Africa into the Sahara Desert, western Australia into the Great Sandy Desert, or northern South America into the Great Amazonian Desert."

Katharine doubted Jane's sincerity. Is she playing the devil's advocate for Andy's sake? "Jane, how can you say that? The Amazon Forest just didn't dry up—it was cut down during the past century. Pierre told me that it barely existed when he departed Earth in 2045. Because the lack of trees changed the climate of the area, the forests can't grow back, either. Their disappearance ought to worry the powers that be, but, unfortunately, short-term profiteering breeds short-sighted reasoning."

"You exaggerate. I haven't seen much forest depletion. The world seems to remain the same."

"Jane, you talk about what you perceive within your own lifetime. During most of the civilized era, resources depleted slowly—with little change from one generation to the next. Early on, people were illiterate, so conditions for later historians to examine and analyze remained undocumented. Prior to the invention of photography, three centuries ago, no graphical records of the Earth's early environment existed. Also, in those early times, the ecosystem had not yet deteriorated to what it is today, so people were unconcerned and didn't bother to write about it. Thus, until recently, people believed that conditions on Earth—those that they had perceived in their childhood—always had existed."

"So, you're saying that, if a person could come back to life again, after having been dead for a century, he would be shocked by the current state of affairs."

"Yes ... well, look at Pierre—he was appalled when he arrived here in 2123 ... but I'm talking about even farther back—say, before the time of Christ. People who read the Bible believe that the Holy Land always was dry without vegetation save for a few palm and olive trees. However, in 4,000 BC the area was a veritable garden—not as pleasant as in 5,000 BC—but nice, nevertheless. Likewise, in Egypt ... for centuries, people believed that the early Egyptians built the Pyramids in a desert. On the contrary, they buried their pharaohs in the most pleasant surroundings possible—again, a garden. What caused the damage to these lands? ... The answer is: ignorant civilizations oblivious of the damage that they had inherited from their ancestors and that they, in turn, added to and passed on to their descendants.

"You know, Jane, humans are, by nature, selfish beasts that are concerned only about themselves and their families and, sometimes ... not even their families. The human species is a blight on the land—a plague—a pestilence—as is any species that multiplies unchecked by natural predators."

Jane shook her head. "Kathy, don't be so God damned melodramatic. Face the facts: Northern Africa and the Near East became desertic when the glaciers retreated after the last ice age. Also, because of the precession of the Earth's axis over the millennia, dry wind patterns gradually emerged within areas bounded by particular latitudes."

"Let me ask you this, Jane—from where and when did Western Civilization emerge?"

"From Egypt and Mesopotamia circa 6,000 BC."

"Okay, now, wouldn't you agree that those areas have been virtual deserts for the past 4,000 years?"

"Oh, more than that—for 12,000 years—since the end of the last ice age."

Katharine smiled. "Still with your 'ice age' theory, uh? ... Look, civilizations cannot spring from deserts. They originate in fertile lands, which they require for their development. In fact, the area from which Western Civilization sprang was called the 'Fertile Crescent'; however, millennia of human excesses caused by overpopulation sucked the land dry of every resource it ever possessed. More recently, in proportion to the rise in population, these excesses have accelerated and spread around the world. Look at Europe, New Guinea, central Africa, North America, and the Asian sub-continent: Were they ravaged by 'dry wind patterns' created by a retreating ice age?"

"No, but—"

"I rest my case."

"What about around here? A few days ago, you told me that forests once covered the whole area."

"Yes, Pierre told me that stands of huge sequoia, redwood, spruce, and fir blanketed the west coast of North America from San Francisco to beyond Vancouver Island. The trees were so huge and numerous, even buildings were constructed from them ... until all were cut down.

"I'm angry that none of those forests remain. How could people have been so selfish, back then? Why didn't they think of the future and leave some for us to enjoy? I suppose it was greed ... pure and simple. The forests existed and, as lumber, were worth much money, so they were cut until gone. With asparagus and tomatoes, no problem exists because they are quickly replaced. However, the biggest trees take centuries to grow. By comparison, human lifetimes are short; therefore, trees can reach maturity only by being inaccessible to human greed. When civilized humans discovered old-growth forests, their extinction soon followed. We will never again see their like because humankind hasn't the patience to await the passage of centuries, which is necessary for their maturity. Humans, like spoiled brats, want their 'supper,' now.

"The same happened in Asia and Europe except that their old-growth forests disappeared during prehistoric times. When Caesar swept through western Europe, unknowingly, he did so through second-growth trees.

The size of the trees that European explorers came upon in America astounded them. The more visionary people wanted the largest ones preserved, so governments set aside protected forests.

"At the onset of the twenty-first century, however, unprotected, old-growth trees existed no more. As the remaining—protected—trees became more and more valuable, the timber industry lusted after them as do foxes before hen houses. Finally, by greasing enough bureaucratic palms with enough money, it succeeded in its goals. The immense sequoia and redwood trees disappeared forever. The last of the tall spruce and fir fell as the drone of the chain saw sounded their death knell. The loggers destroyed the world's oldest and largest creatures and ... their own livelihood. Earth became a sadder place."

Jane exploded. "Don't you blame the loggers—my great grandfather was one—and don't blame the timber industry, either. It was just trying to do its job. Blame the consumer—who demanded its product. Blame the government—which was supposed to be the watchdog, but the loggers? ... Never!

Katharine believed that the pit of her stomach would collapse. She feared that Jane was about to cancel the documentary. "I haven't finished yet. Let me continue."

"Then, be quick about it."

"Jane, I know that any one group cannot be blamed, yet the fact remains that the big forests are gone—have been for decades. I believe that I'm right when I say, our ancestors were responsible—that their society as a whole was responsible. Back then, people believed that the forests were theirs for the taking without concern for the needs of the future. They didn't seem to understand the importance of the benefits of standing forests—clean water, beauty of nature, shelter for fish and fowl, habitat for flora and fauna, recreational areas for humans, ... To them, forests existed to be destroyed. Egotistically, they ravaged the land, making it unusable for anything or anyone else—rich topsoil eroded, ugly gullies appeared, tranquil valleys flooded, climate deteriorated, deserts proliferated, and plants and animals became extinct. Our ancestors were sowers of death and desolation—the great destroyers of Earth's ecosystem."

Jane sighed. "My poor, naïve Kathy—if the forests still existed today, we'd destroy them just like our ancestors did. We work and live in our own, little world without regard for the larger spheres of space and time. We humans haven't changed."

Is she mocking me, or is she trying to steal my thunder? "Yes, greed prematurely destroyed many industries, for instance: hunting an abundant species to extinction—bisons, pigeons, otters, seals, elephants, whales, salmon, tuna, dolphins—to name a few. I cannot understand why people, in apparent frenzies of destruction, decimate their own livelihood for short-term pleasure rather than husband it for long-term prosperity. Humans, like all earthly beasts, live day-by-day and, prompted by limited, myopic intelligence, really don't give a damn."

Jane held up a hand. "Okay, I've heard enough. I'll give you the one A. M. slot."

Katharine saw red. "What! Last week, you were talking prime time."

"I changed my mind ... okay?"

"But, you said—"

"Take it or leave it."

"Dammit, it's Andy, isn't it? He put you up to this."

Jane's lips curled into a sneer. "Don't you—ever again—speak to me about my private life ... understood?"

"Yes, Jane, but first, take some advise from someone with experience: Do not trust the man."

Jane continued as if she hadn't heard. "You get the one A. M. slot because, with your reputation in the Talon interviews, your viewers will readily wait up for you. I reserve prime time for stuffing less-palatable fare down the throats of more-captive audiences."

"Bullshit!"

Jane's eyes widened before they narrowed into slits. She pivoted and walked out.

Revenge is a kind of wild justice,
which the more man's nature runs to,
the more ought law to weed it out.

—Francis Bacon

Three hundred forty-three years into the future, November 11, 2473
Site of the final battle in the war against the Valids
The defunct Republic of Urbane

Flashes of warmth invaded Pierre. He sensed a strength and a vigor that he hadn't experienced in a long while. By contrast to being in John's tortured brain, this new embodiment was ecstasy—without any suffering whatsoever.

Suddenly, he saw, heard, and felt, again. Immediately, his chest drew his attention. Placed high upon it, he noticed … two mounds? *Oh, my God, I've entered the mind of a woman.*

* * *

Breasts erect, General Joan Thorpe strode triumphantly across the battlefield. The long war was over. The Valids had surrendered. Behind rolled her In-valid commanders. Depending upon the particular affliction, each was encased in some type of personal vehicle—ranging from glorified wheelchairs to fully-armed floatporters. Among her In-valid armies, only Joan possessed fully-valid body and mind.

During five years of war, Joan rose in rank to become the Supreme Commander of all the In-valids—impossible for one with validity had she not been the granddaughter of John the Martyr. However, most of her success she attributed to lifelong singleness of purpose—fulfillment of her grandfather's goal and vengeance for the Valids' inhumane treatment of her family. Although free of afflictions, she considered herself a full-fledged In-valid. … After all, truly bona fide Valids issue from Valids.

Most of Joan's enemies were dead; many of her friends were, too … killed in battle. Slain by Joan in hand-to-hand combat only a few minutes before, the leader of the Valids was the last to die. She swung his severed head by its hair as she marched amid her troops to join her father.

The passage, lined with cheering soldiers, reminded Joan of the path to the guillotine her grandfather had been forced to take half a century earlier. During the war—whenever demoralized—she would enter her grandfather's mind and experience his death. Each time, his decapitation affected her differently, but, always, it renewed her resolve. Joan believed that her grandfather's martyrdom was the catalyst that made her victory possible. Clearly, he did not die in vain.

Joan watched a floatporter descend and settle upon a knoll, some yards away. Its canopy slid back, and she recognized her father. As always, his prosthetic eyes, like thick sunglasses, were perched low on his nose—exposing the black patches over his eye sockets. A hatch pivoted down to form a ramp, and his wheelchair rolled out.

The troops yelled, "Long live Alex, son of John the Martyr. ... Long live General Thorpe ... Joan the Liberator."

Her father's grim expression surprised Joan. "What's the matter? You should rejoice. We've won, Father. We've finally won."

"Yes, we've won, but the victors are already squabbling among themselves—like vultures over a carcass. The news is bad."

"How is that?"

"As I speak, the In-valids of Austronia, Russgebiet, and Franqueterre are systematically slaughtering their remaining Valids. Here in Urbane, the War Council, flushed with victory, wants to follow suit. It is even discussing the possibility of making itself the sole governing body. War councils are designed for war. Ours must be disbanded, and new persons, elected to heal the land. ... Joan, warriors make bad rulers."

"Maybe so, Father, but, after wars, victorious soldiers are the only remaining sources of prestige and power. With your guidance, my commanders and I will form an interim government until a democratic one can be elected."

Joan swung the head onto her father's lap. "Here's a souvenir for you."

Her father removed his eyes and held them close to the head for a better look.

"General Beaumont?"

"Yes."

"Who killed him?"

"I did."

"Who severed his head?"

"I did."

"Why?"

"It was expected of me, Father. In my position, I cannot show—even for an instant—any weakness or compassion."

"Seems you've a wolf pack on your hands, Daughter."

"Yes. ... As civilization dies, humankind reverts to beasthood. Perhaps, the mystique of John the Martyr can save us no longer."

"Joan, the War Council has installed itself in the tallest stratoscraper in the area—kicking out the Valid occupants in the process. Its members are caucusing while they await your arrival. Supposedly, they are eager to congratulate you on your final victory."

Joan jerked the head off her father's lap and dumped it on the sand. "Let's go then. I'll get my commanders together."

"They don't want your commanders—only you and me."

"Fine, I'll get my floatporter, and we'll be off."

"Wait! ... Don't you find something amiss in their invitation?"

Joan paused. "No ... why?"

"What happened on March fifteenth, forty-four years before the birth of Jesus Christ?"

Joan thought for a moment. "Julius Caesar, unarmed, entered the Senate and was assassinated. ... I'll not only take my commanders, but a security force as well."

"Good thinking, Daughter."

* * *

Joan and her father entered a tumultuous council chamber. Alarmed by the commotion, they remained near the entrance. Here and there, groups of persons in heated argument yelled and brandished fists at each other. One by one they noticed Joan's arrival, so the room sank slowly into silence.

Joan guessed that they were arguing about her. No doubt, her decision to disarm the Council's guards was unpopular. She glanced at the exits to confirm that her own robosentries—armed with neuron disrupters—were on duty.

Someone called out, "General Thorpe, this is an outrage. How dare you violate the mandate of the War Council. I suppose that, now, we are your prisoners."

Joan turned toward the speaker and recognized Carlos Martinez on his gurney. He had been a major force in obtaining arms and technology for her In-valid armies since before the war broke out. She'd always considered him her friend.

"No, Carlos, none of you are my prisoners, and I am no threat, but I take my precautions … and rightly so, for the real threat lies here in this council. I heard rumors that most of you feel I'm not needed anymore—you believe me too powerful, too dangerous. … If true, you endanger me, also. … How ironic: History repeats itself—coöperation before the kill, squabbling after. Perhaps I should follow history's examples and my own instinct of self-preservation by having you all killed."

Again, the council chamber broke into an uproar—even a greater one than before.

Joan raised her arms, and, slowly, the clamor subsided into pockets of whispers.

"Ladies and gentlemen, as you see, mutual suspicion can only sow anarchy. Certainly, I am the commander-in-chief, but, remember, I am not my own master. My actions are constrained by the memory and goals of my grandfather, John the Martyr, and by the guidance of my father Alex Thorpe, who is a trusted and respected member of this council."

Joan rose to her full height. "So—you want to rule Urbane. Then let it be thus, for all of its surviving movers and doers are in this room." The sighs of relief echoing about amused her.

Carlos yelled, "What about you, Joan? What are you going to do?"

"Unshared power corrupts; therefore, to keep us all honest, my armies and I will share it with you."

"You mean, you'll dictate, and we'll obey."

"You know me better than that, Carlos. This council—the new legislature—will create new laws. I'll execute them. My father will adjudge them. I suggest we get to work—the nation needs healing."

Joan and her father left.

* * *

In the days that followed, Joan became more and more dissatisfied with the new legislature. She knew that, individually, its members were rational and capable persons, but, collectively, they were making unwise decisions.

Apparently influenced by postwar euphoria, each legislator feared condemnation by his peers for what they might perceive to be excessive leniency toward the Valids. Therefore, each successive law proposal became more harsh and extreme until the ones finally adopted were ridiculous—if not abominable.

As chief executive, Joan had committed herself to enforcing the new laws—but she could not accept these. They were counter to everything in which her grandfather had believed and for which he had fought and died. She decided to seek her father's advice.

* * *

"Father, you mean to tell me that the legislature hasn't submitted the new laws to you yet?"

"I've asked for access, but I keep getting excuses. The legislature must know it's passing laws contrary to the fundamental rights of humans. It must know that I will strike them down."

"Well, I received a record of the laws and orders to implement them. Here … listen to them and, if you will, strike them down—for I refuse to enforce them."

Joan approached her father's wheelchair and gave him the record.

He took her hand in his.

She was surprised—her father had shown little emotion since the beginning of the war—fault of the times.

"Joan dear, the stage that is this world is at a critical juncture, and you and I are its critical players. You realize that, don't you?"

Through tears, Joan barely saw. Wiping them away, she looked into her father's eyes. She noticed no tenderness nor even an indication that he was looking her way—such were the characteristics of prosthetic eyes.

"Yes I do, Father."

"After wars, standing armies are threats. Their soldiers become bored, mischievous—even riotous. Are you able to control ours?"

"We're trying—with difficulty. We've discharged many soldiers, but there's nothing for them on the outside, and they're rebelling. Others, we've kept busy guarding the remaining infrastructure and matériel. Some, we've had to put in detention. Foodstuffs are in rare supply, so soldiers pilfer and hoard them. Starvation is rampant, and nothing can be done about it."

"Sounds bad—very bad—but Urbane is a bit better off than the others. We're the only group of In-valids that hasn't yet gone on a rampage after the war—eliminating all of its Valids."

"You'd better take a look at the new laws, Father. The legislature condemned all Valids to death for crimes against humanity … and that's just the beginning."

"Ridiculous … not all Valids are criminals."

"True, but the legislature realizes that half of Urbane's remaining population eventually will die of starvation, anyway. It reasons that, by eliminating Valids, their food can be diverted to In-valids."

"We're that short of food?"

"Yes, Father. The Valids' scorched-earth policy destroyed most of the earth-grown food. Although toxic, it still kept millions of In-valids alive. Now, little remains."

"How about the Valids' food supply on satellites and on the Moon?"

"There's not enough for everybody. The Valids grew only enough for themselves."

"Christ, Joan, the Valids really are a bunch of bastards, aren't they?"

"I'm surprised at you, Father. At your age, you should know that, throughout history, all upper-class minorities have disdained as their worst enemy, the common people, who always have clawed to replace them."

"I do know, but, every time it happens, I'm surprised anew by the virulence of it all. Down deep, we humans are a beastly sort. We pretend civilization for awhile, but, like balls thrown into the air, our natural state of rest is down in the dust among all other God's creatures. ... I don't know, Joan, maybe the effort and the pain aren't worth it. Maybe we should accept the inevitable, and all lie down and die. Maybe the Earth is better off without the human beast."

"Father, we've no time for philosophizing. Please listen to the record, and advise me what to do."

While her father listened to the simulvoice recite the new laws, Joan searched his face. First, he was inscrutable; then, cheeks flushed; finally, lips quivered.

"Outrageous! Sheer madness! These crazy lawmakers have become worse than the Valids. ... Kill all Valids? Invalidate all future embryos? Halt all therapeutic treatment toward validating In-valids? ... These are the death warrants of the human species."

"Father, you and I fought for Grandfather's dream—a fully-valid Earth supporting balanced populations of all species, cohabiting healthfully and harmoniously. Why are they trying to kill his dream?"

"We won't let them, Daughter. They may force the Valids to live off the poisoned land in our stead; they may allow In-valids to take over the Valids' stratoscrapers, satellites, and moon stations; but never may they force the continuing degeneration of human life."

"Then, let us confront the legislature."

* * *

Carlos Martinez, the persuasive president of the legislature, irritated Joan. Apparently, the victory over the Valids had awakened within him a dormant desire for revenge and power. Tardily, she realized that his oratorical fervor had mesmerized and cowed the rest of the legislature. He had converted it into a flock of docile sheep.

Yet, Carlos and she had worked well together during the war. His organizational and managerial talents were phenomenal. Almost singlehandedly, he had accumulated and placed at her disposal the resources necessary to win the war.

Now, however, as Joan and her father confronted the legislature, Carlos's obvious disdain for them reached a feverish pitch. She wondered if he were envious of her military position. Certainly, her act of disarming the Council's guards and replacing them with her own robosentries had set off an alarm in his suspicious head. Whatever the reason for Carlos's irrationality, Joan realized that he had become a dangerous adversary and needed close surveillance. She glanced about the legislative chamber and, with satisfaction, reconfirmed that her robosentries were at their posts near the exits.

Carlos spoke. "Alex, we rule Urbane now. You have no authority to void our laws. They are good laws—designed to redress the inequities heaped upon us by the Valids.

"However, we realize that the law to exterminate the remaining Valids was excessive, so it's been repealed. We will let them try to survive like they forced us to do—down in the dirt, the dust, and the dire survival conditions of Earth's surface. In a few years, radiation, pollution, and malnutrition will alter their genomic sequence patterns until they, too, become In-valids."

Alex said, "Very generous of you, Carlos, but what about the order to invalidate all human embryos and to halt validation operations on In-valids?"

Carlos ordered his robonurse to pivot his forebody up from his gurney.

Joan smiled. ... *Some more of his theatrics destined for the gallery.*

"Alex, we In-valids cannot compete with Valids—neither physically nor mentally. They will always be a threat to us. We are eliminating that threat by eventually making everyone in-valid. ... Those laws will stand."

Alex said, "You go against John the Martyr's principles, Carlos. He wanted the Earth to return to normal—a reasonable population of valid humans and other life forms on an ecologically balanced planet. Around the world, he wanted the establishment and maintenance of optimal habitat conditions through population control and close-cycled production and consumption processes. He wanted the plunder rate of the Earth's limited renewable resources to fall to the regeneration rate."

Carlos snorted. "High-minded talk—I suppose you would have us do this at the expense of the In-valids."

Astounded, Joan interrupted, "Christ, Carlos, you act as if In-valids are a separate race or species of human that should not be allowed to die out. They are an aberration whose root cause is civilization—rather it is the human's inability to properly channel civilization's effects. Existing In-valids should continue to live out their lives, but we must eliminate new In-valids at or shortly after conception.

"The basic cause of our dilemma—overpopulation—has disappeared. The peoples of the world cannot take direct credit for it—they didn't plan to decrease the population. Indirectly, of course, they are responsible—collectively they brought about conditions that forced nature to lower the birth rate and increase the death rate. The Malthusian Method—the most painful way possible to squeeze a species into its habitat—but, after all, it is nature's recourse of last resort."

"Look, no amount of lecturing is going to make us change our minds, so get to the point."

"Sure, Carlos. ... Before the war, the Earth's population dwindled to just over two billion persons. Now it sits at a little under a billion souls gathered in isolated groups near the poles, in alpine plateaux, or atop towering stratoscrapers. Therefore, the planet is getting a well-deserved rest from ten millennia of human vandalization. Perhaps in a couple more, it will again be able to support a few billion people."

Alex added, "Until then, our species must lie low, coddle its environment, and strengthen its geneticism (sic). Toward that end, the legislature must repeal those laws designed to perpetuate invalidity. It must pass new ones that promote validity and natural ways of life compatible to Earth's long-term health."

Joan became impatient. "My father has already voided the offensive laws, so I warn you, Carlos, do what we ask, or we'll dissolve this ad hoc legislature and call a real election.

Carlos chuckled. "I notice that you aren't gurneyed or wheelchaired. You look like a Valid to me, Joan. Perhaps you should join them. Perhaps we can no longer allow a scheming Valid to remain at the head of our military."

Joan ignored Carlos and accompanied her father out of the legislative chamber. Midway across the lobby she heard shuffling noises from behind. Whirling about, she caught four of her robosentries following them—disrupters drawn.

"You will immediately sheathe your weapons and return to your posts," Joan ordered. "Do it, NOW!"

Her father pivoted his wheelchair to face the sentries. Instantly, his body began epileptic-like flailings. His eyes flew off his nose, skittered across the floor, and smashed against the wall. He stood and, zombie-like, remained immobile for a moment before collapsing in a heap—blood oozing from his skull's orifices.

By instinct, Joan went for her disrupter. Before it cleared her holster, she knew that it was too late. An instant before the energy beams slammed into her brain, she thought, *Grandfather, I have failed you. Please forgiv—*

39—PARADISE

Les vrais paradis sont
les paradis qu'on a perdus.

—Marcel Proust

Three hundred forty-three years into the past, October 20, 2130
Informational News Agency
Bellevue, Franklin

Without warning, the wallscreen in Katharine's office projected Jane's holoimage. Katharine was surprised—and worried. Her boss had been avoiding her ever since the projection of the forest documentary the month before. Yet, Katharine had to admit, no pressing reason existed for them to have seen each other. Thanks to Senator Yoshimasa, Katharine continued her free rein over the Talon interviews.

Jane didn't seem to mind. Despite her repeated affirmations to the contrary, the interviews' popularity was enough to have given her agency a hefty profit for the series. However, the interviews did foment bloody confrontations among the world's more-fanatical, special-interest groups.

"Kathy, please come to my office. We need a private talk."

"I'll be right there, Jane."

She hurried down the hall to the executive suites. What did I do wrong? Will she fire me? Her heart pounded in her throat.

Jane's assistant arched his eyebrows and smiled knowingly. "Go right in, Kathy … she's expecting you."

Katharine feigned a grimace of dread. "Yes … I know. Wish me luck." The door slid open, and she stepped into Jane's office, which always had impressed her by its spacious elegance.

"Good Morning, Kathy. Please have a seat … I have bad news." Despite the "bad" news, Jane appeared to relish her role as the dispatcher of it.

Katharine gulped and sat.

Jane continued. "Three more sessions remain in the Talon interview, right?"

"Yes—three."

"Make it one."

Katharine felt a pang of apprehension. "But, why, Jane? … Have I done something wrong?"

Jane smiled thinly. "Senator Yoshimasa is shutting down the series early."

"Why?"

"How should I know? What the senator wants, the senator gets. He informed me of his decision only a few minutes ago, but … he wanted last week's interview to have been the last."

"You talked him out of it, then?"

141

"Of course I did. Even he realizes the importance of having a closing session ... but tomorrow night's interview is definitely the last one. I hope you've enough time to change your format before then."

"I'll be okay." *The bitch doesn't care; she's as happy as a clown.*

Jane accompanied her to the door and, with a surprisingly pleasant tone of voice, asked, "Kathy, how is your daughter coming along?"

"She's fine ... just fine. Thanks for asking."

Katharine left.

* * *

The route through the asylum complex to Pierre's cell was more than familiar to Katharine—it was second nature. The robosentries, which had appeared to be so frightening at first, were, in her mind, benign fixtures no longer meriting her concern. Pierre's futuristic picotechnology had programmed them to ignore her passage.

Katharine walked briskly through the asylum's first checkpoint—Pierre and she had much to talk about before tomorrow night's interview session. One question nagged her—*Why did Senator Yoshimasa want the interviews stopped so suddenly? Was Pierre in danger? ... Was she, too?*

She tried to think of more pleasant thoughts—such as her success with Pierre's interviews. The timeliness of the subject matter, its controversial nature, its very provocativeness aroused great passions and drew a sophisticated, worldwide audience. ... Pierre and she were celebrities.

The interviews resulted in mass confrontations with the huge multinational despoilers of the Earth for their criminal disregard for the health—no, the life—of the human habitat. Again, the corporate giants rallied after brief periods of denials and confusion. Again, their money bought off governmental watchdogs and reversed media propaganda that were against their interests. Again, they continued to plunder and devastate the Earth's resources in the arrogant belief that they possessed the right to exploit them without regard for others or for the future. Of course, those special-interest groups adversely affected by the interviews tried to make Pierre appear to be a fool.

However, Katharine was positive that, overall, the interviews effected an irreversible, positive influence toward remedying the planet's ills. Pierre's forthrightness and dynamic personality certainly contributed to their success. His descriptions of the future were marvels of lucidity and realism.

Katharine's notion of what the future was like—rather, will be like—became a vivid, mental picture. She cried upon listening to Pierre's powerful depiction of John Thorpe's martyrdom, not to mention the demise of his son and granddaughter. However, the greatest impression made upon her was the graphic description of future Earth at the time of Boniface and the extinction of the human species.

The cell door slid open, and Katharine walked into Pierre's arms. She informed him of the senator's decision and of her anxiety about Pierre's safety.

"Kathy, I appreciate your concern, but you should know by now that I remain better informed—here in my cell—than does Jane in her high-tech, solar-system-wide communications center. You see, my picogremlins control her news agency."

"What! Since when?"

"Since the day that Andy and Mario liberated me from the asylum's security system. Thereafter, unbeknownst to my visitors, I ordered my picogremlins to infest their bodies. My tiny soldiers invaded every location that they visited."

Katharine laughed. "So that's how you controlled my wallscreen in my bedroom the day you begged me not to go with Andy—I brought the little critters home myself."

Pierre chuckled in satisfaction. "I've had them infest everyone who has ever visited me—they're like fleas on a dog. Even I don't know how far they've spread, but, wherever they are, they await my instructions—mine alone.

"This morning I listened in on Senator Yoshimasa's conversation with Jane—I knew he would call her."

"How?"

"Well, yesterday, I gave him the final secret about the ignition of hydroxygen. He's a real bastard—I didn't think he'd renege on the rest of his part of the bargain, yet he did."

"What was that?"

"A successful conclusion to these interviews and a public trial for the crimes of which I am accused."

Katharine felt an ache in the pit of her stomach. *Those arsons again—won't they ever go away? I don't want to hear about them, anymore. Please, dear God, if Pierre be my son's killer, hide the fact from me—I could not bear to hear the truth.* "Please, Pierre, don't talk about that. Let's prepare for tomorrow's interview—it will be our last."

"Kathy ... to hell with the interviews—they're history, now. I've got to get away from the senator's clutches. If I don't, he'll put me away without a trial—someplace I couldn't break out of, someplace you couldn't visit."

"Your picogremlins could do the same as they've done here. Then, you could escape easily."

"Kathy, the good senator is suspicious. I believe he's on to my picotechnology. If so, he'll have my next prison guarded by humans. Picogremlins can control robosentries but not life forms. No, I must escape soon—my presence here no longer benefits my mission."

"Where would you stay? The senator would find you wherever you'd go."

Pierre stroked Katharine's hair. "Don't worry, I have taken my precautions. I have a hideout nearby that is impervious to surveillance probes. I must be there before the senator discovers my escape. Then, if I'm lucky, I'll eventually make it home."

"Home?"

"Yes—to Lac Bienville near Hudson's Bay in northwestern Québec."

"Why, there?"

"In 2013, when I was a year old, my father built a hunting lodge on the lake's north shore. My family used it as a summer retreat. When I arrived in 2123 from the future, it was in ruins, so I bought the land and had the lodge restored to what I remembered it to have been like. I am content there—like being a child again—with a child's memories."

"I had no idea ... Pierre, why didn't you tell me about this place before?"

"We had other worries to ponder. Besides, I was afraid I'd never live to see it again—still am, actually."

"Was the area much changed from when you were a child?"

"Yes, quite a bit. The wild animals are gone. The climate is warmer, which allowed the trees to grow big enough to attract the timber industry. I suppose they'll all be cut down in a few years, too—just like on the West Coast. More people, more roads, more pollution exist—in essence, more crowding, more development. ... Back then, we needed less protection from the Sun. ... Everything's worse now, yet, by today's standards, it is still a paradise."

"Will you be safe there?"

Pierre laughed. "Yes, Darling—perfectly safe. The North American government can't touch me in Québec—not legally, anyway. Besides, I'm a hero there—the oldest-living, native-born Québécois, so to speak."

"Can't you be extradited?"

"No—the two countries have no extradition treaty. Ever since the Normans conquered England a millennium ago, French and English cultures have been less than accommodating toward each other."

Katharine felt agitated. "I want to go there with you."

"No, I can't let you ... not now. You are at the peak of your profession. If you came with me, you'd lose everything. You wouldn't be able to return. Like me, you'd be a fugitive for the rest of your life."

"Since my estrangement with Andy, my job security is nil. Besides, I don't care. We'd be together. We love each other, Pierre—that's what counts."

"That's the very reason I wouldn't want you to come with me at this time. I love you too much to see you abandon your career ... and your daughter. She needs you. You need her. Soon, you'll see your grandchild being born. I couldn't let you forsake those pleasures for a lifetime of seclusion and loneliness that would be my fault. ... Later, we'll see."

"If that's what you want. Besides, you're right—at this time, I do need to be near my daughter. ... Let's talk about you. When are you planning to escape?"

"Well, the senator can't yet be aware that I know about his decision to stop the interviews. He has no reason to transfer me to a more secure prison before tomorrow night's session, but he has every reason after. ... I'll escape at three in the morning."

Katharine was startled as his eyes widened in apparent astonishment. "Pierre, what's the matter?"

"Today's the twentieth of October, isn't it?"

She was perplexed. "Yes, it is ... why?"

"Within the next few days, Senator Mizuno Yoshimasa will be assassinated."

"Oh, my God! That's terrible. Can you stop it?"

"I can't—it is a foregone conclusion. I cannot tamper with what is to be."

"But, Pierre—"

"I wish I could, Kathy, but I cannot ... and I should not have told you. Swear to me that you will keep secret what I have revealed to you."

"Pierre, I swear I won't say a word to anyone." She prepared to leave.

Pierre lunged at her, pulled her close, and kissed her hard. "We may not see each other for awhile ... please—spend this last night with me."

Breathless, Katharine said, "Yes, yes, Darling. You know that I will."

A Voice beat more Instant than the Feet—
'All things betray thee, who betrayest Me.'

—Francis Thompson

A few hours later, October 21, 2130, 2:00 A. M.

Katharine cried softly to herself. She didn't mean to awaken Pierre, but he turned on his side, took her in his arms, and kissed her tears away.

"What's the matter, Darling?"

She sniffed and wiped her face on the pillowcase. "Oh, a combination of things—you, escaping ... my job ... my daughter's pregnancy ..."

"She's having difficulty?"

Katharine knew that she was going to cry again—but, this time, she abandoned all inhibitions and bawled like a baby.

Pierre held her tighter and stroked her hair. When she calmed down, he asked, "Is something wrong with your daughter?"

"Oh, Pierre, I've done a terrible thing. I can't sleep, just thinking about it."

"Tell me. Perhaps I can help—even if it's only moral support."

"Against Julie, I've committed an unpardonable crime, which no mother has the right to do."

"What crime? If it was so terrible, why did you commit it?"

"At the time, I believed I was right ... no, that's a lie—I wanted to bend her to my will."

"—about what?"

"Well, after Julie discovered her pregnancy, she imagined the most terrible things about her embryo. She became paranoid because of my own experience with her brother Douglas."

"—your in-valid son who died in the fire?"

"Yes ... she believed that her own embryo might be deformed like mine was." Katharine began to sob, again. "You see, Pierre, my decision to keep and care for my deformed son was based upon what I thought were reasons of compassion, duty, and ... motherly love. Even had I known that my embryo was deformed, I still would have carried it to term. Like my mother and grandmother before me, I abhorred abortion."

"Do you—still?"

In anguish, Katharine grabbed her head in her hands. "That's my dilemma—I don't know. I think that I do, but, more and more, my reasons seem unrealistic—nonsensical. I am torn between the dictates of my upbringing and my more recent experiences—in particular, those with you, Pierre. Your enthusiastic recounts of your life in the future—and in the past—have had a profound impact upon my perspective of ... of ... everything.

"I don't know myself anymore. I've abandoned my code of conduct—my morals. I've experienced a total metamorphosis. I am no longer that uninformed, narrow-minded person my daughter believes me still to be. My horizons have expanded. Now, I am more inquisitive—more aware of the world and its problems. My job has made a difference, of course, but you, Pierre, are largely responsible for changing my outlook on life."

"Kathy, you are an intelligent woman. Eventually, you would have changed on your own."

"Probably so, but I think the change would have been slow. You see, I had fixed moral values—rigid dogmatic ones—believed by my family for generations. ... Yet, you are probably right—in today's world of pollution and overpopulation—they were ripe for change. No longer can the human race retain the luxury of allowing different moral values to each individual's taste. Now, the morality of one adversely affects others. Our moral values must be relative—not fixed—and compatible to the state of our environment."

"So, does this mean, you condone abortion, euthanasia—?"

"Don't be ridiculous ... but, I have only one child ... who needs me—her mother ... and I will do almost anything to keep myself dear to her."

"How about your son? Do you regret having nurtured him?"

Katharine bit her lip and said, bitterly, "Did you say, 'nurtured'?" She uttered a half laugh of derision. "He existed from his feedings—that is all, but 'nurtured?' ... never. I tried to nurture him—I honestly did—but my son never realized that I existed ... that anyone existed."

Pierre touched her cheek to wipe away the tears. "I'm so sorry, so very sorry."

Katharine gritted her teeth. "You needn't be. Those closest to me said that I brought my problem upon myself—that I should have abandoned him. In retrospect, perhaps they were right—maybe, I just prolonged the agony."

"What's this 'terrible' crime you've committed against Julie?"

"I imposed my will upon her in the vilest possible manner: Julie indicated to me that she would reject her embryo if it should prove to be defective. She wanted it examined and, if defects be detected, an abortion."

"That seems reasonable."

"To you ... perhaps, but, three months after the death of my son, I desperately needed a loved one to sympathize with my beliefs, which I had always held sacred. By Julie's actions, she had become guilty of the exact opposite. She might as well have slapped me in the face. She might as well have said, 'Mother, I'm pregnant now, so I'll show you the proper way to start a healthy family.' I was angry. I wanted to force her to do what I had done—to keep the embryo under any circumstance."

"Dammit, Kathy ... tell me what you did to your daughter that was so terribly wrong."

"Pierre, after I found Julie a doctor who agreed to examine her embryo, I bribed him not to notify her should it prove to be defective."

The darkness was pregnant with silence. After a long moment, Pierre's voice came across the gloom. "Do you know what you've done? She trusted you, Kathy. How can—"

Katharine sat up and pounded her fists against Pierre's chest. She screamed, "Shut up! How can you be so god-damned self-righteous about my daughter? You have never ever met her."

"Jeez, I'm sorry, Kathy. I apologize—I should not have said that. ... So, now ... you're upset because the doctor found the embryo deformed, is that it?"

To regain her composure, Kathy lay back and breathed deeply, yet her hands continued to tremble. "Whether it's deformed or not ... I do not know. I asked the doctor to keep the results of the examination to himself. Yet, as her pregnancy progresses, I feel more and more guilty. Every time I see Julie, she is radiant and tells me that her baby is developing normally. She tells me that she is very happy ..."

"When she tells you she's happy, what do you feel?"

"Pierre, I become absolutely terrified. I want to blurt out the truth. I want to take her by the hand, march her into the doctor's office, confess my sin, and try to make things right."

"Why don't you?"

Katharine looked down. Her hands trembled worse than before. "I'm a coward—afraid I'd lose my daughter for good."

"Wouldn't your relations with each other become worse if the baby were born deformed? The truth would have to come out. Julie and you would become irreversibly estranged from one another."

"That thought has tormented me for months, but Julie's chances for giving birth to a deformed baby are very low. I've decided to risk it."

Pierre shook his head. "You are playing a dangerous game, Kathy. The genetic health of our species is worse than you realize."

"Probably, but it's my decision to make, and I've made it."

Katharine thought she heard a noise. She raised her head off the pillow and listened intently but detected nothing more. Pulling the blanket over her shoulders, she snuggled closer to Pierre.

Suddenly, Pierre sat up. "I heard it, too. Quick, get dressed. You've got to leave—now."

Katharine leapt off the cot and, in the dark, feverishly donned her brassiere and panties.

The lights switched on, the door slid open, and Senator Yoshimasa strode in. Behind him, two human guards giggled.

"Shut up!" the senator barked. With hands on hips, he spread his legs and gloated. "Well, aren't you two a pretty picture."

Katharine glanced at Pierre. For an instant, she glimpsed his limp penis protruding beneath his shirttails before he unabashedly thrust his feet into his shorts and pulled them on. "Don't just stand there, Kathy ... I told you to get dressed."

Her cheeks boiled. She reached for her blouse.

Pierre gazed matter-of-factly at the senator and asked, "How did you find out?"

The senator sneered. "You should choose your friends more carefully, Mister Talon."

Katharine's mind raced. "Why that little son of a bitch. Andy! Pierre, it's Andy. Andy betrayed us."

Pierre looked bewildered. "No ... not Andy. He's my friend."

Senator Yoshimasa chuckled. "When it comes to love, young men are so naïve. You are a fool, Mister Talon, but Ms. Carver is even more so. Did you really expect

Mister Drake to let you—his ex-mistress—get away with bedding another man? ... especially one in Mister Talon's predicament?"

Katharine blurted, "How did you know when to come?"

The senator threw back his head and laughed heartily. "Your lover, here, thinks his picotechnology makes him immune to surveillance. He forgot about old-fashioned, hard-wired microphones."

Pierre appeared startled. "That's impossible. My picogremlins would have detected them being installed."

The senator roared. "Oh, my poor, dear sir. This cell block is the asylum's original building. The microphones have been embedded in these old walls for well over a century. Fortunately for me, someone stumbled upon their existence, and I had them reactivated."

Katharine trembled. "What are you going to do with us?"

"To you, my dear ... nothing. Go back to your job, keep your mouth shut, and forget all about Mister Talon."

"What will happen to him?"

"I have an order to transfer him to a maximum-security cell at the Winnipeg Federal Asylum for the Insane, where his 'famous' picotechnology is useless." Senator Yoshimasa turned to the guards and, with a wave of his hand, said, "Take him."

Katharine flung herself into Pierre's arms and wailed, "Oh, no, don't let them do this to you."

41—CATACLYSM

The old world must be destroyed and
replaced by a new one. Our first
work must be the annihilation
of everything as it now exists.

—Mikhail A. Bakunin

Four hundred twenty years into the future, September 23, 2550
The underground home of Earth's last-surviving, true Valid

Pierre's departure from Joan's mind was brutally rapid—one instant he saw four neuron disrupters aimed at him; the next, he again felt that morbid coldness and sense of nothingness. By contrast, he had left the mind of John the Martyr slowly—like a flame winking out after shrinking for lack of fuel.

The momentary nothingness confused him. He forgot what Boniface had told him before he entered the Learning Room. ... Was he to enter the minds of two persons or was it three? He wasn't sure. The thought of experiencing a third death jarred him, but he certainly was not about to display his queasiness to Boniface by cutting short the learning session.

The warmth returned, but not as before. This time, Pierre felt neither strength nor vigor, but peaceful calm. Was he returning to the Learning Room after all? First, his sense of touch returned. He was on his back—possibly on the couch in the Learning Room. Someone shook his shoulder. Was it Boniface? Then, he could hear ... a voice—distorted, garbled, and barely intelligible—a woman's?

"Grandfather, wake up. The sensory recorder is active. The reporter is in the hall, waiting to enter."

Oh my God ... I'm entering a third mind. I hope this one doesn't die on me, too.

Finally, Pierre, again, could see. Slowly, his eyes opened, and he beheld a horribly deformed head, which looked down upon him. It lacked an ear, and its facial features pulled to one side as if an invisible hand tried to rip flesh from skull. Despite the head's grotesqueness, he detected a concerned expression upon its face.

Accustomed to Joan's treble voice vibrating in his throat, Pierre was startled when he heard deep, male mutterings echo through him. "Dammit, girl, why can't I die in peace. You're worse than your mother. Let me be." His eyes closed.

In a pained, yet amused voice, the woman said, "You can't die yet, Grandfather. You have an interview to do."

Pierre swore silently. *I really would like to bail out of this one—that crazy Boniface has put me in a body on its deathbed. ... Oh well, at least this one will die more peacefully than the other two.* He felt strong arms pull him to a sitting position and prop him up with pillows. Through one eye he spied the metallic face of a robonurse. He heard himself say, "Get that bundle of optosynapses away from me."

Coming from a distance, another woman's voice—a sweet one—said, "We're a little grumpy this morning, aren't we?"

149

The eyes through which Pierre looked searched past the foot of the bed and saw the arrival of a huge screen set atop a gurney. It projected the image of a pretty, young woman beneath it. He noticed her artificial eyes and stumpy, flipper-like arms—three of them.

"If you were I, you'd be grumpy, too. ... I don't know why you want to talk to an old man like me, but go ahead—get your questions over with."

The pretty, young woman said, "According to the records, you are the last surviving Valid veteran of the Liberation War. You may well be the last Valid on this planet—period. ... I understand you were the scion of a wealthy family that had lived atop stratoscrapers for generations. Tell me about yourself."

"Well, young lady, what you say is true. At first, my ancestors regularly ventured down to the Surface, but, as it became more toxic, they forsook it. By the time of my grandfather, even if they had wanted, they couldn't have visited it—John the Martyr's guerrillas had cut off Surface access to Valids.

"By then, antineutronics enabled the construction of larger and taller buildings. But, they still needed some structural support from the Surface, thus they remained vulnerable to guerrilla attacks. Fortunately, all of the Valids' needs came from Mars, the Moon, and Earth's satellites, and floatporters eased transportation between stratoscrapers.

"The In-valids started the Liberation War in 2468—we called it the Rebellion—when they discovered that the Valids were attempting a complete break from the Surface by constructing floating cities. They knew that they'd be lost once the Valids floated safely above the Earth.

"The first attack, I remember well—it surprised the Valids completely. At the time, I attended college about ten miles from our family's stratoscraper—a two-mile-high structure. I was looking across at it when it collapsed. The In-valids blew up its support columns, but, because of the antigravity modules, it settled to earth slowly—like a feather.

"The fall hurt many, but few actually died. The real killings began when the In-valids unleashed robots to swarm over the ruins. They slaughtered all within—including most members of my family. Ironically, they killed the one Valid leader who preached compassion and understanding—my father."

"After the war, the In-valids regretted your father's death and, in compensation, allowed you to live, isn't that so?"

"Possibly, but I like to believe that my own efforts were responsible. I was a soldier in the field and fared better than the poor civilians huddled in their stratoscrapers. Yet, at first, I could barely breathe. The food gagged me. The radioactivity threatened me. The heat stifled me—even at night. I realized how pampered we Valids really had been—cocooned in our stratoscrapers with special food and cooled air—free of carbonic and nitric oxides, which so permeate the atmosphere.

"After the war began, the In-valid armies attacked these 'towers of ivory,' which, one after another, came tumbling down. I survived because I adopted the In-valids' methods of survival and drank huge quantities of hydroxygenic water.

"Halfway through the war, the In-valids captured and held me, along with other prisoners, in a deep cavern. At first, I felt relieved—the cavern was cool, without dust and radioactivity, but, like on the Surface, the air was fouled by excessive carbon dioxide—over seven parts per thousand.

"Then, I noticed that prisoners were disappearing. Learning of their executions terrified me—I knew that, eventually, my time would come, too."

Pierre felt faint. His eyes closed. Again, he heard the grotesque voice.

"Grandfather, are you all right?"

His eyes popped open.

"Of course I'm all right, girl—I'm not ready to die yet. ... Where was I? What was I talking about?"

The sweet voice from the screen said, "—about your fear of being executed."

"Right. ... Well, as you can see, I wasn't. Joan the Liberator—God bless her memory—came for an inspection tour and ordered the executions halted.

"After the war, times were terrible. Released from prison, I joined the surviving Valids, who were turned out of the remaining stratocities. We occupied the caves and caverns, abandoned by the In-valids.

"We lacked medicine, food, and water. Millions died. The In-valids refused our pleas for help. Why should they have helped? ... We Valids had never helped them. I became sick and would have died had not a compassionate family cared for me."

Pierre's eyes turned to the side. He saw that deformed head, again. "Its daughter became your grandmother. While she was pregnant with your father, the In-valids deformed the embryo as dictated by their new laws. I was devastated, but could do nothing—all postwar children were being invalidated.

"A year after the end of the war, the In-valids completed construction of the first floating city, which the Valids had begun. Soon, many more replaced the old stratoscrapers, which either were abandoned or relegated to the new In-valids—born of Valids. The years passed, my fellow Valids died off, and nearly all of their descendants left the Surface to live in the remaining stratoscrapers."

Pierre heard the pretty lady again.

"Why do you refuse to leave these caverns? We even have invited you to stay in one of our floating cities for the remainder of your life. Don't you want to savor, again, the cool, clean air of your youth?"

Pierre felt the old man's heart flutter. His eyes blurred. He was dizzy. ... Then, his vision cleared.

"No, I will remain here. After nearly eighty years ... to this dreary place, I've grown accustomed. Perhaps, this dreary place—of so much pain and suffering—I've learned to love. Perhaps, in this dreary place, I stay ... as penance for my people's centuries-long inhumanity toward In-valids.

"Whatever the reason, it is of no consequence, for, when I die, the final days of the human race's stay on Earth will be numbered. Only a short while longer can advanced technology keep away extinction. The Earth is tired ... needs rest—a long rest from the human animal.

"Let the land be swept clean of signs of our passage. Let it subduct into the planet's core and, once sterilized, spew forth to regenerate the Surface. Let the plants grow again to cleanse the air. Let the Sun shine again on the rise of a new and better species. Let us hope that it will be wiser than we, in the management of its evolution.

"Let me rest, for I am tired ... very tired ... oh—so tired ... ."

42—GLOOM

My dear, do not give way to such gloomy thoughts.
Let us hope for better things. Let us flatter
ourselves that I may be the survivor.

—Jane Austen

Four hundred twenty years into the past
October 21, 2130, mid morning
Mario and Julie's apartment
Bellevue, Franklin

In her daughter's embrace, Katharine babbled, "They took him away. They'll kill him. What am I to do? I'll never see him again. Oh, God, Julie, I love him so much."

"Mother ... Please! Try to calm yourself. When you talk crazy like this, I can't understand you."

Katharine pulled away and paced the length of the living room. "It's Pierre! He's done for ... dead. They've taken him to Winnipeg."

"Pierre's dead?"

"For God's sake, Julie—no! ... but, he might as well be. He's in the Federal Asylum. Nobody gets out of there alive. They'll kill him."

"Oh, Mother, you've worked yourself up for nothing. Pierre's just out of one asylum and into another ... no big deal."

"What? You can't be serious. If you think his picotechnology can bail him out this time, you're wrong. Thanks to Andy, they know all about it."

"But, Mario said picotechnology is so advanced that just being aware of it doesn't guarantee being able to counter Pierre's use of it. He will figure something out—always has."

Katharine grew calmer. "Oh, let's hope so. Let's hope that he does it soon."

"Have you eaten yet today?"

"Uh ... no, Dear."

"Then, sit down and have breakfast—you'll feel better."

* * *

Julie was right, of course.

Katharine ate with surprising gusto. She put her fork down and sighed.

"How do you feel?"

"Better ... thanks." Katharine reached across the table and touched Julie's hand. "And how is your pregnancy coming along? Are you well?"

"Yes, I'm fine—in my thirteenth week. Doctor Sullivan said I should deliver a healthy baby toward the middle of April ... why Mother, you're trembling."

The mention of the doctor's name had unnerved Katharine. She bowed her head, put her hand to her brow, and, to hide her feelings, said "Yes, that ugly scene with Yoshimasa—it affected me more than I realized."

Actually, her overriding concern was the forthcoming outcome of her daughter's pregnancy. She realized that, were the fetus badly deformed, Julie could deliver prematurely—possibly with a stillborn. She knew that every passing day increased Julie's chance for a normal baby. Yet, over the past few weeks, the nagging vision that Doctor Sullivan had discovered an in-valid embryo interrupted her thoughts more and more. During frequent bouts of depression, guilt would overtake her, but she'd fight the urge to contact the doctor and learn the truth.

"Yesterday morning, my embryo's physical was perfect. Mario and I are elated, and... ."

To Katharine, Julie's voice seemed to drone on from far away.

"You know, Mother, I must apologize for having criticized you so much in the past about your convictions concerning Douglas. Now, I understand that, all along, you were right. I was so naïve, so selfish ... but youth thinks only of itself. Yet, please understand that the sudden imposition of an in-valid sibling on a small child is cruel."

Katharine's eyes welled with tears, and she stifled a sob. A feeling of panic gripped her. *What is Julie saying? ... that, now, she'd accept an in-valid baby?* Memories of the worst experiences she had endured with Douglas tumbled into Katharine's mind. She felt instant rebellion against the possibility of a similar fate befalling Julie— or, once more, herself: *As the grandmother, I, again, would feel the consequences of having an in-valid family member. I can not bear to repeat that horrible experience.*

Julie was looking lovingly at her. "If Dad had supported your views about parenthood like Mario supports mine, maybe—when I was a girl—our lives would have been better."

Katharine surprised herself—for the first time since Douglas's birth, she felt like defending the memory of her husband. "Julie, are you telling me that you now support my decision to have kept your brother?"

Without a whiff of emotion, Julie said, "Yes, Mother—at his birth, you had no other choice. A mother—no, the parents—must accept the consequences and raise their child as best they can. But, at conception, if nature does not abort a deformed embryo, the mother is responsible for doing so."

"But, I couldn't have. How was I to know—"

"I agree, there was no way." Julie hesitated. "Society didn't help. The laws didn't help and still don't. ... As for me, if I learned—at this moment—that my embryo were defective, I'd be on the horns of a dilemma."

"What do you mean, Dear?"

Julie touched her belly. "This life is now three months old. As we speak, its brain is evolving from animalistic to humanistic, its body, from embryonic to fetal. It is a person. From now on, an abortion would be murder. From now on, I will do anything to protect and nurture this new being within me."

Nausea invaded Katharine. Saliva welled into her mouth. She vomited.

* * *

Katharine sat on her bed and gazed across the room at her future grandchild's crib. *Oh, that a healthy baby will lie there.* She heard Julie whisper from the hall.

"Mother, are you awake?"

"Yes. Come in."

"How do you feel? Better?"

"Yes, thanks."

"Jane wants to talk to you."

Katharine felt a lump form in her throat. "Computer, pipe Jane's call to the nursery."

Jane's image filled the wallscreen. Her demeanor was all business. "As you know, Kathy, the last Talon interview was canceled. Unfortunately, I have no other work for you. The pay due you did not cover the remainder of my loan to you. Please pay the balance as soon as possible, at which time, I will return your belongings to you. According to your pay record, you are due neither vacation pay nor sick-leave pay—you more than used them up caring for your son. For retirement, you are not vested, so your contributions remain in the union's general fund—unless, of course, you should be fortunate enough to find work elsewhere in the media industry. Good-bye, Kathy, good luck."

43—ASSASSINATION

Assassiner c'est le plus court chemin.

—Molière

Eight days later, October 29, 2130
Julie and Mario's apartment
Bellevue, Franklin

Katharine threw herself onto the sofa, kicked off her shoes, and looked up at Mario. "Oof! I've been 'pounding the pavement' all week and have nothing to show for it. You know, Mario, I'm really pissed. My work is known and admired throughout the solar system—or so they all say—yet, I'm offered no job. Apparently, no one dares to buck Jane."

Mario raised his eyebrows. "Well, at least now, we know how powerful that woman really is."

"And vindictive, too. Here I am … flat broke. I owe her—and my bank—a pile of money. I can't find a job. I just don't know what to do." Katharine couldn't keep her chin from quivering. She closed her eyes, covered her face with both hands, and sobbed. A moment later, she felt her son-in-law sit beside her and put his arm around her.

"Don't worry Kathy. What's family for, if not to help each other when times are tough. You can continue to stay here with us … and the money? Well, I can give you some … how much do you need?"

Incredulous, Katharine dropped her hands and stared at Mario. "Oh, no … I couldn't accept. You've already been so kind."

"Look—consider it a loan. With your reputation, you'll eventually get a good job again. Jane can't have you blackballed forever."

Katharine poured herself a stiff drink and took a sip. "You know, Mario … Jane's not the culprit—Andy is. He believes I jilted him for Pierre, so he's putting Jane up to this."

Mario chuckled. "No wrath exists greater than love scorned, eh?" He lay his hands on her shoulders and searched her face. "Now tell me, Kathy—how much? I really want to do this for you."

Katharine looked at the floor. "I need … I need four hundred seventy-eight thousand dollars right away … but, Mario, you are in no position to worry about—."

"Nonsense! I'll transfer half a million immediately. … Computer, transfer money per the conversation. Confirm transaction."

"Source?"

Mario thought for a moment. "Sell Fuerza Cortés stock."

"Destination?"

Katharine was stunned. She had no idea Mario had access to so much cash. *Of course! … How stupid of me—with a father like his …*

"Kathy?"

"Oh, excuse me … ah—to my escrowed account."

"That bad, uh?"

"Uh-huh. … Mario, I feel so ashamed. I don't know how I got myself into this fix. For life's big decisions, I always seem to make the wrong choice. … Ah, Mario?"

"Yes?"

"You don't have to tell Julie about the loan, do you?"

Mario appeared surprised. "Well, no … not if you wish it."

"Thanks, I appreciate it."

The computer voiced, "Transfer of half a million dollars confirmed."

Katharine ordered, "State the nearest-thousand balance of my escrowed account."

"Two hundred twenty-seven."

Mario whistled. "Wow, almost three hundred thousand already gone. Who could have taken it?"

"It's Jane. … Since the day she fired me, the bankruptcy court has allowed her accounts-receivable program to monitor all of my accounts."

"Boy, is she ever brutal. … Look, Kathy, use some of the remaining money to see Pierre in Winnipeg … and how is he? Have you talked to him recently?"

"Yesterday—and, again, they limited us to only five minutes. We could say nothing intimate, mind you—they record everything we say. We're allowed one communication per week and must ask permission a day ahead.

"I asked Pierre about visits. He said that it's useless to ask. I would be granted only limited time through a video port—much like we're doing from here."

Mario shook his head in disbelief. "What's the matter with those asylum people? Even those on death row can receive visitors."

"It's Yoshimasa. He's paranoid about Pierre's picotechnology—afraid he'll use it to escape, again."

Mario smiled wryly. "Kathy, it's not paranoia. The senator's fears are well founded. But, this time, I'm afraid, Pierre will find it difficult to escape."

"Yes—I know. He is quite depressed, and so am I." Katharine's chin began to quiver, again.

Julie burst into the apartment. "Have you heard the news?

"No, Darling, we haven't."

"Yoshimasa's been assassinated."

Katharine gasped and opened her mouth to say, "Pierre's prophesy was right," but thought better of it and remained silent.

Mario said, "Good God! When?"

"Three days ago."

"And we're just learning about it now?"

"Winnipeg imposed a seventy-two-hour security lid on it. … Computer, recount news of the Yoshimasa killing."

The wallscreen came to life with poses of the late senator in various stages of his long political career. "Mizuno Yoshimasa, the distinguished senior senator from the state of Franklin, was brutally murdered on the evening of October twenty-sixth in his Bellevue home. Evidence shows that a bronze statuette, which was found at the scene of the crime, was used to deliver a fatal blow to the back of his skull."

Katharine said, "Who could have done such a thing?"

Mario snorted. "Any number of persons. The man had many enemies—some, bitter."

The computer continued, "... and the evidence against her is overwhelming and more than circumstantial. Several persons stated that they heard Jane Stevens say she'd be happy to see the senator dead, and, more importantly, her presence at the place and time of the crime has been confirmed. This morning, Ms. Stevens was arrested and charged with the murder of Senator Yoshimasa. She is currently free on her own recognizance."

Julie turned toward her mother. "You're very quiet for one who's suffered at the hands of that woman."

"I'm flabbergasted. All I can say is, she didn't do it."

Mario said, "Everyone knew that Jane hated the senator. She could—very well—be guilty."

Katharine said, "In that case, couldn't we all?"

* * *

Over the next few weeks, Katharine tried, without success, for permission to visit Pierre. She had surmised that, once Yoshimasa gone, the consequences of his paranoia would go, too. Yet, his regulations not only stood but became stricter—Pierre was isolated from the outside world. Apparently, the remaining members of Yoshimasa's coterie believed that Pierre had possessed the power to have reached out from his cell and kill their champion.

The new regulations devastated Katharine. The realization that she might never again hear from Pierre plunged her into a mood of despair from which she felt she'd never recover. At first, she abandoned her job-hunting activities and remained in her room. As the case against Jane tightened, her attention was drawn away from her own troubles and more toward Jane's. Almost every day, a new piece of evidence surfaced—more damaging than before. Katharine tried to remain open-minded but, finally, realized that the evidence constituted irrefutable proof that Jane, did, indeed, kill the senator.

The public, which had so admired her before the arrest, now turned on her like a pack of wolves. Evidently, in the minds of the vain and greedy, repressed collective envy of Jane's power and wealth had lain just below the surface, ready to break through should she stumble ... and, now, she had.

Actually, Katharine felt sorry for the woman. Certainly, her precipitous fall from grace shocked Jane. Her only remaining friends appeared to be her vast fortune ... and Andy, who seemed tireless in his efforts to have his dearly beloved exonerated.

Curiously, as the public cooled to Jane, it warmed to Andy—the underdog fighting the evils of The Establishment. Of course, the media pumped him up ... the valiant knight in shining armor—so to speak—had come to the aid of his lover. Andy dismissed the evidence against Jane as being coincidental, criticized the police for a scurrilous investigation, and accused the prosecution of a malicious witch hunt. Andy was a hero in the making, a mentor to be emulated, a warrior for the good, and a crusader for truth and justice.

Katharine knew better.

A blue sky of spring,
White clouds on the wing:
What a little thing
To remember for years—
To remember with tears!

—William Allingham

Six hundred fifty-six years into the future, June 5, 2786
The Learning Room in the floating city of Cumulus
Five miles above Antarctica

Consciousness returned, and Pierre realized that he still lay on a bed—but was drenched in sweat. He wondered if his awareness still emanated from the dying man's mind. He ordered his fingers to move—they did. He ordered his eyes to open—they did. Excitement gripped him. Oh, the feeling—the wonderful feeling of controlling my body again. In appreciation of his returned powers, he continued to blink his eyes while repeating, "The rain in Spain falls mainly on the plain."

He exited the Learning Room and walked toward a smiling Boniface. "Dammit, Boniface, why didn't you warn me that they'd all die on me … and John, in constant pain—which intensity, I've never before experienced. I didn't need that, you know."

"Pierre, don't be so sensitive. Everyone, who visited those persons' minds, came away the better for it—you are no exception."

"I was in the Learning Room for days. How was I fed? How did I relieve myself?"

"Pierre, only an hour passed."

"Only one hour! … It seemed—an eternity. I learned a lot, though … in that hour."

"Tell me, Pierre Talon, what did you learn?"

"Boniface, the beast that is homo sapiens royally fucked up what was once a veritable paradise."

The old man laughed. "You used very earthy expressions back in the twenty-first century, didn't you?"

"Yes, and even they cannot express my outrage for what the human animal has done to our planet."

"Perhaps we can still repair the damage."

Pierre snorted. "That's impossible. From the looks of it, Earth is shot to Hell. Only extinction of our species can enable nature to heal Earth's wounds—and in a hundred-thousand years, at best."

"I'm not so sure … but now is not the time to explain, and I'm not the one to do so. Eat and sleep. We'll continue tomorrow."

Boniface left.

* * *

Pierre awoke refreshed. He washed, ate, and awaited Boniface's arrival by wandering through his quarters. He marveled at the profusion of plants. Lovingly, he touched the leaves. They existed for him—offering to him their life-giving oxygen, accepting from him his carbon dioxide. They were friends of humankind—of all animals.

He blew at a huge leaf. "There you are, my lucky plant—some carbon dioxide for you. Now, give me your oxygen."

He wondered why humans treat plants so shabbily—stripping the land of them, killing the very organisms responsible for sustaining life on this fragile planet. Yes, the day before, he had learned much. *What will I learn today?*

Boniface entered. "Good morning, Pierre. ... Ah, you are ready—then, please, follow me."

Pierre followed Boniface down the corridor to a magneporter. They entered a biplace vehicle, suspended in midair. Like a roller coaster, it sped away—rising or falling and turning left or right.

Although a bit dizzy, Pierre was impressed. He hadn't realized that the city of Cumulus was so huge. "How far are we traveling and to where?"

"About two miles northeast and forty-five stories down. First, we'll visit some of the quarters reserved for those In-valids who haven't yet opted for amputation. Then, we'll see some amputees and, finally, the disembodied—the totally cyborganic."

Upon arrival, Boniface and Pierre toured the residences. The In-valids lived in bungalows nestled among shrubs, flowers, and small trees planted in immense rooms capped by thirty-foot ceilings. Pierre asked Boniface about one of the ceilings—it resembled a real sky.

"The ceilings simulate the skies of the prepollutive era. Notice how the cottony white of the clouds contrast with the clear blue of the sky—an effect not seen on Earth for centuries."

"Do you turn off the 'sun' at night?"

Boniface chuckled. "We're a bit more sophisticated than that. In emulation of nature, all of the celestial bodies rise and set. Wind, rain, fog, snow—the four seasons—exist here. ... In essence, we've established microcosms of Edenic earth."

"Magnificent. Look at those blossoms ... you've captured eternal spring."

"Not at all. Our communities enjoy evolving seasons. This area covers ten acres and, currently, is in Spring. Other communities on Cumulus pass through other seasons. For instance, the dead of Winter rules all twenty floors below us, while Summer warms the eastside."

"Unbelievable! *Incroyable!*"

Pierre visited the homes of several In-valids. The efficiency and cleanliness of their quarters impressed him. Because various deformities handicapped the In-valids, robots and machines cared for their every need. Some In-valids, swathed in antigravity blankets, floated silently in midair, their minds occupied with Dreamworlds of their choice. Others—more "aware"—waited anxiously for Boniface and Pierre's visit.

The enormity and grotesqueness of the In-valids' afflictions affected Pierre more deeply than all else. They ranged from a variety of neurological disorders to seemingly endless sorts of physical deformities. Not only were "standard" body parts misshapen or missing, but other, superfluous appendages protruded awkwardly from twisted torsos.

Boniface took Pierre to another part of Cumulus. Neither bungalows, nor skies, nor seasons, nor any weather existed—only the usual lush vegetation. There, Pierre found amputees existing in many series of small interconnecting rooms where one robot could tend to the needs of many In-valids. Few experienced reality—most "lived" in Dreamworlds.

"Boniface, I've a question that's been bothering me. ... With the apparent sophisticated technology here, why haven't the In-valids developed an effective medical science to deal with their afflictions?"

Boniface appeared surprised. "We have, Pierre. Look at the effectiveness of our organ prosthetation (sic) and transplantation programs. Look at the disembodiment procedure—a marvel of medical technique. Look at these amputees—some no longer need to eat or drink because their blood shunts through nutritioning machines. Granted, their gastrointestinal tracts have withered to nothing, but the need for them no longer exists. Others need no livers, no kidneys, and still others need not breathe. When amputees' bodily functions become completely cyborganic, they usually opt for disembodiment."

"That's all well and good, as far as it goes, but the In-valids' brand of medicine is accommodating their invalidity not curing it."

Boniface sighed sadly. "The issue is complex, Pierre. Because of the way our culture evolved, it permitted some kinds of medical practice while forbidding others.

"After the In-valids won the Liberation War, those with advanced levels of invalidity gained more respect, became more popular, and acquired more power. In fact, a sort of invalidic fanaticism spread until an elite cult, which extolled the values of invalidity, entrenched itself. Eventually the less in-valid vied among themselves by undergoing operations that rendered them more in-valid than their peers. Invalidity had become a badge of honor."

"I assume that most In-valids are highly educated, so shouldn't they have realized that, by remaining in-valid, dire consequences could occur ... dire to the human species, I mean."

"Pierre, your argument is academic. Periodically, some of our ancestors did try to reverse the increasing invalidity, but they never succeeded."

"Why?"

"Their efforts were too little, too late, that's all. ... However, you, Pierre, really are in no position to criticize."

"I can guess what you mean: In the twenty-first century, had we addressed our efforts to eliminating the nascent causes of invalidity, the human species might not now be in eclipse."

"Yes, but the world needed the effort from the advent of the Industrial Revolution—not from your own era, two centuries later. ... Come, we travel to the top of Cumulus."

Again, Boniface and Pierre's magneporter zipped through Cumulus at high speed—missing beams and columns by inches. Minutes later, it braked to a halt in a blaze of light.

Pierre was flabbergasted: In every direction, as far as he could see, meadows, orchards, and forests bathed in sunlight. A myriad of fauna grazed contentedly, while a variety of primates gamboled in treetops. Birds chirped and flitted about, and huge animals waded knee-deep in streams and ponds. Overhead, clouds drifted by, and, in the distance, lightning flashed followed by rolling thunder.

Have I entered the mind of Adam? Is this the Garden of Eden? Immediately, Pierre dismissed the idea. *Perhaps, we've descended to the Surface.* He rejected that one, too. *I've got to be in a Dreamworld. ... Hey, it's not so bad—maybe those In-valids are on to something, after all.* Then, he glanced about and noticed Boniface at his side and the dark hole in the "earth" through which the magneporter had emerged. Reality returned.

"Good God, Boniface, where are we? Is this real?"

"This is no simulation, Pierre. We are in Cumulus's wildlife park atop the city."

"It's beautiful—even idyllic, but how did it get here, and how is the atmosphere maintained? Even clouds, rain, and wind occur."

Boniface appeared amused. "Pierre, you see before you the remains of Earth's life forms. Over the centuries, as the habitat shrank, zoological gardens came to shelter the threatened species. When the Surface became uninhabitable, we built gardens and parks atop stratoscrapers and floating cities. This is the last one remaining."

"We're floating at an altitude of twenty-five thousand feet, aren't we? How can you maintain the air quality so high up?"

"A dome holds the air in."

"I didn't notice any, but—if one exists—what holds it up?"

"Air pressure."

"It must be tremendously huge."

"It caps the full diameter of Cumulus—six miles."

"What's your energy source—the Sun?"

"Partly. Cumulus's power plant is six hundred feet below us. The same microscopic spheres of concentric neutrons and antineutrons that make up the antigravity modules supply its fuel. The matter-antimat—"

"Let me guess. ... You inject the matter-antimatter spheres into the combustion chamber where high-frequency energy beams force neutron-antineutron intermixing, so ... poof! ... 'annihilation'—and all the energy you could possibly need."

Boniface laid a withered hand on Pierre's shoulder. "Young man, I am convinced that you are the right person for the arduous mission we have planned."

"You don't have much choice, do you?"

Boniface chuckled. "No, I guess not ... you are it."

"You've mentioned this mission earlier ... something about going back into the past. How is that possible?"

"Believe me, Pierre, it is possible—but, difficult. You will travel across the Universe into an anticluster of antigalaxies."

"Boniface, a voyage like that would take hundreds of millions of years—maybe billions—and I'd be long dead."

"The trip would seem to take that long, but only in relation to time on Earth. You'll travel at very near the speed of light, so the trip will take only a month plus another month to return to Earth of the year 2045—to your own era."

"No, you mean to an earth, billions of years in the future—if it will still exist."

"You are rather stupid after all, Pierre Talon. Why do you think you'll be traversing the Universe in the first place? ... to travel through antispace and, thus, through antitime, that's why. By judiciously controlling the balance of velocity and duration of stay between matter and antimatter environments, a mass can be made to arrive at any place at any time."

Pierre's mind raced. "Yes—of course—it makes perfect sense, now. ... Has anyone ever done it before?"

"Nope."

"Dammit, Boniface, you expect me to be your guinea pig? No way! I'm staying right where I am. For the rest of my life, I'd be perfectly happy to pitch a tent out there on that meadow among the elk."

"Pierre, you will go, and you will arrive back on an earth of the past—that's a promise."

"How can you be so sure?"

"History told us so. History told us that, centuries ago, a man named Pierre Talon came from the future to save the world from its imminent demise."

"Are you sure that he was I?"

"Well, he mentioned me by name and the year 2786 plus ... another year."

"Which one?"

"2789."

"That's over two years away—what happens then?"

"History says that you will begin your return to the year 2045."

"If the trip is already a foregone conclusion, why can't I leave now?"

"Your spaceship isn't ready yet—it's being built in moon orbit. Besides, don't forget—your departure date, 2789, is also a foregone conclusion."

"Then history revealed to you my identity and arrival time."

Pierre smiled. "Yes—that's what I've been trying to sink into your hard head. ... You see—everything we do is preordained."

"I'd like to see the spaceship. Can we visit it?

"Not so fast, young man. Come—we must first visit the disembodied and, then ... Strata."

> What hangs people ... is the
> unfortunate circumstance of guilt.
>
> —Robert Louis Stevenson

Six hundred fifty-six years into the past, December 18, 2130
Julie and Mario's apartment
Bellevue, Franklin

Week after week, Katharine continued her inquiries about Pierre's well-being. Always, they landed on deaf ears. Her two trips to Winnipeg produced nothing either. Every morning, she prayed for Pierre, but, after two months, hope of being reunited with her beloved was dim indeed. She mourned his absence as she would his death, knowing full well that the probability of his demise was high.

The second day of Jane's murder trial came to a close. Katharine had considered attending but, at the last moment, decided not to. From the time, two weeks ago, that Andy had publicly accused her of being the real murderer, Katharine had been continually hounded by the media. She could just imagine her arrival at the courthouse—a real circus, an experience she could do without.

"Mother, you needn't worry about Andrew's accusations—the prosecution's case against Jane is open-shut. You really should go. You'd be amused. I would've thought that you'd want to see Jane get her comeuppance."

"Julie, I'm tired—hunting for a job consumes my entire day. Besides, I'm in no position to gloat—look at me, I exist at the largesse of my daughter and son-in-law."

"Don't worry—once Jane's in prison, that'll change."

Katharine snorted. "Think again. With her wealth, she'll find a way to control her empire from within."

"Like buying off the prison staff?"

"Absolutely."

Again, Julie's profile distracted Katharine. Her daughter's pregnancy was five-months along, yet it didn't show. Many questions bombarded Katharine's soul, but she knew of no discreet way to satisfy them: *Had Doctor Sullivan discovered an in-valid embryo? Could he be trusted? How much did Julie know? Was she suspicious? And, what about Mario? Should the baby be deformed, what would he do?*

The computer disturbed her musing. "Someone at the door wishes to see Ms. Carver-Howe."

"What? Who could that be? ... I dropped Howe from my name years ago." Katharine approached the door. "Open."

The door slid open. A shiny, new robot faced her. "Are you Katharine Carver-Howe?"

By now, she was quite curious. "Years ago, I was."

In an impatient tone of voice, the robot said, "I ask you, 'Is your legal name Katharine Carver-Howe?'"

Julie ran to the door. "Who in hell do you think you are? Since when have robots turned surly?"

The machine moved smoothly to face Julie—more smoothly than Katharine had ever seen one move before. "Be aware, Julie Carver-Pavía, I can—and will—defend myself."

"Well, I never—"

"You needn't answer my question. My DNA scanner indicates that you are the person whom I seek." The sleek robot reached into its purse, extracted a sheet of paper, and held it out to Katharine. "Take it."

Flabbergasted, she did as it ordered.

The robot turned and vanished.

Julie said, "What is it?"

Feverishly, Katharine unfolded the paper, then caught her breath. "It's a subpoena. I'm to appear tomorrow morning at Jane's trial."

* * *

From the witness box, Katharine gazed over the courtroom crowd with a stoic air of disdain and indifference, yet her entrails quivered with fear and rage. To avoid eye-to-eye contact with anyone—particularly Jane and Andy—she forced her glances to dart from face to face. Yet, when they lit upon Andy's, his staring at her in obvious contempt prompted her, in turn, to stare back with as hateful an expression as she could muster.

"Ms. Carver-Howe, you detested both Senator Yoshimasa and the defendant, isn't that so?"

"Objection—leading the witness."

"Sustained. ... The defense will rephrase the question."

"Your honor, I have a hostile witness here."

"I said, 'Objection sustained.' "

"Jane Stevens fired you five days before the murder of Senator Yoshimasa—is that correct?"

"Well, she had no more work—"

"Ms. Carver-Howe—just answer my question—yes or no."

"Yes."

"By the time of the victim's murder, were you failing to get another job and blaming your problem on the defendant?"

"Objection!"

"I withdraw the question. ... The fact is, you owed the defendant a considerable sum of money and were searching for a way to renege on your debt. The fact is, you knew—in advance—when and where the senator would be murdered because you killed him. Isn't that so?"

"Objection—your honor, this line of questioning is going nowhere—in fact, it's ridiculous."

"Overruled."

"You killed him and planted evidence to point to the defendant—lint from the defendant's clothes, traces of her perfume, dust mites containing her DNA ... very astute of you, but crudely done."

The prosecutor rose. "Your honor, Ms. Carver is not on trial here—besides, absolutely no corroboration for these wild accusations exists, even in the slightest."

"Your honor, I'm establishing reasonable doubt here."

The verbal duel transpiring before Katharine confused her. Yet, its continuance relieved her of answering many of the questions put before her. To those that the court required her to answer, she did so in complete confidence, for she knew that Senator Yoshimasa was not slain by her own hand.

Whenever Jane did not avoid Katharine's gaze, she looked straight through her—as if she were nonexistent.

Andy, on the other hand, continued to stare at Katharine during her entire testimony. Toward the end, when the revelations boded ill for Jane, Andy's lips curled to form a curious, little smile. Evidently, he wanted to refuse Katharine the satisfaction of knowing that he knew she had beaten him.

The court broke for lunch. The crowd streamed into the lobby. The media converged upon the principals with a bombardment of questions, and—yes—quite obnoxious ones blared forth. Katharine was thankful to Mario, for he blazed a trail for Julie and her through the crowd to the top of the courthouse steps. There, she suddenly came face-to-face with Andy and Jane.

Apparently taken by surprise, no one spoke. Even members of the media held their breaths—ready to train cameras on the next tidbit of news.

Katharine noticed Andy's glance at the cameras before he fixed his eyes upon her and say loudly, "You think you fooled everyone, don't you. Well, you can't fool me. Senator Yoshimasa was my friend, and you killed him. You'll get caught, you'll see."

Katharine ignored Andy. She looked at Jane, who appeared to be in a daze. "Jane—I'm sorry … I'm sure that you are innocent, as am I."

Jane glanced up. Her eyes seemed vacant—distant. They held neither hate nor contempt. She said nothing.

Mario took Katharine by the arm, "Come, let us go home."

* * *

Days later, the jury found Jane Stevens guilty of the murder of Senator Yoshimasa.

Der Gedanke an den Selbstmord ist ein
starkes Trostmittel: mit ihm kommt man
gut über manche böse Nacht hinweg.

—Reinhold Niebuhr

A week later, December 24, 2130
Julie and Mario's apartment
Bellevue, Franklin

Christmas Eve was upon them, and they had all but forgotten the excitement of Jane's trial. Under Julie and Mario's tree, few presents lay—not for lack of a holiday spirit but for, a child.

Julie beamed. "Next year, we'll have plenty of toys 'n' stuff wrapped in fancy paper and tied with pretty bows."

Mario glanced at Katharine and winked. "Well, not too many—we don't want to braticize the kid."

"Nonsense, you can't spoil a baby as young as it will be," Julie said, in mock wisdom.

Mario finished preparing the drinks. "Here, Kathy ... be careful, it's hot. I hope the rum isn't too strong."

"Never during Christmas." Katharine laughed and took a sip.

"Here's yours, Julie ... no rum for you."

Katharine was surprised that she could feel such gaiety for she still had found no job, still lived under her daughter's roof, and, worst of all, still had no news of Pierre. At Mario's urging, she had interrupted her job-search efforts until after the holidays. Both Julie and he were trying to make her Christmas pleasant. She appreciated the gesture.

Mario said, "Computer, time."

"Twelve oh seven."

"Show INA news."

The newscaster's holoimage filled the center of the living room.

Katharine recognized her. "That's Nourra Akhemed—I guess that, now, she's the noon anchor."

"A friend of yours?"

"Yes. ... I hope she still is."

"... and, now, for a lighter side of the news: After a thirty-year, cleanup effort, the Snohomish and Stillaguamish river valleys are finally ready for resettlement. Winnipeg has stated that the radioactivity in the soil there has returned to benign levels. The majority of the former residents died long ago of leukemia or cancer, so most of the survivors are afraid to return. They suspect that the government continues to lie about the radioactivity levels—just as it has always done—they claim. The land is dirt cheap, pun intended, so many young families—despite the possible hazards—are moving into the area. Let us wish them good health.

"News flash, just in ... Doctor Bruce Sullivan, renowned therapist for deformed children, was found dead this morning—slumped over his desk."

Katharine dropped her mug, which shattered upon hitting the floor. "Oh, God! ... No!"

"A heart attack was suspected, but, moments ago, the cause of death was confirmed to be suicide by poison. Apparently, the man's profession caused him to suffer bouts of depression. However, the impetus for his fatal act of desperation appears to have been an impending indictment for having euthanized his more wretched patients. A holograph, left behind, confirms the tragic events ... in a most dramatic fashion."

Mario said, "I didn't care for the man, but I'm sorry to see his life end like this. His soul must have suffered great pain."

Katharine trembled uncontrollably. She glanced at Julie, hoping that her daughter hadn't noticed. ... She feared that, eventually, the authorities would examine the doctor's records. She wondered if Doctor Sullivan had documented the existence of their verbal contract. She had paid in gold. No payment record existed, yet apprehension of eventual discovery invaded her. *Will my agreement with Doctor Sullivan be exposed?*

"Mother, why are you so upset? I didn't know that you and he were so close."

"Well, er ... you see, we did work together for many years ... to keep Douglas alive—you know. I've lost a friend—a good friend ... and so have the in-valids." Nourra's holoimage regained Katharine's attention.

"Ladies and gentlemen, as an INA exclusive, we now transmit the holograph of Doctor Sullivan's last moments."

The image of the doctor shocked Katharine.

The man sat at his desk, his face—haggard. His hands trembled. He seemed thinner than she remembered. When he spoke, she forced herself to remain calm in Julie's presence, although her survival instinct screamed that she flee—away from her daughter ... far, far away. *What did he say? Did he bare all?* She bit her lip and closed her eyes.

"My dearest Carol, I speak only to you. ... Always remember that ... I love you very much.

"Long ago, I justified my actions to myself and feel that no justification is due society ... what I did was right. Yet, I cannot leave this horrible world without trying to make you understand. I love you, Carol—I always have—although I seldom took time to tell you so during our thirty years of marriage.

"Early in my career, I became resolved to sacrifice myself and, in the process—you—to help the deformed, retarded, and maimed. That help was expensive. I charged the rich as much as they would bear, but never was there enough money. Occasionally, I'd dip into our savings to help a poor family. I believed that my efforts were making a better world. Many times, I did improve the lives of my patients and was happy for them.

"Yet, as the years passed, the influx of hopeless cases became a flood. I tried—I truly tried—but, eventually, I realized that I was not curing them but merely keeping them alive—much like a torturer prolonging the lives of his victims so as to increase his morbid sense of pleasure.

"I came to abhor my work. Morning after morning, leaving home for Pineridge to attend to my suffering patients and their tormented families, I'd be nauseated. Oftentimes, before entering Pineridge, I'd retch in some hidden corner.

"Then, one day, a child died in my arms. I looked down upon him. He seemed, so at peace. A warm feeling permeated my being—even an instance of ecstasy. I realized that death is the ultimate cure. God meant it to be so.

"Later, when I notified the parents, their reaction to their child's death appeared to be as was mine. A heavy responsibility was lifted from their souls." Doctor Sullivan paused to wipe his eyes.

Katharine could not keep her voice from wavering. "Oh, my God! The poor man! … I thought he was heartless and greedy. All along, he was helping others while hiding his torment—holding in his anguish."

The doctor continued. "From then on, my dear Carol, death held no terror for me. I realized that death is as natural as birth. So, one time, while treating a badly deformed child—who was suffering horribly—I, quite naturally, put a stop to it. I became giddy. I had become God. Perhaps you remember the night you awoke and found me crying, and I tried to convince you it was nothing. That was the day I became God to those children.

"Later, I felt twinges of guilt, but only fleeting ones. I rationalized my actions in a logical manner, otherwise, I'd have gone mad. I reasoned that we were keeping these children alive artificially. In essence, we were usurping the role of the real God—the One in Heaven. We were preventing Him from deciding who should die and who should live.

"These deformed children were destined to die—as are we all—but we wrongfully assumed the burden of keeping them alive, while God tried to pass them onto a better world. What manner of egotistical creature are we, that we should have the gall to interfere with God's work."

Doctor Sullivan looked into his hand. Its palm cradled a capsule. "I hear the police in the outer office. They come to arrest me. I have finished my life's work. I fear death no longer. Farewell, Carol … I love you." He placed the capsule between his teeth and bit down. Eyes wide, his throat emitted a short gurgle before his body slumped forward.

Nourra's holoimage returned. "In other news … several persons were found guilty of—"

"News off," Mario ordered. "Good Lord, the man had courage."

Julie said, "He seemed irrational—perhaps, even mad."

For fear of betraying her emotions, Katharine dared not utter a word. She turned to seek the haven of her room and managed to croak out, "I'm sorry … I must lie down for awhile."

* * *

With the holidays over, Katharine returned to job hunting, but, again, with no luck. "What shall I do, Julie? I can't even find a menial job—robots or retards get them all. The Informational News Agency won't have me back either—Jane rules her empire from prison. I've heard that, with her fortune, she buys leaves of absence from her cell whenever she wants. What a laugh—she uses prison only as a bedroom."

"Don't fret, Mother, something'll surface, and you can always stay here until you're back on your feet."

Katharine noticed that Julie's pregnancy was beginning to show. "You look magnificent, Dear. How do you feel?"

"Fine ... of course I haven't been examined since before Doctor Sullivan's death, but nothing would have changed—I'm too far advanced. Yet, I do need to find a new doctor."

Katharine felt as if a lead weight had fallen to the bottom of her stomach. *What will the new doctor find?*

Mario entered the living room. He carried a quizzical expression. "Kathy, two policehumans are here ... to see you."

Immediately, Katharine "knew" why they had come. She had been expecting them. She turned toward Mario. "Please, leave me alone with them." Her calmness surprised her.

As Julie left the room with Mario, she turned and asked, "Mother, what's this all about?"

"Nothing, my dear—it's—uh—well ... it's probably about my testimony at Jane's trial."

Sad, and very tired, Katharine was certain that her worst fears were becoming reality—Julie and the whole world would soon know about her secret with Doctor Sullivan.

A man and a woman approached. "Ms. Katharine Carver?"

"Yes ..." Her heart pulsed in her throat.

"I'm Lieutenant O'Connell and this is Sergeant Mendoza," the woman said, indicating her partner. "Ma'am, we won't take up much of your time. We're here about Doctor Sullivan."

"Yes, I've been expecting you."

The lieutenant appeared confused. "You know, then?"

"Well, yes—I ... you see—" Something in the back of her brain told Katharine to shut up.

"Doctor Sullivan was your late son's physician—was he not?"

"You mean my daughter's?" *Shut the hell up, dummy.*

"No, ma'am ... your son Douglas's. ... Was he your daughter's doctor, also?"

"Uh—no ... of course, I meant Douglas." *What is going on here.* Katharine hoped that she had caught herself in time.

"We have evidence that Doctor Sullivan killed your son."

The lieutenant's statement took time to penetrate Katharine's brain. "You mean that Doctor Sullivan is the arsonist? Why ... that's incredible! That is fantastic!"

Again, Lieutenant O'Connell appeared bewildered. "Ma'am, we still don't know who the arsonist is, but we do know that your son was not killed in the fires."

Katharine became dizzy. "Not killed in them? Then, how—"

"Ma'am, five hours before the fires broke out, while your son slept, Doctor Sullivan suffocated him. The arsonist merely cremated his body."

As consciousness faded, Katharine caught a glimpse of the sergeant rushing to catch her.

Old age hath yet his honor and his toil;
Death closes all: but something ere the end,
Some work of noble note, may yet be done,
Not unbecoming men that strove with gods.
—Alfred, Lord Tennyson

Six hundred fifty-five years into the future, June 6, 2786
The floating city of Cumulus
Five miles above Antarctica

A visit to the disembodied of Cumulus emotionally moved Pierre. At first, he thought he'd entered a library, but, instead of books on shelves, he noticed human brains—row upon row of them submerged in a clear liquid, which—in appearance—resembled white wine. The place was eerie—hot, dim, and silent except for blood gurgling through tubes to thousands of brains.

Boniface and he stayed for only a moment, but it was enough time for Pierre to grasp the morbidity of the scene. He believed, with difficulty, that each brain was experiencing a normal life, simulated though it be, with only a dim recollection of the grotesqueness of its sloughed-off body. He remarked that these "beings" no longer could give to their species or to their environment—they could only take. They had become blood-sucking parasites.

* * *

Pierre noticed the large, double, bronze doors at the end of the corridor long before Boniface and he actually arrived at them. He was surprised by their ornateness because everything else that he had seen in Cumulus was strictly functional.

Boniface stopped before the doors and motioned for Pierre to follow suit.

A sweet feminine voice surrounded them. "Boniface, Mister Talon and you may enter."

Pierre was startled—he recognized the voice. A glance at Boniface told him that the old man understood.

"Yes, Pierre, my mother was the young woman who interviewed the last Valid—on his deathbed, 236 years ago."

The massive doors opened slowly, and Pierre followed Boniface into a circular room. Plunged in darkness, it appeared to be empty. Then, high up, in the center of the room, he noticed a ring of optical fibers whose converging beams shone down upon a large, transparent bowl that rested upon a small, circular platform. Beneath, he barely discerned its tall pedestal and the four surrounding robots whose blackness blended into the platform's shadow.

"Welcome to Cumulus, Mister Talon. I hope that Boniface's efforts to acquaint you with our little world and its problems satisfy you."

"Yes, ma'am, but I'm confused as to how I fit into your scheme of things."

"My scheme is quite simple: You return to your era and effect changes in human civilization that save it from extinction."

Pierre was really confused, now. "How can I do that? I wouldn't know where to begin."

"Do not worry—we are grooming you for your mission, Mister Talon."

Pierre looked up at the bowl. Within, he saw Strata's brain. Under the bright lights, it glowed a grayish pink. Without thinking, he stepped toward it.

A robot responded by stepping out from under the platform's shadow.

Pierre gasped and stopped short.

The robot was gigantic and looked evil and menacing. It's lenses flicked left, right, up, and down in seemingly eager attempts to seek out all possible dangers to the well-being of its mistress. Then, as if nothing had happened, it backed itself into the shadow and returned to alert status.

"Jeez, Boniface, that thing scared the crap outta me. Why does Strata need guards, anyway? The In-valids seem harmless enough. I certainly hope Strata doesn't feel she needs to guard herself against me. I've no reason to harm anyone. I just want to get back home in one piece."

Boniface put a reassuring hand on Pierre's shoulder. "She doesn't fear you—it's her own people, she fears. Occasionally, an In-valid or a robot goes berserk and tries to harm her."

"Why should it want to do that?"

"Strata has absolute power over life and death in the Solar System. Inside that bowl, atop that pedestal, in the middle of this room, her mental processes connect to everything of importance in our culture. If she so chose, she could transmit a mere thought to the Moon and destroy everything upon it. Others are envious of her powers and would take them from her ... if they could."

Pierre leaned toward Boniface and whispered, "Strata hasn't said anything for awhile. Is she still listening to us?"

"Possibly not—sometimes she becomes preoccupied with a problem that suddenly crops up either here or on the Moon or on Mars."

"Can't the robots and computers handle the problems without her?"

"Most times—yes, but Strata knows the importance of staying on top of developments, especially to let the competition know that she's aware of what's going on."

The room filled with Strata's voice. "Sorry, Mister Talon, I was detained elsewhere. ... Before your departure date, you cannot learn all that you need to know, so, tomorrow, you receive a memory implantation."

"A what? Pierre started to panic. You're not going to let her operate on me, are you, Boniface?"

"In your own words, you said, 'I want to get back home in one piece.' Well, an enlarged memory is essential for the trip and for the success of your mission. No danger exists—Strata has one, and so do I."

Pierre felt reassured but remained apprehensive about the risks involved in a medical procedure about which he knew nothing. "What will it do—make learning easier, faster, or make me smarter or what?"

Strata spoke. "None of those things. The memory contains information that you can access as needed. However, you cannot access it as randomly and quickly as your natural memory, but, by concentrating on what you want to know and if that information exists, it comes to you in ultimate detail."

"What kind of information?"

"Everything that's happened in the world since you departed your own era—well, almost."

Pierre inhaled sharply. "Good God, you mean I'll have over seven centuries of human experience at my fingertips—just like that?" He snapped his fingers.

"That is correct, Mister Talon; however, some information held in your supplemental memory is not available to you."

"Why not, ma'am?"

"Because your premature knowledge of it might compromise the success of your mission."

"Like what, for instance?"

"Like anything that might upset you or cause you to stray from your mission—such as the circumstances surrounding your own death. On the other hand, whenever you become discouraged, information pertinent to uplifting your spirits is released to your consciousness."

Pierre's dread of undergoing the surgical operation receded. "Then, in addition to information, I get an interactive program, which analyzes my thoughts and doses out information on a need-to-know basis."

"Exactly. In that manner, your brain is not cluttered with extraneous data at a time when the full capability of your intellectuality must concentrate on one particularly difficult problem. ... Now, I must leave you—some amputees are complaining about their robotic help, and I want to solve their problems personally. Go to your quarters, relax, and prepare yourself for tomorrow's memory implantation. Good-bye, Mister Talon."

"Good-bye, ma'am."

Si libentir crucem portas portabit te.

—Thomas à Kempis

Six hundred fifty-five years into the past, January 17, 2131
En route to Julie and Mario's apartment
Bellevue, Franklin

Katharine felt terrible—both mentally and physically. She was sure that the day's frustrations in trying to crack the job market were responsible for most of her ailments. Yet, her head spun, and her forehead was hot to the touch. She was anxious to arrive at the apartment—a bath and bed beckoned her. *How much longer will my children welcome me there?* she wondered. *I've got to find a job before their baby arrives. Lord, what am I to do?* Panic plunged her spirits into despondency. The pounding in her head was incessant. She felt her brow again.

The cabin slowed to a stop. Katharine descended. She raced to the apartment's entrance, but the door remained closed. "Computer, open the door—I'm Katharine Carver."

"Access denied."

"What? That's impossible. No—check again. … Let me talk to Julie."

"Access denied. Your daughter does not wish to speak with you."

Oh, my God! … Somehow, Julie knows the truth. Did the police tell her? Worse— what if she saw a new doctor, who discovered a deformed fetus? Lord, no, don't let such a horrible possibility be true! Katharine pounded on the door. "Let me in! I must know! Is the baby alright?"

"That answer is unavailable."

Katharine shuddered at the computer's response. She slammed her fists into the door until their aches became unbearable. Dizziness overwhelmed her. She closed her eyes and leaned against the door. She slid to the floor and cried over and over, "Let me in. Please, let me in." Her incoherence degenerated into a series of moans and sobs.

With a swish, the door slid open, and Katharine's forebody slumped backward into the entry way. She stared at a pair of feet a few inches from her nose.

"Get up."

The voice sounded harsh. Befuddled, Katharine tried to place it.

"I told you to get up."

It's Mario. He has never spoken an angry word to me before. She felt his toe nudge her shoulder.

"Come on, come on—stand up."

With difficulty, she stood. Her hands shook as she tried to slick hair—wet with tears—away from her eyes.

"Clean yourself up, pack your belongings, and get out."

Katharine's head was on fire. Breathing pained her. She knew that she was sick. "Mario, please! I need to see a doctor."

173

From behind, she heard a snort and turned to see Julie standing—legs apart—fists on hips. Her expression was contemptuous.

"You've seen one-too-many doctors, already. ... Oh, Mother, how could you? Why? ... For God's sake, why?"

Mario chimed in. "It was stupid ... and sneaky, Katharine."

She shot back, "Don't butt in, Mario. This is between my daughter and me." As she spoke the words, she regretted having uttered them.

Mario's cheeks reddened. He stepped toward her.

Julie strode between them and pushed him back. "Darling, I'll take care of this." She turned and confronted her mother.

Katharine realized that, this time, she was not to hear one of her daughter's childhood tantrums. She shuddered and steeled herself for the fury of a mature woman.

" 'Don't butt in.' Is that what you just told Mario? Well, what the hell do you think you've been doing all your life?" Julie was almost screaming, now. "You prolonged my brother's agony. You ruined Daddy's life. You're doing a hell of a good job ruining mine... . How dare you! How God damn' dare you! Just who in this world do you think you are?"

Feverish and dazed, Katharine lashed out. She mustered her strength and struck her daughter across the face.

Julie staggered backward. She touched a hand to her mouth. It came away bloody.

In one stride, Mario was upon Katharine. He seized her arm and held it in an iron grip.

She saw his eyes flash, then glow—like smoldering embers. She was afraid for her life. "Mario ... don't." Her arm throbbed. She felt herself being propelled across the room. She stumbled and fell.

Mario tightened his grip.

"Please, you're hurting my arm."

Silent to her pleas, he dragged her across the floor toward the exit. "Door, open."

Katharine heard the door swish. She felt Mario lift her and throw her across the threshold. The welcome mat broke her fall.

For a long time, she remained in a heap, sobbing. *Why did I hit Julie? My own daughter ... I struck my own daughter? I must be going crazy.* She crawled to the door. Listlessly, her fist banged it once. "I'm sorry, Julie. Mario, I'm sorry. Please, forgive me. Let me in. Is the baby alright? What have you learned about the baby?"

The computer answered. "This terminal no longer transfers Katharine Carver-Howe's messages to the Pavía household."

What can I do? ... I'll go to the Agency—someone there will help me. "Get me a monocabin."

"You are not listed on the Pavía account."

"Then, charge mine."

"Yours is on hold for lack of payment."

Katharine fought a rising tide of hysteria. "I've got to have a cabin. Please! ... Get me a cabin."

"Sorry, Ms. Carver, no active account lists you."

"Oh, God, don't make me go down to the surface—I couldn't stand it down there. I'd die."

"Ms. Carver, this system no longer responds to your queries. For further information, please contact your account representative."

"Computer, get me the Informational News Agency."

The speakers remained silent; the wallscreen, dark.

Katharine raised a fist. "Damn you! Damn you all!"

She shuffled over to the fire exit and tried to force open the iron gate, but, long ago, rust had gripped its hinges. She pushed harder and squeezed through a crack to the stairwell. It was gloomy. Many of the lights were broken. Some were off. *God, how far above the surface am I? ... must be a couple thousand feet.*

Slowly, she wound down the stairs toward street level. Dust, dirt, and scraps of garbage littered the steps. On one landing, she trod upon the dried-up remains of a rat and, in a rage, kicked it down the stairs. An hour passed—maybe two. Often, she stopped to catch her breath. Her mouth was parched; her tongue, thick. Her heels throbbed. She gripped the railing harder and continued to hobble downward.

Perhaps another hour passed. Katharine's pace slowed. No longer could she bend her ankles—her Achilles tendons flexed with difficulty.

At the next landing, a huge fire door barred her path. She pushed it hard, yet it would not budge. She sat on the steps and cried. Total exhaustion overcame her. She slithered to the floor and closed her eyes.

* * *

Katharine awoke with a start. Something had brushed her hand. She shook it frantically. A small spider crawled away. *How long have I slept?* "What time is it?"

Her aural receptors remained silent.

"Are you against me, too." She was forced to look at her wrist terminal for the time. *It's already four in the morning.* Beside the fire door, she noticed a red button. *The lights are on—so this thing must work, too.* She pushed the red button and heard the whir of a motor and the grinding of gears. Then, the noise became labored, as if the mechanism were under great strain. She saw the big door shudder, heard a cracking sound, and felt escaping air rush past her. The blast of a hot, foul-smelling gas hit her full in the face. Grains of sand invaded her eyes and nostrils and lodged between her teeth. *Oh, my God, air from the surface!*

The door opened slowly. Beyond it, Katharine noticed signs of habitation—blankets on the floor and, nearby, empty food containers. Odors of garbage and death gagged her. In the hollow of a blanket, she spied a grimy doll with one arm ripped off. Feverish, giddy, and fearful of stumbling on the broken liquor bottles, she grasped the railing and, despite the pain, tiptoed down the stairs. She raised a sleeve to her nostrils to ward off dirt borne by gusts of wind blowing up the stairwell. Yet, grit and sand whipped through to attack her eyes and mouth.

On one landing, a crumpled-up blanket moved, which startled her. As she drew near, a pack of rats fled from under it and scurried down the stairs. To Katharine's horror, their flight exposed the corpse of a baby, which the rats had nearly transformed into a skeleton. She uttered a soft cry, pinched her nostrils, and pressed onward.

At the bottom of the stairwell, Katharine encountered another fire door. It hung precariously from its guide rail by one roller—half blocking the exit. She stopped and tried to rub the sand from her eyes. She peered through the opening at the outside world, to which she had not ventured in many a year. The thought of exposing herself to the elements terrified her, yet what difference would it make—she hadn't much to live for, now.

Gingerly, Katharine crept from the stairwell to the sidewalk. Clouds of dust blew down the street, which seemed to be deserted. A huge, computer-controlled, recyclation (sic) truck drove past. It roiled up a cloud of filth, which engulfed her. Grains of sand crackled between her teeth. She coughed and spat a brown mixture of spit, phlegm, and dirt. *I feel faint ... I must lie down.* She glanced up and down the street. At one end, she noticed a break in the buildings. *Is it an alley? Perhaps I can find shelter there.*

Katharine hurried across the street, but another truck almost ran her down. At the last instant, a leap into the gutter saved her. For some time, she lay in the dirt—coughing. Then, the sound of yet another truck grew louder. She rose to her knees and, on all fours, scurried into the alley.

Eyes closed, Katharine panted to catch her breath. A putrid stench wafted up her nostrils. Her eyes popped open to stare into a black puddle of stinking, oil-covered water garnished with scraps of rotting garbage. Forearms submerged, she could feel the wet filth permeate her clothing from breast to thigh.

She struggled to her feet and vomited into the puddle. Without thinking, she raised her sleeve to wipe dribble from her chin but began retching instead. She staggered over to a wall, leaned against it, and slid to the ground. Her fever seemed to be worse; her breathing, more labored.

She gazed upward and realized, this was the first time since she was a young woman that she had seen an unfiltered sky and been forced to breathe unfiltered air. The stratoscrapers sheltered her from direct sunlight, and, for that, she was grateful, but she could do nothing about the air. Its noxiousness burned her throat—gagging her. A coughing fit beset her and would not stop. Dust choked her. Her coughs became continual heaving retches of black spittle.

A movement from across the alley startled Katharine. She noticed a wizened, old man in rags stare in apparent amazement from atop a torn, grease-stained mattress.

Perhaps, he believes that I am dying.

His skinny arm beckoned to her.

She shook her head—No!

He stood up—on one leg; the other was lacking. With much effort, the old man crutched himself over to her and offered her an almost-empty bottle.

She cringed against the wall.

"Don't be afraid," he said gently. "Wash out your mouth with this—it's brandy."

Hesitatingly, Katharine reached for the bottle and took a swig. The stuff was strong. The alcohol stung her fever-cracked lips yet felt good against her parched tongue. She swished it, gargled it, and spat it to the ground.

"Take it all and, this time, swallow it."

She obeyed and felt the better for it. "Thank you."

"You've got to get out of those wet clothes—you're catching your death."

"No, no, I've got to go."

"Suit yourself, lady ... I'm only trying to help."

Katharine scrambled to her feet and fled the alley. She ran down the street in the direction of the Agency. From time to time, she'd glance upward, check the direction the stratocabins were taking, and try to follow. *And to think that I've taken those cabins a thousand times and never looked down. ... See no evil.*

She slowed to a trot, then to a walk. She tried to catch her breath, but the foul air prompted more coughing. Her wet clothes seemed to have turned to ice. She began to shiver. Her teeth chattered. Her head felt as if it were going to explode. *The old man was right—I've got to get out of these wet clothes.*

Katharine staggered from door to door, pounding on them as she went. No one came to her aid. Obviously, the lower floors had been abandoned long ago. Looking through cracks in dirty, boarded-up windows, she perceived no signs of life—nothing but dust-covered trash. She shivered uncontrollably. Her eyes kept rolling up into her head. She tried to yell, "Please ... someone help me," but only a croak escaped her cracked lips. Then, as her will to remain conscious faded, she felt her knees buckle.

49—DEATH

We all labour against our own cure,
for death is the cure of all diseases.

—Thomas Browne

Two days later, January 19, 2131
Second floor of an old warehouse
Bellevue, Franklin

"Virgil, I believe she's conscious."

Katharine marveled at the size of the timbers overhead. She coughed. Phlegm exploded from her lungs.

"There, there, my dear. Cough hard—it'll clean you out."

She did so—not to obey the strange voice—but because her body demanded it. She sneezed. Her ears hurt. Her eyes watered. All sorts of vile stuff streamed out her nostrils.

Someone wiped her nose.

As would any snotty child, she thrashed her head in avoidance of the helping hand.

"Ssh, ssh, calm yourself, you'll be okay, now."

Katharine heard it again—that unknown, yet soothing, voice. She obeyed it but continued to stare at the ceiling. She could not imagine trees big enough to have produced those timbers.

"How is she, Sammy?"

The voice was a man's.

"Can't tell—her eyes are open, yet she seems unaware of her surroundings. Her fever was pretty high, you know."

Katharine searched for the voice. She glanced to the left and noticed a plump face smiling down on her. "Who are you? Where am I?"

"Look, Virgil, she is conscious."

"Notify the doctor, dear—she will be anxious to hear the news."

Katharine tried to raise herself up on one elbow but fell back. She had time enough, though, to catch a glimpse of a gaunt, black man with sunken eyes—slumped in a wheelchair. Her awareness increased. "Who are you people? Why am I here?"

The fat lady with the pleasant face, blue eyes, and curly-blond hair said, "I'm Samantha, but everybody calls me Sammy. Here is my husband Virgil, and you are Katharine Carver. I recognized you when I first saw you—you're the lady from the holovision."

Katharine touched her head. "I remember now—I was on the surface. What happened?"

"Two days ago, Virgil and I found you unconscious on the sidewalk. I lifted you onto his wheelchair, and we brought you home."

Katharine looked around her—the room was enormous, bare, and decrepit. "This is home?"

"It's an abandoned warehouse. The owners let us live on the second floor. Virgil worked for them before he got sick." Sammy leaned over with a cup. "Here, drink this—you are still dehydrated."

Katharine pulled back.

"Don't worry ... this is hydroxygenated water, like you're used to drinking up in your towers. You can thank Doctor Wong for it."

"Is he your doctor?"

Virgil's reaction startled her. "Good God, no. We can't afford to see doctors ... and he is a she."

"You had her come especially for me?

Sammy said, "No ... she showed up on her own."

"How did she know to come here?"

Sammy seemed perplexed. "I don't know. You were dying. I contacted someone at your agency for help. The woman there said you no longer worked for them. I told her that you were dying—that your lungs were failing. That's when she broke the connection. I tried over and over to talk to someone else, but I couldn't get past that same woman, who finally became angry. Then, I asked my friends around here, but they've no money for doctors, either. A couple of hours later, Doctor Wong showed up. She said, she'd heard that a dying woman was hereabouts and wondered if she could help."

By the time Sammy finished talking, Katharine's eyes had closed. She vaguely heard the big woman say, "Good—go to sleep, my dear."

* * *

Katharine awoke with a start. Someone was shaking her shoulder. She opened her eyes and again saw those huge beams overhead. "Trees must've been enormous back in those days," she murmured.

"I thought that you said, she was coherent."

"She was, Doctor ... before she went back to sleep."

Katharine was fully awake, now. She turned her head to gaze at a tiny, impeccably-dressed, asian woman. "You must be Doctor Wong. You needn't worry—my mind is clear. I was just remarking how big the trees were back when these beams were hewn." She pointed to the ceiling.

They all looked up.

Virgil said, "This warehouse is over two hundred years old. You won't find many timbers like these around anymore."

Doctor Wong seemed disinterested. She shifted her attention to Katharine. "You almost died on me. You required oxygen infusion while I shut down your lungs for drainage. The high fever could have damaged your heart or brain, but my scans show you'll be alright after you regain your strength. ... Yoo hoo! ... Ms. Carver? Are you still with us? Did you hear what I said?"

Katharine was thinking about Julie and Mario. She shook her head and wiped away a tear. "Uh? ... yes. Look, Doctor Wong, I'm not ungrateful, but you should have let me die." She heard Sammy suck in air and say, "Now, now, Ms. Carver, I'll not permit any gloom and doom talk around here. You're gonna get well ... I know it."

Katharine failed to suppress a sob. "You don't understand. ... I have nothing. ... I have no one. My life is finished."

* * *

Katharine's health improved despite her desire to die. Sammy amazed her. The woman was always cheerful, always helping others, always with something good to say about the most trying of circumstances. Early on, Katharine discovered that Sammy was not only fat but in an advanced state of pregnancy. She was mortified to learn that only one bed existed and that she, Katharine, was sleeping on it. No amount of urging could persuade Sammy and Virgil to take it back.

After a week, Katharine was strong enough to walk to the building's only toilet—on the ground floor—without having to use the ancient freight elevator. The flight of stairs was rickety, but, by gripping the railing, she could navigate it okay. The cubicle was filthy and in disrepair, yet Sammy kept the toilet, itself, immaculate despite the crack, which seeped water onto the floor.

Katharine began to watch Virgil. The man was wasting away. After awhile, she realized that he was in constant pain. Yet, he never complained. At night, though, he'd moan in his sleep, and Katharine could hear Sammy crying softly from her pallet in the corner. In the morning, the sweet lady would be as cheerful as ever while she hovered over her husband—washing and shaving him.

One night, Virgil fell out of his wheelchair.

In the morning, Sammy found him in the fetal position on the old, creosote-stained floor. A splinter of wood had grazed the poor man's cheek, which was caked with clotted blood.

Katharine helped Sammy put the unconscious man to bed. The big woman amazed her by performing her washing-and-shaving ritual on Virgil in her usual happy mood, as if nothing had happened.

A few days later, Doctor Wong arrived with her weekly gift of food and water.

Katharine took her aside and whispered, "Virgil can't hold anything down anymore. He's in and out of consciousness. Can you help him?"

The doctor sighed. "He is riddled with cancer. We could feed him intravenously for awhile, but why prolong the agony?"

"What about his pension?"

"You mean, after he goes?"

"Yes."

"Well, it'll probably go, too."

"Sammy sells very few of her wood carvings—and, for practically nothing." Katharine bit her lip. "Oh, God, she'll be alone with a baby to feed—without money."

"She'll be one among millions." Doctor Wong shrugged her shoulders, as if to say, "I can do nothing." Then, she faced Katharine and said, "You have recovered fully, so I won't be coming back. Good-bye and good luck."

"Just a minute ... how am I to pay for your services?

"Ms. Carver, you owe me nothing."

"You appear to be a doctor for the rich. Why did you come here? Who sent you?"

"Well, I, ah ... I, ah, ... spend a few hours a week with the poor. It is every doctor's duty—no, an obligation—to society." Doctor Wong turned and departed.

* * *

A week later, Katharine approached Sammy, who sat on the edge of the bed. She noticed that Sammy gazed at her husband with an expression of serenity and contentment. "Is Virgil better?"

Sammy smiled her little smile and said, "Yes, Kathy, dear—much better."

"Oh, I'm so happy for you … and for him."

"Thank you. … Death is so much better for him."

"What?" Katharine glanced at Virgil, whose eyes, now glazed over, stared unblinking at the huge, timbered beams. She squatted to Sammy's level, cupped the plump cheeks in her hands, and looked into tearless eyes. The tranquility in them shocked her.

Sammy stared back—unflinchingly.

"My God, Sammy, what sort of creature are you? Does nothing bother you? Have you no grief? Your husband is dead, for Christ' sake!"

Sammy was slow to speak. "To grieve is a selfish act, Kathy. Virgil's death makes me worse off, but he is the better for it … why should I grieve for the end of his suffering? Why should I grieve now, when, months ago, I knew that he was dying. Make the life of a suffering beloved one as pleasurable as possible by letting him die quickly. Birth engenders death. Every birth pairs with a death. We rejoice at birth, yet death is soon to follow. Why not despair at birth and rejoice at death?"

Both squatted before the death bed awhile longer, staring silently at Virgil's peaceful face. Then, Katharine grabbed Sammy around the neck and buried that lovable face in her bosom. "Jeez, Sammy, life really isn't worth living, is it?"

Sammy did not answer.

* * *

There was no funeral. The county took Virgil's body away, and that was the end of it. The owners of the warehouse gave Sammy ninety-days notice to vacate. Katharine realized that, were she Sammy, she would have panicked long ago.

Instead, all day long, Sammy hawked the wooden figurines, which she carved at night.

Katharine got work in the kitchen of a hospice that fed the most wretched mass of human beings she'd ever seen. Her only pay was room and board, but the space allotted to her was so dilapidated, she decided to stay with Sammy until they were forced out of the warehouse. Her boss loaned her a mattress—a well-peed-upon one—which Katharine put in a corner of the huge room. Sammy strung a cord with draped sheets around the area. The arrangement offered little privacy, but Katharine now possessed a space of her own.

Sammy appeared unconcerned about the imminent birth of her baby, yet Katharine was worried. "You've got to slow down. You're hardly sleeping."

The big woman laid her chisel and mallet aside and turned to face Katharine, who noticed that her normally cherubic cheeks were gray and drawn. "I must earn as much as I can now—before the baby arrives. Afterward, I have to take care of it."

"I'll help you with the baby—you should know that."

"Of course you would—at first—but, Kathy, you've your own life to live."

"My life is your life and the baby's. I have no one else now, Sammy."

* * *

Katharine awoke with a start. She listened. … All was silent. She went back to sleep.

Again, she awoke and heard, from across the room, lungs frantically expulsing air. For an instant, she thought little of it. Then, her mind raced. *The baby's coming.* She leapt to her feet and bounded to Sammy's side.

Katharine noticed that the woman's skin was flushed—especially her face. Sweat soaked the bed. Sammy didn't appear to be agitated, but Katharine suspected that she was trying to minimize her condition for her sake.

"Why didn't you awaken me? How long have you been in labor?"

Sammy smiled faintly. "It just started. Go back to bed … I'll be alright."

" 'Go back to bed'? Are you crazy? Jeez, Sammy, you look exhausted." Katharine spread Sammy's legs and thrust her fingers up her vagina. "My God, you're dilated. You've been in labor for hours."

Katharine fought rising panic. "We need a doctor. Maybe Doctor Wong can come."

Sammy reached out to her. "You still don't understand, do you? Doctor Wong was only for you. I am on my own. Do not worry—the baby will come soon. … Kathy, hold my hand. Please—hold my hand!"

Katharine's heart pounded. "We must get someone else."

"There is no one else." Sammy clawed for Katharine's hand, arched her back, and bit her lip. She moaned and squeezed Katharine's hand. "Stay with me, Kathy. Don't leave me."

"I'm here. I'll always be here." Katharine stroked the poor woman's head and wiped away her sweat. She whispered, "Don't fight it. Get plenty of air then push—hard."

Several times, Sammy breathed deeply and pushed. Minutes later, she breathed deeply and pushed, again. Then, she breathed deeply and pushed harder … ever harder. Breathe deeply … breathe deeply … and push harder… .

* * *

As the hours passed, Katharine became more concerned—Sammy's usual expression of sweetness gradually evolved to one of anguish. "I can't push any longer … Oh, Kathy, I'm so tired."

"You're doing fine. Relax. Get some rest."

"But the contractions keep coming, and nothing happens."

Katharine examined her again. *Oh, dear God, she's been fully dilated for hours—why doesn't the baby come?* "Sammy, I think the baby's almost here. Give another push." She felt Sammy shudder and heard her utter a brief cry, then … silence. Frantically, Katharine scrambled onto the bed to cradle Sammy's head in her lap. She stared into her eyes. To her horror, those soft eyes no longer twinkled but were fixed upon the huge beams overhead … as had been Virgil's. She rocked to and fro with Sammy's head in her embrace and cried in despair.

With a start, Katharine released her grip, and Sammy's body fell back onto the mattress like a limp, rag doll. *The baby! What'll happen to the baby?* Katharine planted her ear onto Sammy's abdomen. *Do I hear a heartbeat? I don't know … yet … yes, I do—a faint heartbeat.* In a frenzy now, she bounded from the bed to Sammy's workbench. She fumbled for a carving knife. *I must do it. Sammy would want it.*

Katharine realized that little time remained, yet, poised above the bed, she hesitated ... nervously twisting the knife in her fist. *God, please ... give me strength.* She knelt over Sammy and gritted her teeth.

She cut rapidly, trying to miss the baby. Sammy's blood flowed lazily onto the sheet. Slowly, the mattress sucked it up—sponge-like.

Sammy's life blood—ending up in a urine-stained mattress. Katharine bit her lip and wept. She could barely see, still her weapon hand worked relentlessly. She threw the knife aside and ripped open the placenta with her bare hands. Desperately, she groped for the baby. She felt it squirming for its life. From Sammy's gaping womb, Katharine pulled it—slippery with blood.

The baby did not breathe.

Katharine pursed her lips around the tiny mouth and gently sucked fluid, which she spat to the floor. She felt the little chest heave and heard the crackling sound of a newborn fighting for its first breath of life.

Tiny lungs swelled with air, and the staccato cries of Sammy's baby echoed from the shadowy reaches of the warehouse to assault Katharine's ears.

She held the infant up to the light and examined it. Under its mother's drying blood, its brown skin glistened crimson red.

"I name you Douglas." Katharine glanced down upon Sammy's gutted body and caught her breath. "No, I name you Sammy ... Your name is Samuel Virgil ... Samuel Virgil Carver."

La distance n'y fait
rien; il n'y a que le
premier pas qui coûte.

—Marie de Vichy-Chamrond,
marquise du Deffand

Six hundred fifty-eight years into the future, July 14, 2789
The floating city of Cumulus
Five miles above Antarctica

The results of the neural implantation overjoyed Pierre. In his enhanced memory, he found a new toy. Every day, for months, he traveled to the top of Cumulus and, while exploring its vast, veldt-like park, probed his enormously-improved intellect. He fantasized about what impression he might have made upon his professors and peers had he, as a graduate student, possessed such super memory. He speculated, *I would have been world famous—probably more so even than Einstein, Feynman, or Hawking.*

Boniface criticized Pierre for his hermit-like habits and persuaded him to visit those "aware" In-valids who were so anxious to meet him. Earlier, Pierre was reluctant to circulate among the In-valids because the experience depressed him, but Boniface eventually shamed him into it.

As Pierre grew more accustomed to his new intellectual powers, the construction of the spaceship claimed more of his time. His first moon trips, one every two or three months, began as little curiosity visits. However, after completion of the spaceship's frame, Pierre's brief visits evolved into lengthy lunar sojourns until, eventually, it was Cumulus that he visited rarely. In particular, the matter-antimatter reactor fascinated him. It was "light years" ahead of the crude engine, which had powered him into the future.

* * *

One day, Pierre discovered why his spaceship from the past had accelerated so rapidly to near light speed. He was anxious to tell Boniface.

"I've learned why our spaceship accelerated faster than planned."

The old man smiled knowingly. "I wondered when you'd figure that one out."

"Since I arrived here, I've pondered the problem to no avail. Then, today, a possible solution came to me—no doubt from my extra memory. So, I ran some model simulations, and they worked."

"How?"

"Boniface, inertial force varies throughout the Universe."

"That's good, Pierre, but be more specific."

"Well, the inertial-force potential at any point in space is proportional to the scalar sum of the pulls of gravity from the masses surrounding that point. I've an example that enables a lay person to understand it."

"Well, then, let's hear it," Boniface ordered.

184

"Suppose that an unpowered spaceship floats in space such that all of the masses of the solar system—the Sun, Moon, Earth, and all of the other planets, moons, and asteroids—surround it. Each mass applies a gravitational pull on the spaceship, and, if the pulls are more from one direction than from the others, the spaceship moves—or, rather, accelerates—toward that one direction, right?"

The ancient one stroked his beard. "Right."

"Okay, suppose, further, that the spaceship is so located that all of the gravitational pulls upon it cancel each other, such that it remains immobile. Of course, so long as gravitational forces are the only ones applied to the spaceship, it and everything within it don't feel them—everything is 'weightless.'"

Boniface smiled. "Of course."

Pierre smiled back. "Now, let us make an analogy, so that we can more easily understand our little thought experiment or, as Einstein would have said, Gedankenexperiment.

"Let a corral at a horse ranch replace the solar system, and, a wild horse, the spaceship. Let wranglers' lassos be the members of the solar system.

"The wranglers surround the horse with their lassos around its neck. Each pulls back to keep the horse immobile, so that the vector sum of the lassos' forces equals zero. Should the horse try to move in any direction, it must exert much force, which, if many wranglers exist, it might not possess. The horse must overcome the scalar sum of the forces, not the—zero—vector sum. Of course, the scalar sum is the sum of the forces' magnitudes irrespective of the directions from which the forces might be applied."

Boniface continued to stroke his long, white beard. "Yes."

"The horse feels the lassos bite into its neck because they apply their forces at a few points. Contrarily, gravitational forces apply themselves evenly throughout a mass in direct proportion to each component's contribution to the aggregate mass, thus the spaceship detects no force. However, should the spaceship try to move, it—like the horse—must overcome that scalar sum of forces created by all those surrounding celestial bodies. In other words, it must overcome inertia."

"An excellent example, Pierre, but how does it relate to the navigational error made by your crew?"

Boniface's condescending attitude irritated Pierre, but he decided to let the old one continue to enjoy his role of devil's advocate.

"You know how it relates … you just want to see whether I do.

Boniface chuckled. "Naturally."

"Well, we calculated our acceleration by relating it to what—we believed—was a constant—inertial force. However, as we left the solar system behind and entered deep space, unbeknownst to us the inertial-force potential decreased. We had shed those restraining 'lassos' and, in blissful ignorance, accelerated into the future."

"Very poetic, Pierre. … Now, had you invented another Gedankenexperiment before your departure from the year 2045, you might never have made your error, and we, at Cumulus, might never have known of a Pierre Talon."

"What kind of Gedankenexperiment?"

"To make my point, I use a force that is related to inertial force—centrifugal force. … First, I set up the apparatus for the experiment: Suppose that you are weightless in a spaceship in the deepest reaches of space—the farthest that you can be from any mass—let us say, midway between the two superclusters of galaxies the most distant from each other.

"You mean, billions of light years from the nearest speck of matter?"

"Yes, Pierre—and even, from antimatter. ... All energy sources in your spaceship are turned off. You look out a porthole and see the infinite blackness of deep nothingness. With a powerful telescope, you barely see a faint white dot, which is one of the two superclusters. Likewise, from an opposing porthole, you barely discern the other supercluster. With your telescope, you sweep the Universe in all other directions, but the panorama yields no other points of light."

"Jeez, Boniface, I get your point ... I'm really alone out there."

"Right. ... Periodically, you check the two points of light. They remain at the same locations relative to their respective portholes. You still float inside your spaceship in midair—weightless. The experiment is ready to be performed.

"You fire rockets that are tangential to the sides of the spaceship. It begins to spin about its longitudinal axis. You know that it is spinning because the two points of light now appear to revolve about it. Faster and faster the ship spins until the two, white dots blur to create a faint circle of light around it. You shut off the rockets. Again, all power sources are off; all man-made forces, gone; yet, the two points of light continue to blur in their rapid revolutions about the ship.

"My question to you, Pierre, is: Are the items in your spaceship still weightless, or has centrifugal force pushed them against the hull of your spaceship?"

Pierre thought for a moment. *Logic tells me that centrifugal force pushes them ... then, again, from where would the centrifugal force come? If my spaceship is, indeed, rotating, it rotates only in relation to other matter in the Universe, and the closest is at one of those two points of light, billions of light years away.* "I don't know, Boniface."

"Shame on you! Why didn't you search for the answer in your new memory? ... It is there."

"I'm sorry. I forgot." Pierre closed his eyes and covered his face with his hands. The answer came to him. "Almost weightless."

"Right. ... Why?"

"Because, rotation relative to other masses creates centrifugal force, and the spaceship rotates only in relation to the distant superclusters, which are too far away to have much of an effect."

"Bravo, Pierre—correct again. Incidentally, do you believe that places exist in the Universe where no inertial force can occur?"

Pierre concentrated for a moment. "Yes ... at the boundary between a galaxy and an antigalaxy, where the scalar sum of gravity and antigravity cancel each other."

Pierre saw admiration in the old man's eyes.

* * *

The last few weeks of preparation were tough on Pierre. He wanted to remain in the thick of the work that was needed to ready the spaceship. Although Boniface insisted that no need existed for his presence at the work site, Pierre wasn't able to conquer his fear that a robolaborer might lose a screw and sabotage the whole project.

Finally, the great day arrived. The spaceship had received its final inspection three days before, and, since then, Pierre rested from his labors in the soothing environment of Cumulus's wildlife park. He walked alone through the vast, sun-drenched meadow, which was bedecked with bright flowers of every sort—a sight that might have awed Claude Monet, himself.

Then, he received the shock of his life—his mother's voice echoed through his brain as if she were talking to him from a few feet away. He could not actually hear her, but ... *yes, dammit, I do hear my mother—I really do.* Then, the meadow blanked out, and he saw the brain in the bowl under the lights and the outline of the pedestal and the robots beneath. By some magic, had Strata transported him into her control room? Yet, Pierre still felt the warm, soft soil of the meadow underfoot. He realized that she simply had bypassed his eyes and ears with sensory inputs of her own choosing. *My God, she's powerful.*

His mother's words were, "Mister Talon, your spaceship is ready, and we, the In-valids of Cumulus, are ready for your departure. Are you?"

Pierre realized that, like the time he had heard his father's voice, this one only sounded like his mother's.

"Yes, ma'am, I'm ready."

"I know. I scanned your brain and found knowledge enough to assure the success of your mission. Boniface accompanies you as far as Moonbase Twelve. Go, now, to the launch complex—he awaits your arrival. ... Farewell, Mister Talon. Good luck."

"Good-bye, ma'am."

The meadow returned.

* * *

The moonship shot through the opening in the side of Cumulus and, under the influence of antigravity modules, rose silently into the sky. When clear of Earth's troposphere, its matter-antimatter reactor ignited, and Pierre felt the familiar "kick in the butt" that he had come to enjoy.

He looked over to Boniface and was taken aback. Tears streamed down the old man's cheeks—they matted his beard. *I didn't realize he had grown so fond of me—he hates to see me leave—the poor man.*

Boniface glanced at him. "You're surprised at my tears, aren't you? Some are for your departure, but most are for my mother. You see ... I shall never see her, again."

"What? You can't be serious. Why not, Boniface?"

"She will be dead. All will be dead."

"But ... but, why?"

"Pierre, the In-valids are tired ... bored. They have experienced every Dream-world. They have seen, heard, and felt all. For the past few years, only the anticipation of your arrival kept Strata and the others alive."

"How will they die? ... and what about you? You can't come with me to the past—the spaceship's too small. And the poor animals—the last of Earth's plants and animals? ... Oh, my God!"

"Please, Pierre, remain calm. Don't upset yourself before departure. All on Cumulus are resigned to their fate. They realize no future awaits them. Now that the time has come, they want to die in peace. Please … let them. Strata, probably, already has begun the process—blood deoxygenation and withholding of other life-support essentials."

"What happens to you?"

"I'll spend the remainder of my life on the Moon. In my old age, I enjoy its lesser gravity. When I become lonely, Dreamworlds will lessen the monotony."

"What about Cumulus … will you ever return to it?"

Boniface sighed. "No … never. Without Strata, any reason to visit Cumulus no longer exists. After the In-valids are dead, the robots will dispose of their remains and, after a fashion, continue to manage a Cumulus devoid of humankind. Eventually, of course, the robots will fall into dormancy—their programmed task of caring for humans having become obsolete.

"The remaining plants and animals will then be alone to face their fate—whatever that might be. Cumulus could continue to float about the Earth for years—its life-support systems intact. Then again, it may settle to the Surface or against some mountain-side and disgorge the surviving life forms onto the poisoned land. Possibly, some could adapt, but most would succumb. Whatever happens, Pierre, will be beyond our caring."

The moonship arrived at Moonbase Twelve. The time for farewells had arrived. Pierre turned to face Boniface.

The old man laid a trembling hand on his shoulder. "In one of your months, you will have traversed the Universe and arrived in an antisupercluster of antigalaxies hundreds of millions of years in the future. After two months there, at near light antispeed, you will be hundreds of millions of years in the past. Another month back in the matter side of the Universe will put you back on the Earth of your era. What say you to that, Pierre Talon? Are you properly impressed?"

Pierre sensed that Boniface's banalities were meant to conceal his real emotions. They both knew that, not only would they not see each other again, they were witnessing the demise of the greatest epoch in Earth's history. Pierre had difficulty finding the proper words for the occasion. "Boniface, if I succeed in my mission, I might change the course of history, right?"

"Right, Pierre."

"Well, in that case, the In-valids might not evolve into a dominant society. Hell, few In-valids might exist in the first place. John, Alex, and Joan might never be born. How can you cope with the prospect that Strata and you might never exist the second time 'round?"

"We do exist. We have experienced long lives. Nothing can change that. Your return to the past gives Earth a second chance for survival. How can Strata and I not be content to receive in our second lives whatever role fate has in store for us—even not to be born. If we would be born again, we would have no knowledge of our former lives, in which case, we would be different persons, isn't that so? After all, only memories make the person."

"I guess you're right, Boniface. Permanent amnesiacs, in reality, have died, and new persons have taken over their bodies."

The two men looked at each other for a long moment.

Pierre broke the silence. "I suppose that we can't delay the inevitable any longer." Welled-up tears blurred his view of the old man's face. He took Boniface in his arms and hugged the frail frame. "Farewell, my friend."

Boniface's expression took on a stern aspect. He spoke resolutely. "Your goal is to return to the past and make as many changes as you possibly can that will benefit the future of our species as a whole. Changes for anyone's personal aggrandizement are forbidden except when necessary for your goal. Good-bye, Pierre Talon. ... Good luck."

Pierre turned, entered the shuttle, and departed for his spaceship in moon orbit.

* * *

Pierre finished the last checks of his spaceship. He realized that the beginning of his trip would be arduous. His body must withstand ten days of continuous, thirty-five g-force acceleration until the spaceship was near light speed. Normally, a short exposure to a fifth of that force crushes a person, but, for Pierre, the application of magneto-biosis would solve the problem.

Courageously, Pierre inserted the intravenous needle into his arm. The magnetizing fluid flowed through his blood vessels and permeated his tissues—even his bones. He felt weird—the small magnetic fields generated by the spaceship's equipment pulled his body parts in various directions.

Strapped into his couch, Pierre ordered the powerful electromagnets located in the nose of the craft to test themselves. Pierre's flesh pulled forward as the magnetic-force field applied to his body increased to four 'g's.' His arms felt like they were being pulled from their sockets.

The remaining systems checked out, too. Boniface and he transmitted final farewells—Pierre was ready for blastoff.

Begin acceleration, Pierre thought.

Immediately, the immense reactors exploded into life, and the spaceship began its long climb toward light speed. Pierre couldn't feel the crushing acceleration—magnetic force automatically canceled inertial force.

The Sun became a tiny dot behind him, and the Centaurus star system soon flashed by. Pierre was happy. He was going home.

In poverty, hunger, and dirt.

—Thomas Hood

Six hundred fifty eight years into the past, March 20, 2131
The hospice for the poor
Bellevue, Franklin

Katharine, not yet inured to the bleak decrepitude and stifling heat of the hospice's maternity ward, sighed and wiped gritty sweat from brow and neck. She watched the mothers—haggard and gaunt—breast feed their babies. Occasionally, she'd hear a woman cough in a pathetic effort to expel persistent phlegm.

Gretchen, an emaciated young mother with pendulous breasts, tried to suckle Katharine's little Samuel—apparently, without success. The baby refused the nipple.

Katharine chuckled to herself. *Good! He's not hungry. Thank God, I've finally found formula for him.*

* * *

After Samuel's birth, Katharine was desperate to find milk. Gretchen, new at the hospice, offered to wet-nurse Samuel in return for special privileges on the food line.

At first, Katharine was reluctant to accept the offer—she could have been fired if she were caught serving more than each person's ration—but finding milk for Samuel was imperative. Reluctantly, she risked asking her boss if Gretchen could be allowed a larger ration of food if she would suckle two babies instead of one. Fortunately, her boss was a compassionate woman who had suffered as much as any of the hospice's residents … she approved.

Samuel grew rapidly from the wet nurse's milk, but Katharine always was reluctant to give him up at feeding time. He was all she possessed, and she hated sharing him with the warm breast of another woman. When he became round and plump, she hastened to put him on her precious, new-found supply of formula. In particular, she'd fill him up just before he was to suckle.

* * *

Gretchen covered her breast and wiped Samuel's mouth.

Katharine felt a rush of satisfaction. She leaned over and snatched her cherished son from the wet nurse's embrace.

Gretchen looked up—eyes brimming with tears. "Does this mean, you'll be taking Samuel for good?"

"Yes, my dear. He won't need you anymore. From now on, I can feed him myself."

"Please!" A scrawny hand clawed at her arm, which, Katharine noticed without concern, was almost as spindly as Gretchen's.

190

"Yes?" Katharine studied the sallow face, which marked the young woman as decades older than her real age. Eyes encircled in black pleaded from sunken sockets.

"Please, Kathy," Gretchen whispered, "can't we go through the motions? I can fake it. Nobody'll know … please!" The woman gripped her arm so desperately … Katharine feared she'd draw blood.

Gretchen's eyes, her face, her whole being implored, and, suddenly, Katharine's little, self-serving world crumbled. She averted her gaze and cried softly, *Oh, my God! How could I have been so blind … so selfish?* She lay Samuel on the cot, cradled Gretchen's head in her arms, and sobbed into her ear, "I'm so sorry, my child. Please forgive me. I was jealous—no, envious—of you. I guess, subconsciously, I was afraid you'd steal Samuel away from me."

Gretchen looked up at Katharine almost reverently, "Oh, I could never do that." Her voice wavered. "My own baby is too much for me, as it is." Tears streamed down her cheeks. She whispered, "I'm hungry, Kathy—I'm always hungry. You won't have to cut my ration, now, will you?"

"Ssh—be quiet!" Katharine whispered. She glanced about the ward. Apparently, none of the other women had heard—they were still busy feeding their babies. She thought, *Perhaps, I can share some of Samuel's formula with her. … No, I can't risk running out.* She murmured into Gretchen's ear, "We'll go on as before: I'll feed Samuel before you pretend to suckle him, and you'll continue to get the extra ration."

"Oh, thank you, Kathy … thank you."

"Be careful, girl … don't show so much emotion." Katharine checked her wrist terminal. "I've got to get ready for lunch duty." She strapped little Samuel onto her back and strode between the double row of rickety cots to the ward's exit.

* * *

While Katharine set up the food line, she thought of Julie and again tried to muster enough courage to contact her. She knew that her daughter's time was near and needed, from Julie, news about her grandchild—if not forgiveness for the unpardonable act she had inflicted upon her only surviving child.

Yet, Katharine still hesitated to act. Over and over, she had resolved herself to contact Julie, and, over and over, she had done nothing. She would rationalize: *I'm tired. I've barely the strength to perform my work. Caring for Samuel consumes all my spare time. Besides, my wrist terminal refuses to transmit.* At other times, she believed that her martyr complex was controlling her. Yet, Katharine knew that she was only making excuses. *Am I still punishing myself? Do I still want to punish Julie?*

Katharine glanced at her wrist terminal. *Jeez, only fifteen minutes before security unleashes the poor wretches.* She worked rapidly to transfer the last of the meager amount of food into the serving pans. Her hunger was always at its worse when she worked with food … food that—she knew—was not hers to eat. She remembered well the time she had sampled it—swift punishment followed: Two days without a morsel.

Katharine placed the pans in the steam table and passed the ancient Geiger counter over them. Radioactivity levels acceptable, she signaled security to open the door and steeled herself for the stampede.

Not to be born is the best for man.

—Wystan Hugh Auden

Three weeks later, April 6, 2131
Olympicview Maternity Hospital
Bellevue, Franklin

"Your breakfast, Ms. Pavía." The roboserver set the tray in front of Julie and left the room.

Julie couldn't eat—she fidgeted with the hem of her bedsheet. She had no more tears. She had cried them all and felt resigned to the catastrophe of her daughter's birth. An inner force of resolve and fortitude prompted her to deny herself the luxury of grief and self-pity. Now, she was mature—an adult, mindful of adult duties and adult responsibilities.

However, Mario worried Julie. The reality of their daughter's condition seemed to be almost too much for him to bear. The day before, she saw near panic in his eyes. A man talks bravely, but, when a once-in-a-lifetime tragedy strikes, a woman is required to cope with the situation.

Julie compared Mario's reaction, yesterday, to her father's, when her brother was born. She found Mario's to be more compassionate. He had told her that he didn't want to reject the baby outright—to put her in a state-run institution for in-valids and forget her—like Julie's father had wanted for Douglas. On the contrary, he said that he wanted to place her in an expensive, private home with lavish care—said, he didn't want his wife to ruin her life taking care of their deformed daughter—said, she should soon be free to have another baby ... supposedly.

Although Julie was alone in her maternity room, her thoughts turned vocal. "Well, I refuse to do it. I will care for my baby myself, and ... I'll never have another ... never!" Her outburst surprised even herself.

Julie remembered that only a few months before, she would have kept an in-valid baby only to please her husband—and not a badly deformed one, at that. Now, Mario no longer wanted to keep the child at home, and, suddenly, she had insisted upon doing so. *Why? Do I want to punish Mario ... or Mother? ... or myself? Perhaps I've acquired a martyr complex. Perhaps my maternal instinct is aroused. Perhaps, subconsciously, I want my life to parallel my mother's—that of the mother of a deformed child.* Perplexed, she shook her head.

Julie realized that the most amazing aspect of her attitude was that she already had experienced the great sacrifices that must be made for an in-valid child. She knew that familial activities are centered around him. She knew that familial wants and needs are suppressed for him. She knew that his siblings—and parents—become psychotic martyrs for the remainder of their lives. Often times, retention of an in-valid child costs unconceived or unborn siblings their lives—a sort of retroactive murder. Julie was numbed by memories of these dilemmas yet irresistibly drawn to emulate her mother's martyrdom.

She tried to rationalize into insignificance her daughter's defects vis-à-vis Douglas's. Granted, the baby possessed a horribly deformed body, but her brain is intact. *As her mind develops, I must be near to help her.*

Julie had finally accepted the risk of losing Mario should she persist in insisting that she keep their daughter at home. She felt certain that her husband was less selfish than had been her father.

Mario strode into the room.

His grim expression of determination unsettled Julie. Possibly, she had misjudged him.

He approached and, with neither a gesture of love nor regard for her grief, said, "Well, have you made up your mind?"

Mario's insensitive attitude prompted her into more stubbornness than before. "I already told you last night, Mario: 'I'm taking my baby home.'"

Her husband raised his arms in frustration then let them drop in defeat. "Julie, the baby is going to die—maybe not today—or tomorrow—but, soon. Why invest your emotions—my emotions—in a baby that possesses no future?"

"You don't understand … I already have eight-months' worth of emotion invested in our daughter, and, no matter what her condition, she's still ours. Perhaps she will die, but I will give her my motherly love until that day arrives." Julie could see Mario's frustration mount—he seemed on the verge of tears.

In an apparent change of tactics, he took Julie's hands in his. "Look, honey, it's not as if we're abandoning the child. She'll get just as good care in a private institution as she will at home—perhaps, better. You can visit her every day, if you wish." He kissed her on the forehead.

She pulled away. "No! … and don't treat me as if I were a child."

Abruptly, Mario turned toward the window and slammed his fist into the palm of his hand. "Dammit, Julie, for years you criticized your mother because she kept Douglas. Now, you do the same."

"Just one minute, dear husband. Don't try to compare the two cases. Big differences exist: First, we are not bringing her home to impose her upon an existing, valid sibling who is allowed no say in the matter. Second, unlike Douglas, she is not a vegetable without feelings."

"Yes, but, like Douglas, she will die young."

"Christ almighty, Mario, Douglas didn't just die—he was killed. If you can find my mother, ask her what the proper course of action to follow is. She did it for Douglas."

Mario turned and raised his eyebrows. "I might do just that."

"Do what?"

"Find your mother, that's what. It's long overdue. Maybe she's dead—how long has it been? … almost three months, now? Don't you even worry about her?"

Julie shot back, "God, Mario—of course I worry about her, but, since the time I found out that my baby was in-valid, I feel no compassion for her. She deliberately let me carry a deformed embryo into the fetal stage. I can't forgive her for that."

"But, she didn't know that the baby was deformed."

Julie trembled with anger. "Christ almighty, are you trying to find excuses for my mother's behavior?"

"No, but—"

"Look, Mario, what's done is done. All I'm saying is, had I known that our baby was deformed when it was in the embryo stage, I'd have readily aborted it to give our second child a clean start—to give us a second chance at happiness. Now, it's too late—I must concentrate on this baby, like Mother did with Douglas."

Mario rushed to the bed and grabbed her hands. "No, no—it's not too late! Julie, Julie ... give up the baby. We'll have another one."

"No, I will not! We're going to—"

The brisk arrival of a matronly woman in starched whites interrupted them. To Julie, her broad smile seemed donned as part of her uniform.

"Good morning, ma'am," the woman singsonged, "and how are we today?" Before Julie could answer, the woman—apparently disinterested in any response—turned toward Mario. "Ah, you must be the lucky father." Immediately, she pivoted to face Julie again. "Ms. Carver-Pavía, you are to leave the hospital now." She swung back to Mario. "Sign where indicated, please." She shoved a displayboard at him and impatiently tapped her foot.

Julie caught Mario's eye and arched her eyebrows in feigned astonishment.

Mario returned the gesture as if to say, "I'm just as confused as you." He asked, "What's this?"

"A mere formality, sir ... necessary before departing the hospital." The woman's, porcelain-like smile never faltered.

"Who are you?"

"Oh, haven't we met? I am sorry, sir, one sees so many people, one forgets whom one has met and whom one has not.

Mario said, "Well, I'm one whom you haven't."

"I'm Ms. Jourdan, administrative assistant for departures. Please ... could you sign the release order—I've my rounds to make, you know."

"No, I did not know." Mario pointed at the displayboard's screen. "What's this for?"

Ms. Jourdan glanced disdainfully at what Mario indicated. "—permission for the disposition of your son."

"She's my daughter."

"Sorry ... daughter, then."

Julie asked, "What disposition?"

"Well, we can't transfer your child to a Franklin state facility without this release, and he—er, she—can't remain here ... naturally."

"I don't need to sign," Mario blurted. "Tomorrow, a medical team transfers our daughter to a private home for the deformed."

"No, Mario," Julie screamed, "she is coming home with us. You cannot take her from me."

Ms. Jourdan raised her voice. "Ma'am, regardless of what you may decide, the child and you must be out of this hospital by tomorrow afternoon. We're over-crowded." She wheeled around to leave.

"Just a minute. Surely a doctor is coming to consult with us?"

The woman turned back and irritably scanned the screens on the displayboard. "No ... nothing about it here, but I do notice that your daughter is inflicted by a typical—yes, very common—class H-17 deformity: dissolved vertebrae and no limbs, indicating that her ancestry was exposed to a particularly virulent type of radioactive poisoning." She turned toward Julie and, with an air of superiority, said, "Ma'am, I wouldn't recommend keeping your child at home. With this type of deformity, the parents usually abandon their fetal issue to the state."

" 'Fetal issue'? ... oh, God." Julie choked up and felt that she would vomit.

The matron rambled on. "Well, they are in constant pain, you know, and often must be sedated. Later, nervous spasms occur, which would cause them harm should they not be restrained. Because they lack a backbone, only professionals can handle them. Of course, most die before the age of ten—usually of a severed spinal cord. ... If that is all you require, I must be going." Ms. Jourdan pivoted and marched briskly from the room.

Julie was dumbstruck. She glanced at Mario, who looked as if he were about to faint.

He spread his hands. "Julie! ... Now, won't you change your mind?"

"Mario, that horrible woman can't make me ... and you can't, either."

For a moment, her husband neither spoke nor moved, but his lips blanched and his chin trembled. He opened his mouth as if to speak. Then, his eyes turned steely, and he stomped from the room.

Julie buried her face in a pillow.

> For many a time, I have been
> half in love with easeful death.
>
> —John Keats

That same day, after lunch
The hospice for the poor
Bellevue, Franklin

Finally alone, Katharine sat exhausted. Quietly, she sipped dandelion coffee. The concoction was bitter, but the herb rendered the water potable. Cheeks in palms, she stared at the shambles of the food line, which, as always, was scraped clean. Courage mustered, she rose to clean up the mess.

A noise from behind prompted Katharine to turn. She gasped in surprise. Piercing black eyes glared at her from behind a mask. *Why is he hiding his identity? Has he come to rob us?* Then, she realized that the mask framed an air filter. *He can't be one of us*, she thought. *Besides, he's too-well dressed.* Suddenly, she recognized him. "Mario? Is that you? Why are you here?"

Mario approached and eyed her from head to foot. For a moment, his scrutiny paused at the sight of Samuel on her back before moving on. He said nothing.

Katharine's mind raced. *Julie isn't with him. What's going on?* The situation, finally, dawned on her, and her blood ran cold. Staccato-like, she blurted questions. "Julie had her baby, didn't she? How is she? How is the baby? Tell me, Mario … please, tell me! … For God's sake, tell me!"

Mario stared at the floor. His chin began to quiver. "Kathy, I … uh—"

She grabbed his shoulders. "The baby was stillborn. Is that it? Something happened to Julie?"

Mario continued to avert his eyes. Except for a sob, he remained silent.

Katharine shook him violently until his air filter flew off and skittered across the floor. "Tell me, damn you … tell me what has happened."

To her surprise, Mario didn't resist. He said quietly, "Julie's fine." Then, he burst into tears. "The baby's alive, but she's … oh, God, Kathy, she is horribly deformed."

Katharine's head spun. She screamed, "Mario, what's wrong with my grandchild?"

Mario wiped away a tear then spoke with words that seemed to flow like honey. "Kathy, listen to what we have as a daughter: She possesses no arms … no legs … her vertebrae … useless cartilage—like gelatin and … ."

Katharine moaned and tried not to listen, yet she hungered to know. She had to know.

"—and, after much suffering, she will die young. Kathy, your son's body was intact without a brain to control it. He could not have suffered as much as our daughter will suffer—her brain is intact without a body to control. I ask you, Kathy, when all is done, who will have suffered the most? ... your child or ours? ... and who will have caused her suffering? ... and who caused his?"

Katharine could not bring herself to answer these ghastly questions. She was fully awake, yet she was having a nightmare. *Horribly deformed? Her brain—intact?* She covered her face with her hands then clasped together her fingers, tilted back her head, and gazed at the ceiling. "Go away, Mario. Do you hear me? Let me be. Please ... leave me in peace." Her closing eyes cascaded welled tears down her cheeks.

Mario uttered a scornful grunt. "After what you have done to my family, I cannot leave you in peace. You owe me, Katharine Carver. You owe your daughter, and I have come to collect."

Startled, she glanced at Mario. "Collect what? As it is, I'm allocated barely enough food to keep me alive. What else would you have from me?"

"Your influence over your daughter."

Katharine failed to suppress a chuckle. "Goodness ... that died long ago."

"Julie's emulating you, Kathy. I don't know why she is, but it's tearing our marriage apart."

"So, she wants to keep the baby, like I kept Douglas?"

"Yes—and she refuses to consider having another one."

"And, you do want another baby?"

"Of course! I want healthy children. Doesn't everyone? Julie needs to have another baby—a valid one—who can fulfill her motherhood dreams in a healthy fashion, but she wants to keep this one in our home and sacrifice herself for the rest of her life."

"So ... you want to abandon this child, is that it?"

"Of course not. I have the means to keep it comfortable in a private home with professional caretakers until it dies, but I cannot allow Julie to be a slave to it."

Katharine eyed Mario with suspicion. "Like Douglas's mother was to him?"

"Exactly! ... Look, Kathy, Julie is donning the cloak of a martyr—a masochist, even. We both love her and have got to stop her—you and I."

Katharine was exhausted. She could not fight Mario and Julie any longer—and, curiously enough, she wondered why she ever had. She sighed and faced Mario. "What do you want me to do?"

Mario rushed to her and grabbed her hands. "Go to her. Tell her you love her and want the best for everyone concerned, but don't bluntly advise her to abandon the baby. I tried that—the effect was the opposite intended."

"Well, I wouldn't do that anyway. Perhaps, I should apologize to her."

"That couldn't hurt, you know." Mario put his hand to his nose. "Jeez, Kathy ... how can you breathe this stuff?"

"After awhile, you get used to it."

"Come to the hospital with me now, Kathy."

"I can't—I've dinner duties to attend to."

"Please! She needs you. Our marriage needs you. ... I need you. You've got to see Julie by tomorrow—before she leaves the hospital."

Katharine hesitated a moment, but she knew that she would go. "Mario, I'll be there after breakfast."

"Thank you, Kathy." He embraced her then quickly released her and stepped back. "Good God, Kathy, you feel like a bag of bones. What's happened to you?"

Katharine suppressed a smile. "Most people on the surface are worse off than I. Despite my appearance, I do eat from time to time—and so does Samuel."

Mario said "Computer, reinstate Katharine Carver on my transportation account."

"No, Mario, I want nothing from—"

"Nonsense! If you walk, you'll never get there."

Katharine noticed a quizzical expression on Mario's face.

"Did you say—Samuel? Who's he?"

Katharine pointed to the baby on her back.

"You're carrying a sick woman's kid on your back while working yourself to death for bare subsistence? Kathy, that's crazy!"

"Samuel is mine. I brought him into this world—such that it is."

Mario's mouth fell agape. He stared at Samuel in disbelief. "Yours! But, when did you have the time ... where did you ... who could be the father?" He smiled wanly. "You're joking—right?"

With a straight face, she said, "No, Mario ... I am not."

"Then, for Heaven's sake, tell me about it."

She did.

* * *

Katharine, sopping in sweat, sat bolt-upright in bed. Her eyes snapped open, yet images continued to dart in front of them—disembodied faces and fingers floating in the dark. She saw faces leering at her, felt fingers jabbing at her, heard voices shrilling at her, "Guilty! Guilty! Guilty!" Her neck pulsated in harmony with her heartbeat. Invoking calm thoughts solved nothing. The sneering persisted ... and the pointing ... and the accusing.... .

She cupped hands over ears and cried out, "Guilty of what? Please, dear Lord, tell me of what I am guilty." She hesitated. "No ... don't tell me—I know already. I must save Julie—but, how? The baby—yes, the baby. It cannot live—Julie's only way out— a dead baby" ... *A dead baby.*

Katharine, in a daze, leapt from bed and jumped into her clothes. While strapping Samuel to her back, she tiptoed from the hospice.

A deserted street greeted her. She was certain that a hot, grit-laden wind swirled around her, yet it felt like a cool breeze buffeting her hair.

Normally, she'd guard Samuel against the harshness of the elements, but, tonight, the air seemed benign.

"Where am I going? I don't recall." *A dead baby!* ... "Oh, yes ... to see my daughter. She needs me."

Katharine set a rapid pace toward the Olympicview Maternity Hospital—several miles away. She began running. Her lungs filled with air—cool, clean air ... good air. The omnipresent phlegm had vanished. She breathed deeply. *A dead baby!* She felt good. She glanced back at Samuel.

He grinned, as if to say, "Go, Mother. Fly like the wind."

She looked up toward the stratoscrapers. Their brightly lit tops hid behind the clouds, yet they glowed silk-like through the mist, betraying their presence.

Katharine lengthened her stride. Her legs felt good. *A dead baby!* They were powerful. The decaying buildings and heaps of trash flashed by at an astounding rate. She glanced back at Samuel. He was having the time of his life.

"So, you want Mother to run faster, eh?" Effortlessly, her legs strode farther and pumped faster. Each time a foot struck the ground, she felt it squish something. She glanced down. "Oh, my God, I'm stepping on babies." *A dead baby!*

Katharine tried to sidestep the babies, but, each time a foot slammed to the ground, a baby would appear beneath it. To put the babies behind her, she ran faster. It didn't work—babies now blanketed her path.

Then, Katharine realized that her feet no longer touched the ground. She was flying ... flying over a carpet of babies! Soon, she neared the bottom of one of the hospital's emergency stairwells. Its old, rusty gate, sealed shut with cobwebs, loomed rapidly.

"I can't stop—what shall I do?" *A dead baby!*

The gate exploded open, and Katharine sailed up the stairs. The climb to the top was easy—a half mile up in seconds.

Katharine burst into one of the hospital's reception areas. She breathed slowly—as if she had just arisen from bed. People and robots alike stared at her in dismay.

A robosentry said, "We've been expecting you, Ms. Carver."

It gestured straight ahead to a door, above which, a sign read: Preemie Ward G, Deformed. "You will see your granddaughter, now." *A dead baby!*

"First, I'll see my daughter."

"No, Ms. Carver, your granddaughter is waiting for you ... has been, since she was conceived, go through that door and perform your duty."

"My duty?"

The robosentry seemed annoyed. "Yes, your duty to Julie, of course. You should have performed it sooner, you know."

Perplexed, Katharine entered the room, which was long and narrow. My duty—*a dead baby!* At the far end, she noticed two robonurses working near an incubator. They didn't seem to notice her. Despite the room's large size, she found her granddaughter quickly ... row 187, column 24—like on a chess board. Her tag read: Carver-Pavía daughter, 241 days of gestation, 685 grams. *My God, barely over a pound.*

With vision partially obscured by tears, she gazed through the incubator's dome—down upon a naked mass of flesh and bone. Its arms and legs ended short of elbows and knees. Evidently to protect the spinal cord from damage, its torso lay encased in a sausage-like sheath. Tubes of various sizes protruded from most of its bodily orifices. *A dead baby!* As if fighting for every instant of life, its chest heaved up and down, like a runner's after the 100-meter dash. Periodically, the infant's whole being quivered, punctuated by spasmodic jerks and twitches.

An acrid taste filled Katharine's mouth. She felt faint. She sank slowly to the floor and lay there for several minutes—Samuel atop her belly. Apparently, no one noticed. When she felt better, she struggled to her feet and again gaped at her granddaughter. Soon the child's macabre movements mesmerized her. *A dead baby!* Her thoughts turned to better times. In her mind's eye, Katharine saw the day of her wedding:

Al and she loved each other deeply. In their youthful naïveté, they were confident of leading an idyllic life together with happy, healthy children. At first, life fulfilled their expectations. In harmonious togetherness, Al and Julie and she lived and played and loved. Then, she birthed Douglas.

She wondered what her life—and the lives of her loved ones—would have been like, had her moral upbringing and the laws of the land been different. Certainly, an examination of Douglas's embryo would have detected its invalidity early, and she would have aborted him. At that stage, it would have been an abortion much like God's abortion—as Pierre was so fond of saying. Her family would not have led such tormented lives, and … she would have birthed another child.

Katharine was convinced—at last—that her preoccupation of caring for Douglas kept her from being a proper mother for Julie and from having a third child. *Did I unknowingly murder my third child? Or … did Douglas's survival murder him?* Suddenly, hideous visions of Julie's future flashed through her mind. *No, no … I cannot let my Julie suffer. I cannot let her baby suffer.*

Barely able to see through her tears, Katharine thrust her hand through one of the incubator's armholes. *A dead baby!* Tenderly, she pressed her palm against the tiny mouth and nostrils. She dreaded having to witness the baby's inevitable struggle for life, but the baby didn't struggle. Katharine closed her eyes and pressed harder. The mass of flesh gave up its life easily—the little chest heaved once or twice, then stopped, as if to say, "Thank you, Grandma, for sending me to a better world." She withdrew her hand. From the incubator, no cry came—no sound, no movement. The baby lay still. Its chest heaved no more. Its stumps jerked and twitched no more. Katharine knew it was at peace, yet she uttered a moan of grief.

Then, the enormity of what she had just done, hit her. *Oh, my God—I've murdered my granddaughter. I can't face Julie, now—not after what I've done. I can't go on living.* A silent scream of agony swept through her brain. *I wish I were dead. I must be punished. I've got to die! Sammy said to rejoice in death … yes, yes—sweet death—let it come! Let me embrace it!*

Katharine barely understood what she was doing. She unstrapped Samuel and placed him in an empty incubator. Zombie-like, she shuffled into the corridor and headed for the exit. She felt tears streaming down her cheeks yet did not attempt to wipe them away. She stared straight ahead. Her arms hung loosely at her sides. Several persons passed and glanced curiously at her before continuing on their way.

Yes, death is my only relief. For the good of my daughter—for everyone—I must vanish. I give her my Samuel—a healthy baby—like the one she would have birthed had I not interfered.

With eyes fixed upon the huge iris diaphragm at the far end of the transport platform, Katharine dragged her feet toward it. *The next time the diaphragm opens to let a cabin pass through, I'll jump.*

As she reached it, it opened, and she craned to peer into the nebulous void beyond—a gray mass of roiling mist. Before she could see much, a cabin swished through, and the diaphragm closed.

I've got to jump next time—I can't stand myself any longer. I'm useless to my daughter—she's better off without me. The next cabin left, but Katharine still teetered on the edge of the platform. She heard, "Ms. Carver. Stop! Don't do it." She turned to notice a robosentry weave through waiting travelers as it raced across the platform toward her.

Another cabin sped through the opening diaphragm.

Katharine dived into the void. At first, the weightlessness exhilarated her. Then, thoughts and movements slowed. *Has the passage of time slowed, also?* She stretched out her arms and legs and dived like an eagle. The cool wind streamed past her. It lulled her into a delicious state of hallucinative ecstasy. She reveled in her freedom. Life was good.

Suddenly, she broke free of the womb-like clouds. Reality smacked her. She found herself tumbling end over end. The ground magnified itself in a slow, but continuous, zooming action.

Will Julie and Mario care for Samuel? What will he be like when he grows up? Will Julie have another baby? Is Pierre dead? … Oh, God—please let me live to know the answers.

Before Katharine smashed into the Earth, she expelled a long shriek of terror.

Round and round the sand,
As far as eye could see,
The rolling mist came down and hid the land:
And never home came she.

—Charles Kingsley

An instant later
The hospice for the poor
Bellevue, Franklin

"Kathy, be quiet! Your screams are awakening the whole place. We can hear you from our ward—way down the hall. What's the matter? Are you sick?"

"Wha … ? Gretchen?" Katharine raised herself up on one elbow. Sweat dripped from her. She focused her eyes on the silhouette of a head.

It whispered, "Yes, I'm Gretchen."

Katharine moaned. "Oh, I just killed my granddaughter and … and … I committed suicide—I guess …"

"Ssh! You've killed no one and certainly not yourself. You're talking to me, aren't you?"

Katharine rubbed her head. "Yes, but, it was so real that—"

"Nonsense, you had a nightmare—that's all."

Reality surfaced slowly. Katharine wiped the sweat from her face. "It was terrible, Gretchen. I thought—"

"Never mind what you thought—it wasn't so. You are in the hospice; it's four in the morning, and you need sleep."

"Four? … I've got to go to the kitchen."

"It's too early yet. Get some sleep."

"No, I've got to prep for lunch, too. After breakfast, I must visit my daughter in the hospital."

"Do you mean … the one up there?" Gretchen pointed to the ceiling, as if Heaven itself were beyond.

Despite herself, Katharine smiled. "Yes … the one up there."

Gretchen said reverently, "I wish my baby could have been born there."

How ironic … her perfect baby—born in wretchedness, and my wretched grand-daughter—born in luxury.

* * *

Katharine's "second" trip to the hospital was different. This time, she possessed no superpowers. This time, Samuel slept in his pouch. This time, she availed herself of Mario's transportation account. In seconds, the turbolift whisked Samuel and her up to the transport platform where they caught a monocabin to the hospital.

202

En route, Katharine speculated as to what must have gone through Julie's mind when she discovered the truth about her baby. For what seemed the millionth time, Katharine regretted having made that "malicious" contract with the doctor and wondered why she had done so. *In God's name ... why? Had my grief over Douglas's death caused me to become irrational? How can I make things right to Julie, now?*

Katharine tried to visualize what might have happened had she not made "that devil's pact" with Doctor Sullivan: Her Julie—most certainly—would have had an abortion—although a criminal act it would have been. Perhaps, by now, she would have been pregnant again with a valid embryo—this time to birth a normal, happy baby.

However, Katharine realized that, perhaps, time had run out for her daughter ever to have another child. She would always remember Julie's words to Mario after her dinner party last August.

Her daughter had said, "You see, if our first child is in-valid and you decide to keep it, I would support your decision for the sake of our marriage, but I would never have another child—possibly the very one that could have been valid."

Ironically, her threat could now become a reality. Katharine bit her lip and cried in despair. *Perhaps the nightmare was God's way of prompting me to perform an abominable, yet necessary, act—that of really killing my granddaughter.* She shook the thought from her head.

The cabin approached the hospital's transport platform—straight at the iris diaphragm, which popped open at the last instant to let the cabin zip in.

Katharine passed through the pollution barrier and, with trepidation, entered the hospital. She breathed deeply. *Aaah, at last! ... The sweet odor of clean air. This time, it's for real.* She felt self conscious for she was dressed in what, only a few months before, she would have considered to be rags.

Samuel was secure in his pouch, which she slipped 'round to her chest. He slept the sleep of innocents.

A robosentry passed them through the first checkpoint.

Katharine followed its instructions—the second corridor to the right, then the first one to the left. She passed though the second checkpoint and entered the Premature Wing beyond which she could find her daughter's room.

Samuel stirred for a moment then slept on.

Katharine noticed that she was walking past Preemie Ward G. She stopped and leaned against the wall of the corridor. *Mario said that my granddaughter is in this ward. Should I stop to see her, first?*

Katharine looked at the ceiling. Silently, she sobbed. Then, she bawled out loud. She glanced at Samuel to see whether she had disturbed him—he continued to sleep. Minutes later, she composed herself, turned, and took one step after the other toward the incubator room. At the entrance, she hesitated. *Dare I enter? ... Yes, I must see what manner of monster I have inflicted upon my children. Will its condition be as horrible as my nightmare depicted it to be?*

She entered. The room appeared to be smaller than the one in her dream. At the sight of a robonurse, an overwhelming urge to flee invaded her.

"May I help you, ma'am?"

Katharine began to tremble. "No, I, uh—"

"Have you a family member here?"

"Well, yes, I, uh—"

"The parents' name?"

"Pavía ... Julie and Mario."

The robonurse hesitated a moment. "I am paging the father now."

"No, you misunderstand. I want to see the baby."

"I am instructed to notify the father—if you should arrive."

"Fine, I'll visit the baby until he comes."

"No, you must wait for the father."

"Kathy, thank goodness, you're here."

She pivoted to face Mario.

He seemed weary—his face, haggard. He stared at her for a moment. "The baby is dead."

Katharine heard ringing noises and rhythmic pounding of blood. She felt a sudden hunger in the depth of her stomach. Through welling tears, Mario's image blurred. She averted her gaze. She fumbled for a tissue. She wiped her eyes. *Why am I crying? Is it the baby's death? Is it Julie's freedom? Is it reflex action to society's need to witness grief? ... but, I'm not grieving. No, ... I'm relieved—so very relieved.* "What can I say, Mario? Frankly, I'm not sorry about the baby's death, but I am profoundly sorry for what I've done to both of you. I hope that, some day, you can find it in your hearts to forgive me." She sighed. "Thank God, this ordeal is behind us."

Mario grunted. His expression hinted of a smile. "Not quite ... Julie is very depressed. She's just as hostile as before—says that she's been cheated, says that since I got my way, I'm 'too arrogant for words.' "

"Got your way?"

"Yes—not taking the baby home. She had insisted upon doing so." Mario took Katharine by the arm. "Come. Talk to her. I don't want to leave her alone too long."

Katharine pulled back. "No, Mario ... maybe, now's not the time."

"If it's not now, it'll never be the time. Look, she's your daughter. You've got to face her sometime, and the sooner, the better."

Reluctantly, Katharine followed Mario toward the Maternity Wing, yet apprehension permeated her being. *What can I say to her? Any words of consolation on my part, no matter how well chosen, will seem insincere—even cavalier. Yet, Mario is right—I must face Julie.*

Mario entered his wife's room. "What are you doing? Why are you up?"

"I've been told to leave—that's why I'm up. This room is for mothers, and I, certainly, am not one of those."

At the sound of her daughter's voice, Katharine tensed up and hesitated to enter the room. From the corridor, she gestured silently to Mario that she would not make her presence known to Julie.

Mario ignored her and said, "You need your mother, don't you, Darling?"

Katharine heard only a sigh. She turned to leave, but the words, "Yes, I guess I do," followed. She turned back and entered the room.

Instantly, Julie stopped her packing to gasp and stare in surprise at Katharine. Then, apparently remembering that her foul mood was justified, she turned away to continue packing. "I didn't invite you here."

"Julie, I'm sorry. I know that I—"

"Please! Leave!

"Darling, I invited her."

Viciously, Julie turned on Mario. "You had no right. This is my room. I receive only whom I want."

Mario rushed to his wife, gripped her shoulders, and shook her. "Stop it! Stop it! The baby is dead. Had your mother not done what she did, it still would be dead—you'd have aborted it. We've suffered enough—all three of us. Look at your mother. She's suffered plenty. It's time to start over."

Julie began to wail and let her head collapse on Mario's chest. At each sob, her body shook.

Mario embraced her, pursed his lips against her forehead, and stared at the ceiling.

Katharine watched them stand there—together in each other's embrace—for a long moment. She resisted the urge to run and join them. *It's not my place. I must leave them alone—let them make up.*

Samuel stirred. He began to cry.

Katharine scurried into the corridor. *My baby's hungry. I must return to the hospice.* She hurried toward the exit.

"Mother!"

Katharine stopped in her tracks—not by that one word—but by the manner in which her daughter uttered it—a little girl, pleading for her mother's help. No—Julie's tone is more like, "I forgive you. Let us start anew."

Katharine pivoted to see Julie standing in the middle of the corridor. Her expression was somber, yet her eyes were pleading.

Katharine ran to her daughter and enveloped her in a groping embrace. She sobbed into her ear, "I am so sorry for what I have done to you. I had no right. It was inexcusable. Please—try to forgive me."

Squeezed between mother and daughter, Samuel screamed at the top of his lungs.

Mario rushed out. "What are you doing to that poor kid?"

Katharine stepped back and wiped her eyes. The incident seemed to clear the air. "Don't worry, Samuel is husky. Besides, he's hungry. I was just returning to the hospice to feed him."

"Kathy, we're not going to let you leave, now. I'll get a robonurse to feed him."

Julie said, "Try if you want, Mario, but the hospital won't feed visitors."

"Darling, he's just a baby."

"They don't care about that."

"Then, I must return to the hospice."

"No, Mother. ... I'll nurse him."

Katharine witnessed Mario's mouth literally drop open as she, herself, was stunned beyond words.

"Well, what's the matter with you two? The baby is hungry, and I've got milk. It's as simple as that. Give him to me. What's his name, again? ... Manuel?"

"No, Samuel."

"You are right, Mother. He is husky ... and healthy, too."

* * *

The weeks passed slowly for Katharine. Although her duties in the mess hall remained the same, they became more and more of a drudge for, without Samuel, life itself was a chore. To see him, she'd periodically visit Julie and Mario, but, upon each departure, her despondency worsened. She tried to hide her moodiness, yet Julie and Mario seemed to sense it. Each time that they tried to cheer her up, their efforts degenerated into increasingly awkward conversations.

Consequently, Katharine visited them more briefly and less frequently. She realized that Julie and Mario could raise Samuel better than she. Eventually, she vowed to keep out of their lives as much as possible and pass the remainder of her life in penance for her sins.

One day, Katharine awoke and found Gretchen hovering over her.

"What's the matter? Why are you looking at me like that?"

"Don't you remember?"

"What?"

"Look at your wrists."

Katharine raised her arms. "My goodness, why are they bandaged?"

"You slit them with a kitchen knife. Luckily, you severed no tendons."

Katharine groaned. "I remember nothing. How could this have happened?"

"We don't know except that we found you lying in a pool of blood shortly after you returned from your visit to see Samuel."

"Oh, Gretchen, each time I must leave Samuel, I'm so miserable, I could die. Maybe, in a fit of depression, I did slit my wrists, but, I can't remember doing it. Am I becoming insane?"

"I don't know, but you've got to find a way to snap out of these depressions of yours—they're getting worse. Perhaps, you should take back Samuel."

Katharine glanced up at Gretchen. "Oh, I dearly want to, but I can't."

"Why not?"

"To raise him in this world of filth and want? My daughter can better care for him."

Gretchen's eyes watered. "You are fortunate. I can't keep my baby from harm's way. I have no one to go to—up in those towers—up in those stratoscrapers."

Katharine felt helpless. She touched Gretchen's arm. "I'm sorry."

* * *

Katharine was tired. She had consumed her dandelion coffee and was hunched over a mess-hall table with her head cradled in her arms. Eyes closed, yet awake, she daydreamed about Julie and Samuel.

Her aural receptors crackled. She sat bolt-upright. She listened intently. ... Nothing. "Mario? ... Julie? ... Is that you?"

A long hum invaded her ears then, "Kathy, can you hear me? This is Pierre."

Epilogue—REWARD

So also is the resurrection of the dead.
It is sown in corruption;
it is raised in incorruption.

—1 Corinthians 15:42

Eighty one years into the future, April 25, 2212
Pierre and Katharine's villa
Lac Bienville, Province de Naskapi, la République québécoise

The great day had arrived. Katharine was ready. Her home was ready. For all her one-hundred-twenty years, she felt quite spry and alert. She glanced at her husband, bent over in his wheelchair. "For Heaven's sake, Pierre, don't be so gloomy. Today is your two-hundredth birthday."

Slowly, Pierre raised his eyes and, again, started his phlegm-clearing ritual.

Katharine tried not to wince, but, each time he coughed, a shiver snaked up her spine.

Finally, he burbled, "That's why I am gloomy. Besides, I feel more like three hundred."

"Then, why keep resisting the lung prosthesis? Mine's half a century old and only hurts when I laugh."

Pierre grinned briefly before going into another coughing fit. "... No, I'm too old to go through all that. Besides, I've too much hardware in me as it is. *Je suis une vraie quincaillerie.*"

Their granddaughter Rachel stood combing the few-remaining, gossamer strands of her grandfather's white hair. "Pépé, the media from North America are interviewing you. Please, don't lapse into Québécois—they won't understand it."

Pierre's face took on that stubborn look, which, in the last few years, was all too familiar to Katharine. "Girl, I'll do as I God damn' please."

Katharine sighed. "How many times must I tell you, Pierre, 'She's not a girl anymore.' She's almost eighty, you know."

Pierre's eyes misted, and he muttered, "Yes, I know."

Katharine and Rachel followed Pierre's wheelchair as it navigated itself through the rambling house to the conference room. Much of the family was already gathered there.

Katharine scanned the crowd and noticed that most persons were ambulatory. To the left, she barely recognized her great granddaughter, who lay on a gurney. Some years had passed since she had last seen her—with hair already gray and skin already wrinkled. *My God, she's barely forty!* She surmised that the young man standing to the right of the gurney was the woman's son. Behind, Katharine made out the bald head of Rachel's son. *He must be about sixty, now.*

In front, with piercing black eyes and flowing white mane in striking contrast to his dark skin, stood her beloved Samuel. Most of the others, she did not know—her great, great grandchildren, no doubt. She was neither able nor disposed to keep track of them all anymore.

Samuel came forward, kissed all three on the cheek, and took up his position beside Pierre's wheelchair opposite his sister Rachel.

Katharine glanced at the long table in back. Everything seemed to be in order—the wine was being chilled, and the birthday cake was awaiting the knife. To her right, she heard whispers. She turned to see what the commotion was about. The crowd split to enable the passage of a tall, thin, old woman attended by her retinue.

The woman, dressed entirely in black, walked slowly toward them. At first, Katharine could not make out who she was—a wide-brimmed, black hat shielded her face. Then, she noticed Pierre gasp and feverishly try to stand.

Visibly befuddled, he looked up at Rachel, then, at Samuel, and groped for their arms. *"Aidez moi, les enfants."*

Although both were eighty, Rachel and Samuel stooped and pulled Pierre up by his armpits.

Finally, the old woman stood opposite them. Her brown eyes twinkled, and her large mouth broke into a familiar smile—one they had not seen in, perhaps, thirty years.

Katharine tried to keep from shaking but was too excited not to. She noticed that Pierre trembled also. She marveled at the old woman ... those teeth still flashed white against her black skin. *My God ... all these years have passed, and, yet, she appears to have barely aged.*

"Hello, Kathy ... Pierre. Congratulations on your bicentennial, young man."

Pierre emitted a short chortle. "Why thank you, Jane. I am deeply touched by your presence here, but you shouldn't have come. You're a couple of years older than I ... physically speaking, of course."

Jane's teeth gleamed. "Ah ha, so you've kept track, too. Well, I'm going on 128 and never felt better—except for these damned legs of mine. For the past thirty years, they've kept me cooped up in my 'ivory tower' ... or so I believed—but, when I learned of your special birthday, I was determined to break out of my shell and see the both of you one, last time ... we've not many years left, you know."

An aide arrived with a chair, and Jane sat. She turned to face Katharine. "You've barely changed since I last saw you, Kathy—a little thinner, perhaps."

"Well, thirty years does make a difference—and before that, the summer of 2142, I believe ... Andy's funeral. Did you ever forgive him, Jane ... for what he did to you?"

"Good heavens, yes. I even forgave him before he was killed. Every Christmas, I'd go to the prison and visit him. He was very repentant—couldn't believe I forgave him or would want to see him again."

"Pierre and I visited Andy in 2137 ... when we returned to Franklin for the children's funeral."

"Julie and Mario's ... ah, yes, that turbolift accident was horrible. As I recall, the murder allegation came to nothing."

Rachel spoke up in dismay. "My parents ... murdered? Who could have killed them? I never heard about this before."

Katharine sighed and looked at Jane, reproachfully.

Jane appeared startled. "I'm sorry—I thought they knew."

Gently, Katharine touched her granddaughter's arm. "When you were little, your Pépé and I didn't want to upset you unnecessarily. Anyway, at the time, the sleaze media were just inventing wild speculations ... no one ever discovered any evidence of murder."

"But, I have the right to know what happened, Grandma—we all do." Rachel gestured to the others for support.

Most nodded or murmured in assent.

Katharine glanced at Pierre then at Jane.

In obvious tired resignation, Pierre shrugged his shoulders.

Jane said, "Has the time come?"

Katharine hesitated for a moment, then said, "Yes, it is long overdue. Since you broached the subject, Jane, you tell them."

Jane removed her hat. Her luxurious head of long, black hair, which Katharine had admired so long ago, no longer existed. Jane licked her lips and said, "A few of you history buffs already know what I am about to reveal—most of the others, probably, do not.

"After Senator Yoshimasa's assassination, the police speculated that Pierre and I would gain the most from his death, but Pierre was in maximum security in the Winnipeg Federal Asylum for the Insane.

"After my arrest for the senator's murder, I learned of the contrived evidence against me. Andy appeared to be outraged and claimed that he was doing everything possible to organize my defense—like seeking out the truth and trying to get me a good lawyer, which I already had—under retainer ... you know—things like that. But, the evidence proved to be overwhelmingly against me, and, on January 28, 2131, I entered prison for life."

Katharine remarked, "Yet, you spent only six months there."

Jane smiled wanly. "Yes. By some miracle, irrefutable evidence surfaced that exonerated me and condemned Andy. He replaced me in prison and, after ten years incarceration, was killed during a prison riot."

"Why did he do it?"

"The senator had discovered that Andy and Mario plotted to help Pierre. He threatened to have Andy fired from his job."

"Not only that," Katharine interjected, "Andy knew that Pierre had revealed the secret of hydroxygen ignition to the senator. Andy demanded to get a share of the profits, but the senator refused. They argued, and Andy hit him with a statuette."

Rachel asked, "But, what had my parents' deaths to do with all this? What was this 'sleaze media inventing wild speculations' all about?"

Katharine sighed. "Nothing, really. The media created those rumors. You see, no one could discover the origin of the evidence against Andy, so the press 'gave' the credit to Mario."

Rachel said, "Then, Andy must have contracted for my father's murder ... and my mother, being with my father at the time, was killed, also."

Pierre roused himself from his stupor. "Stop it! Stop it—all of you. You act like the media you disparage—spreading around rumors, guesses, and sheer gossip."

Katharine became upset and, admittedly, a bit testy. "But, Pierre, what else has one to spread around, when one hasn't the facts? I suppose you possess them."

Pierre stared ahead for a moment then said, "All I can say is that Mario did not furnish the evidence against Andy, and that, indeed, an accident killed Mario and Julie— not murder."

Suddenly, Katharine saw the light. She should have known that Pierre had supplied the proof against Andy. Pierre saved Jane, and Jane had guessed it. For years— ever since the children's funeral—Katharine had been perplexed by Jane's new-found friendliness toward Pierre. *Now, I know why.*

Rachel seemed dissatisfied with Pierre's answer. "Pépé, how can you tell? How do you know?"

"I just can … leave it at that."

"But, Pépé—"

"Rachel," Katharine bellowed, *"N'as-tu pas entendu Pépé?"*

"Oui, Mémé."

A stir at the door drew Katharine's attention. The governor of Naskapi Province, accompanied by members of the media, entered and minced briskly toward them.

With a flourish, the governor kissed her hand. *"Ah, chère madame Talon, je vois que vous êtes aussi charmante que jamais."*

Katharine saw through his compliment and politely told him so. *"Monsieur le gouverneur, vous êtes trop flatteur pour une pauvre, vieille femme comme moi."*

After a few more mock exchanges of mutual admiration, the governor began his speech. He elocuted a brief introduction in Québécois then continued in English for the benefit of the foreigners. "Ladies and gentlemen, today the world celebrates the two-hundredth anniversary of the birth of Doctor Pierre Talon, a great scientist and a great humanitarian. His glorious fight to control Earth's surpopulation has been… ."

Katharine tried to listen, but her reminiscences were too powerful to ignore. The presence of Jane had awakened memories of her youth:

… For the most part, Pierre's and her life together had been long and happy. It began, however, on a note of sadness. She remembered the day well—so very well, so many years ago… .

* * *

For Katharine, the trip had been arduous. The meager diet and foul air at the hospice had weakened her, so her resistance to the effects of acceleration was low.

She was relieved when the shuttle empadded at the new port city of Baleine-Est on the east shore of Hudson's Bay, its rising waters having, long ago, engulfed the old port of Poste de la Baleine. After traveling two-hundred miles up the Grande Baleine River, she arrived on the shores of beautiful Lac Bienville located in the vast interior of Naskapi, Québec's northernmost province.

Although tired, Katharine felt jubilant—only a few minutes remained before she'd see Pierre in the flesh. Her heliocar rounded the last bend, and there it was … an old log cabin nestled under the trees. She saw Pierre. Her heart leapt.

Sporting a stubby beard, he awaited her arrival in front of his cabin. The blue-denim jeans and heavy, wool shirt in red and black plaid made him look like a *coureur de bois* of old Nouvelle France.

The car braked to a stop. Katharine leapt out and into Pierre's arms. They kissed with the passion of long separation. Pierre's beard scratched her cheek, but she didn't mind.

"Oh, Kathy, I'm so glad you're here. I was really lonely without you."

She stepped back and examined him. "My God, Pierre, you look like you stepped out of a page from a history book."

"You should talk—you're positively desiccated."

Katharine sighed, "I know."

She found the cabin to be rather quaint. The old furniture made the place homey. Except for the robosentries stationed outside, the wallscreen in a corner was the only incongruity. "I see you appreciate the warmth of antiques."

Pierre laughed. "Antiques? Albeit hard to find now, these sticks of furniture are my contemporaries."

"I like this place, but those robosentries out there make it look like a fortress. Do you really need them here?"

"My dear, during my absence, they kept it from being vandalized."

"And the trees—they're so big."

Pierre sighed. "How sad. ... You've never seen and never will see really big trees. Teeming humanity has consumed them all. Just thinking about it renders me nauseous."

"Did you have trouble escaping?"

"A little, but their security had become lax enough for me to exploit its failings *et—me voici!* ... and—here I am!

"Where were you when you contacted me at the hospice?"

"Here."

"Couldn't you have called sooner?"

"No, darling—that I leave North America first was urgent. Besides, I didn't know about your situation until I contacted Mario."

Katharine gripped Pierre's arms and stared into his eyes. "I almost killed her, you know."

"Who? What are you talking about?"

"My granddaughter. Had she not died, I probably would have killed her. Can you imagine? ... I, the mother of poor Douglas, euthanizing my own granddaughter? Had I done so, I would have betrayed my upbringing—my code of ethics."

"Kathy, darling, ethics are not constant. They are relative to the society that spawns them. They change with time and circumstance. They did with me. I experienced the same torment as you—admittedly, to a lesser degree because my own family wasn't involved. Yet, I was required to kill."

"The arsons?"

"Correct ... and Kathy?"

"Yes."

"I am ... I'm responsible for the death of your son, Douglas."

Katharine studied the anguish in Pierre's face. "No, my darling—you did not kill my son. Doctor Sullivan euthanized him the evening before the arson occurred.

* * *

Yes, it was a long time ago.

Katharine gazed at Samuel—still a handsome man. The governor was eulogizing Pierre, and Samuel listened in rapt attentiveness. *What a fine father he had become— with two healthy children of his own.*

Upon hearing her name, Katharine returned her attention to the governor's voice: "During the past century, Pierre Talon and his wife, Katharine, lead the struggle to create a reasonable abortional and euthanasic policy. Their fight was a valiant one, and, worldwide, you can see much of what they accomplished for the human race... ."

Although the governor's words lauded Pierre and her, she knew that someone in her own family had written them. In fact, the governor—certainly in deference to his power brokers—ignored the part about the primary role Pierre and she had played in decreasing pollution, reducing radioactive contamination, and preserving natural resources.

Katharine was proud of the results of their lives' work but saddened to think that, in the three decades since their retirement, society at large had reversed many of their accomplishments. With bitterness, she realized that neither old age nor advancing poor health caused Pierre's melancholy of late. The real cause was the realization that he had failed to wholly succeed in his mission.

At first, whenever he'd be moody, she would ask about it, but he'd always answer the same: "I haven't changed the future. I've changed nothing. I've failed Boniface. I've failed the human race. In 2789, our kind will be no more." Eventually, she stopped asking.

She noticed that the crowd was stirring, and her thoughts returned to reality. The speeches were over. Their guests gravitated toward the refreshment table.

Jane stood. "I am tired. I must leave—no, please, don't get up."

Katharine was amazed by Jane's spritefulness and told her so.

"Well, Doctor Wong did take good care of me over the years. Poor woman—she died only a few months ago."

Katharine was dumbstruck. "Did you say Doctor Wong?"

"Yes," Jane said innocently, "she was my private doctor. Why do you ask?"

"She saved my life ... no, Jane, you saved my life."

No one spoke for a long moment.

Jane continued to stare at Katharine, then she spoke, "So, now ... you know."

"Yes, now, I know." Katharine leaned toward Jane, pulled her down, and kissed her on the cheek. She whispered into her ear, "I thank you for my life at a time I wanted to die."

Eyes moist, Jane stood straight, touched Katharine's shoulder then, Pierre's. "We may never see one another again ... in this life. Good-bye, dear friends."

Pierre shook uncontrollably and tried to speak.

Through tears, Katharine looked up, but Jane was only a blur.

* * *

During the weeks following Pierre's bicentennial celebration, Katharine noticed that her husband was growing weaker by the day. When he lapsed into a deep sleep, she gathered her loved ones around her.

"Oh, Samuel, I'm so happy you could come so soon. For the moment, he's resting peacefully." Distraught, Katharine led her grandson to the sitting area outside Pierre's bedroom.

"Have the others arrived yet?"

"Only Rachel. She came yesterday."

Upon seeing Samuel enter, Rachel arose and embraced her brother.

Katharine was relieved to hear the beeps continue in the same rhythmic fashion as before. *Thank God! He is still alive.*

Samuel asked, "How long has he been like this?"

Rachel said, "Last night, after sleeping a whole day, Pépé awakened, became incoherent and babbled about his failed life—his failed mission. He mistook me for Grandma then argued with a nonexistent being. Finally, he fell asleep again."

"And, today?"

"He hasn't awakened yet—might be in a coma. This morning, his lungs failed. He's undergoing oxygen infusion as we speak."

The robomedic exited Pierre's bedroom and approached Katharine. It said, "Your husband is resting well. I have done everything possible for him. Only time will tell. To monitor his status, I'll put myself in dormant mode over there in the corner." The machine walked to the corner and became immobile.

Katharine sat down next to Samuel. All was quiet—except for the beeps. She listened intently to them and, after awhile, tried to measure the delay between them. The beeps seemed to evolve into hammer strikes against an anvil, which got closer and closer until her brain was ready to explode.

"What happened to my sister?"

The hammer and anvil vanished in a flash. Katharine's blood felt like ice water. Her eyes darted to Rachel's face. "How long have you known? ... I have tried to keep it a secret."

"Several years."

"How did you find out?"

"Pépé told me."

Katharine was annoyed. "Why are you bringing this up now? Your Pépé is dying, for Christ' sake."

Samuel interrupted. "We had a sister?"

For a moment, Katharine stared at the floor. She sensed her grandchildren's eyes upon her. She looked at her grandson. "Yes, you did."

Again, Rachel asked, "What became of her?"

"Pépé didn't tell you?"

"He said that only you could."

Despite Pierre's condition, a pang of anger shot through Katharine. But, an instant later, remorse followed. "And I will, too." She began her story:

"When your mother was a little girl, I gave birth to a horribly-deformed son. I was young and naïve, and... ." As her story progressed, Katharine watched the expression on Rachel's face evolve from disgust, revulsion, and—sometimes—horror to sympathy, understanding and—finally—approval.

Rachel interrupted, "My existence, then, is a frigging miracle."

"Yes—and your validity is even more so. Had your in-valid sister not died, you never would have been conceived. Relieved of the burden of raising an in-valid child, your parents were free to try again. Yet, fearful of a repetition, they took their precautions. Julie proved to be healthy, but an examination of Mario's geneticism (sic) revealed that someone in his ancestry had been exposed to high levels of radioactivity. Nevertheless, expensive—and quite illegal—genetic engineering managed to extract enough of Mario's few healthy sperm for a valid conception, which resulted in a beautiful, baby daughter ... you."

"Mémé, you, then, are responsible for my validity ... even, my survival."

Katharine was confused. "What do you mean?

"Don't you see? By forcing my parents to endure the pain of birthing a deformed baby, you caused them to assure that their next baby would be a healthy one."

Katharine was elated that Rachel could see some good in a terrible act, which Katharine had condemned herself for committing. "I never thought of it that way; however, they would have taken precautions, anyway."

"I don't believe so, Mémé. You see, because of my father's defective sperm, my mother would have had one abortion after another, which wouldn't have been enough of an impetus to do what my parents had to do to birth me ... only birthing a deformed baby would."

Katharine sighed. "You're probably right." She glanced at Samuel.

For some time, her grandson had been uncommonly silent, but, now, he spoke. "Grandma, had I been born like your first granddaughter, how would you have dealt with me?"

Katharine's tears gushed forth, and she bit her lower lip. "I would have killed you, as, no doubt, your natural mother Sammy would have wished—then I'd have killed myself. You see, back then, only you kept me alive. You needed me. To care for you, I forced myself to live, although I wanted to die ... and I almost did—after Julie and Mario began caring for you."

The beeps—the rhythm of Pierre's heartbeats—startled her. They were accelerating.

In the corner, the robomedic came to life and turned to address Katharine. "Currently, your husband experiences an abnormally high level of neural activity in an unlikely area of the brain. Never before has this phenomenon been observed ... hmm, most curious. I wonder what's causing it."

* * *

"Pierre Talon. Listen to me. This is Boniface, the Valid of Cumulus, speaking to you. You are asleep, and the program in your supplemental memory is releasing this particular message because you succeeded in your life's work and are, now, near death.

"You believe that you failed in your mission, but historians documented your wife's and your accomplishments in detail. During the six centuries following your deaths, they credited you for keeping the human race alive until your arrival in the year 2786.

"Pierre, without your tireless devotion to your mission, John, Alex, Joan, Strata, I, and all the others never would have existed. The human species would have become extinct long before your arrival in the future. Your spaceship would have arrived on a dead earth, and you would have perished along with your crew.

"Strata and I knew that, when you would return to the past, a navigational error would put you in 2123 rather than in your own era of 2045. However, had we compensated for it in advance, you would have returned to 2045 and not fulfilled your mission.

"Your knowledge of the Monnetville-Stock-Market results and of the locations of those three, archaeological sites was based upon our historical records of what you did in the past. You did not change the past—you created it in the first place. Strata's and my role in saving the Earth was to assure that your predestined life not be altered.

"… Little time remains—you are getting weaker. I now reveal to you—your greatest achievement. I apologize for having kept it secret, but its premature revelation would have diluted your resolve to succeed in your mission:

"My dear Pierre, by allowing Strata and me to exist and by bringing your spaceship to us, you saved the human species from extinction. You see, when it crashed, not one, but three crew members survived—you … and Dimitri Adam … and Evelyn Chang."

* * *

"Oh, my God, the beeping stopped." Katharine rushed into Pierre's bedroom. She knelt beside him and searched his face. She found it set in a serene smile. She turned to her grandchildren. "Rachel, Douglas … at last, Pépé has found peace."

"Douglas?"

About the Author

The Fetal Issue is the author's first novel after being a technical writer for many years. His other salient experiences occurred as: a USAF pilot; a construction camp manager in Nigeria and at various sites in Alaska; a restaurateur in France, Florida, and Seattle; an instructor of business applications of computers at various community colleges; a professor of computer systems technology at Memphis State University; and a professor of computer science at Western Washington University.

* * *

The content of *The Fetal Issue* exposes the feelings and beliefs of members of the author's family as arrived at by life's experiences, but the author does not attribute any one belief to any particular one of them. In addition to his wife and him, these members include their three children (all sons), his mother, and his sister. His wife's parents died before this book was written.

The author's wife is Roman Catholic. Upon marriage, the author converted from Lutheranism to his wife's religion and agreed that their children would be raised as such. Had he not done so and his fiancée still married him, she would have been chastised or, perhaps, excommunicated. Even though the author converted to Catholicism, he was baptized Lutheran, so his fiancée and he were not allowed to be married at the central altar but off to the side. Also, only close family members were allowed to attend the wedding—friends, acquaintances, and the public were forbidden to attend.

At the beginning of his wife's first pregnancy, she contracted a kidney infection with a high fever. The doctor did not alert them to the possibility that the fever might affect her embryo, which was to become Franck Guy Myhre to whom this book is dedicated.

Franck was born with a double cleft palate and hare lip, which, as he grew, required a series of twelve operations to correct the defects as much as possible. Before his parents learned that the kidney infection might have been the culprit, the author's father-in-law urged them not to have any more children because he feared that his son-in-law possessed defective genes. Had the author and his wife taken his advice, their two normal sons would not have been born.

Their son, Franck, agrees that, had his embryo been detected to be deformed and his parents decided to abort it, their decision would have been the right one to take. However, at the time, an abortion was unthinkable because it was illegal.

Franck designed the image on the cover of the soft-bound copy of this book.

www.ingramcontent.com/pod-product-compliance
Lightning Source LLC
Chambersburg PA
CBHW030312290526
45785CB00001B/324